JOY ADAMSON

BEHIND THE MASK

JOY ADAMSON

BEHIND THE MASK

Caroline Cass

WEIDENFELD and NICOLSON
LONDON

First published in Great Britain in 1992 by
George Weidenfeld & Nicolson Limited
91 Clapham High Street, London SW4 7TA

A catalogue record for this book is available from
the British Library

ISBN 0 297 81141 X

Filmset by Selwood Systems, Midsomer
Norton, Avon
Printed in Great Britain by
Butler & Tanner Ltd, Frome and London

To Tara and Tasmin
with love

'The credit belongs to the man who is actually in the arena, whose face is marred by dust and sweat and blood; who strives valiantly, who errs and comes short again and again, who knows the great enthusiasm, the great devotions, and spends himself in a worthy cause; who at best knows in the end the triumph of high achievement, and who at worst, if he fails, at least fails while daring greatly.'

Theodore Roosevelt

Contents

Illustrations

All photographs from the author's collection, unless otherwise indicated

Between pp 50–51

Joy with her mother
Collecting mushrooms in Seifenmühle
1920. Joy aged ten, with Traute, ready for a fancy-dress ball
1922. Victor and Traute Gessner with their three daughters, Joy, aged twelve, Dorle and Traute
1924. Joy and Traute
Joy having killed her first roebuck, aged 15
Joy dressed as a 'Russian candlestick' wooden doll for the Gschnas Ball in Vienna
Oma, Joy's adored maternal grandmother
Joy. Summer, 1931
Viktor von Klarwill
Joy on board ship travelling to Kenya, 1937
Joy and Peter Bally
Joy and Pampo, her orphaned baby elephant, at Isiolo
1936. George Adamson on top of Marop
May 1946. George and Joy on safari
Joy bottle-feeding Elsa at Isiolo
Elsa and Makedde
Elsa out hunting with George and Makedde
Joy and Elsa, close companions
June 1960. Siesta – Joy and Elsa on the banks of the Ura river

Between pp 114–115
Follow my leader – Joy and Elsa
A crocodile killed by George on a trip to South Island
Joy with Sir William (Billy) Collins, her publisher
Virginia McKenna with 'Elsa' in *Born Free* (Rex Features)
Joy during the filming of *Born Free* (Hulton-Deutsch Collection)

Her Majesty the Queen and Joy wearing identical dresses at the royal command performance of *Born Free*, London, 1966

Pippa, with a broken leg, at the animal orphanage in Nairobi (Camera Press)

Elsamere on Lake Naivasha

Joy at Elsamere (Camera Press)

Joy's favourite companions at Elsamere, her family of colobus monkeys (Camera Press)

Joy aged 66 (Camera Press)

George aged 71 (Camera Press)

George's assistant Tony Fitzjohn with two young lions at Kora (Camera Press)

Joy's assistant Pieter Mawson at Shaba (Duncan Willetts/Camerapix)

Joy's kitchen at Shaba (Duncan Willetts/Camerapix)

George at Joy's funeral in Nairobi (Duncan Willetts/Camerapix)

Joy's cairn at Shaba

Between pp 178–179

One of Joy's flower paintings (Collection of Lord and Lady Percy)

Joy at an exhibition of her tribal paintings (Rex Features)

A watercolour of Lord and Lady Percy with Joy and George Adamson done by Lady Percy (Collection of Lord and Lady Percy)

Joy with her least favourite animal, an elephant, at Naro Moru (British Film Institute)

Joy and George with Virginia McKenna and Bill Travers on the set of *Born Free* (British Film Institute)

Virginia McKenna and Bill Travers with Girl at Malindi (Ronald Grant Archive)

George and one of his lions with his assistant Tony Fitzjohn at Kora (Gerald Cubitt/Bruce Coleman Ltd)

George at Kora (Gerald Cubitt/Bruce Coleman Ltd)

Joy with her leopard cub Penny at Elsamere (Gerald Cubitt/Bruce Coleman Ltd)

Penny up her favourite tree at Shaba

Shaba camp

Joy with Bill and Ros Hillyar and their son, Charles

Joy, Pieter Mawson and friends at the swimming hole at Shaba

Joy and George. The fondness remained to the end

Acknowledgements

I must express my deep gratitude to everyone in Kenya, Europe and America who has helped me over the past two years. Special thanks must go to Enid Dawson, who acted as a valuable Kenya consultant for certain aspects of the book, Lord Weidenfeld for his support, Lady Powell, my editor Christopher Falkus, whose idea it originally was, Anne Engel, my agent, for all her interest and suggestions, Peter Marrian for his generous hospitality in Kenya, and Dorle Cooper, who talked to me at length about her sister and with whom I kept up a lengthy correspondence. I am deeply grateful to Lesley Baxter for all her hard work and encouragement. Lastly I must thank my mother, Dinah Pritchard, whose help and love throughout the writing of the book made it all possible.

Others I would like to thank are: Bunny Allen; Petal and David Allen; Tony Archer; Jack Barrah; Jonny Baxendale; Peter Beard; Muff Becker; Sieukwe Bisletti; Esmond and Chryssee Bradley Martin; Diana Bunny; Dr Reginald and Mrs Bunny; Mervyn Carnelly; Georgio Cefis; Katherine Challis; William and Annette Cottrell; Jack Couffer; Mervyn Cowie; the late Sir John Cumber; Jock Dawson; Dean Close School; John Eames; Alexander Edukan; Mrs Tiokko Ekai; Rodney Elliott; Kim Ellis; Albino Ewoi; Mary Anne Fitzgerald; Tony Fitzjohn; James Fox; Lyn Fry; Eleanor Gall; Sandy Gall; Terence Gavaghan; J. B. Gilet; Ted Goss; Rod Grainger; Anthony Gross; Freddy Gross; William and Morna Hale; Rene Haller; Jolyon Halse; Jean Harvey; Jean Hayes; Brian Heath; Richard Hennings; Ros Hillyar; Robin Hollister; Philip Hook; Lady Mary Howick; Pat and Ronnie Hughes; Alison Hutton-Wilson; Elspeth Huxley; Lady Huxley; Michael Hyde; Dr Ernst Illsinger; Lady Jeans; Peter and Sara Jenkins; Peter and Mary Johnson; Jo Kendall; Tony Kennaway; Prof. Wolfgang Koos; Prof. Lang; Franz Leubner; Sir Frank Lloyd; Peter Lokali; Loshua; Lois Low; Bobby Lowis; John MacDonald; Melody MacDonald; Julia McCall; Virginia McKenna; Jill Megson; Harry Minitree; Maeve and Barry Mitchell; Mohammed; Anne Morson; Millicent Morson; Gerald Nevill; Robert and Pat Nimmo; Verena Nowotny; Bill Oddie (lyricist of 'My Pride and Joy'); David Odhiambo; Desmond O'Hagan; Perez

Olindo; Hon. Patricia O'Neill; Ian Parker; Dr Fritz Pendel; Gerald Percy; Suzanne Pesche-Schmutzer; Tim Piccolo; Mary Pike; Patricia Powys; Leslie Pridgeon; Philip Ransley; Alys Reece; Mirella Ricciardi; Peter and Sue Robertson; Dorian Rocco; Edward Rodwell; Joan Root; Monty Ruben; Paul and Elma Sayer; Emil Schembera; Otto Schungel; Daphne Sheldrick; Ken Smith; the late Sir Tony Swan; Phil Synder; Sarah Tennant; Brian Tetley; Thoitanguru; Anne Thurston; Sir Richard Turnbull; Bobby Tyers; Errol Tzrebinski; Cunningham von Someren; Maria Wall; Roy Wallace; Peter and Ayesha Walters; Duncan Willets; James Willson; Kathleen Willson; Nick Wood; Ambassador Woschnagg; Ruth Wurstemburger-Bally; Denis Zaphiro.

1

Fifi

On 20 January 1910, in an imposing town house in Troppau, Austria, a daughter was born to Ober Baurat Victor Gessner and his wife, Traute. With little enthusiasm, they named her Friederike Viktoria. The Gessners had desperately wanted a son and the birth of a second girl was an acute disappointment which did nothing to bolster an already ailing marriage.

The maternal side of Friederike's family were influential citizens of Troppau. Her great-grandfather, Carl Weisshuhn, the owner of a number of paper mills, was a titan of a man who possessed an equally colossal personality. His fortunes had risen rapidly. The son of a game warden in the forests of southern Germany, he had started on his path to success by acquiring a wife who would tolerate his romantic encounters, devote her quiet strength to counter-balancing the needs of her dynamic husband and subsume her individuality in the breeding of many children. Weisshuhn charmed presidents, peasants and pretty women with the same easy manner and interest he showed in his burgeoning family. As his business flourished, he and his family took up residence in an elegant, four-storey house in Troppau. He used the ground floor as his business offices; the remainder was occupied by a menagerie of children, governesses and servants.

Friederike's maternal grandmother, and her namesake, was Weisshuhn's second daughter. As soon as she came of age, she was married off to a suitable but dull bourgeois, Herr Greipel. Within a year she presented him with a daughter, Traute. Ten months later she became a widow.

The young Traute, Friederike Viktoria's mother, had a pert nose and a determined chin, set off to advantage by a pair of luminous, blue-grey eyes. Thick, dark blonde hair was caught up in a loose bun at the back of her shapely head, in the current fashion. Although photographs of her as a young woman show her to have a rounded face with full-blown cheeks and a jaw too large to be thought conventionally beautiful, she is remembered by all who knew her as a pretty young woman. Traute was popular, with an adventurous and independent side to her nature and a heady passion for life. She was blessed with a clear soprano voice and her talent for music was matched by her abilities as a watercolourist and draughtsman. When she was not revelling in being the centre of every party and enchanting her numerous local admirers, she indulged her creative spirit by filling her sketchbook, with a record of the area in which she lived.

In 1908, in the age-old tradition of arranged marriages, which offered women security but also imposed the wifely duties of 'subjection, help-fulness and gracefulness', Traute, aged twenty, was wedded to Victor Gessner, a middle-class civil servant many years her senior. Compared to her family's social standing, his parents were considered of little import-ance in Troppau. In the young girl's eyes at the time, however, it did not bother her that she had married beneath her. Gessner had a handsome, finely structured face, appeared considerate and was approved of by those closest to her. He sported a moustache, was of medium height and his charismatic eyes could quickly change from a soft, concerned blue to a steely grey. (He was later to be accused by his wife and daughter Friederike of harbouring a sadistic nature.)

While Victor and his wife shared a deep appreciation of music, their differing ages, natures and aspirations ensured that, within a decade, the tenuous links of affection would be ineluctably weakened. Victor Gessner was a clever man, conscientious in his job and concerned about his wife's creature comforts, but his cloistered spirit was too serious for Traute. A combination of separate social gatherings and increasing financial pres-sures began to take their toll on any connubial bliss that might have existed. The couple's first two children were born in quick succession. A year after the birth of their eldest daughter, Traute, named after her mother, Friederike Viktoria was born in the Weisshuhn house in Troppau.

Although her parents had bestowed upon her the Christian name given to every second daughter in Traute's family, they found difficulty in accepting that she had not been born male. She was called Fritz by her disillusioned father, encouraged to wear boy's clothing, and brought up like a son. The shy young girl with her mop of pale blonde hair was nicknamed 'Fifi' by the rest of her family and friends. Although she was respectful of her father she remained guarded in her relationship with him. His attitude towards his two daughters appears to have been ambigu-ous. On the one hand he could be engagingly affectionate, enjoying the rituals of storytelling and patiently introducing them to the habits and behaviour of woodland creatures. Yet his moods had a habit of changing swiftly and he would suddenly round on the two girls, admonishing and punishing them on the slightest pretext. The feelings this unpredictable behaviour produced in Fifi were reticence and even fear, although it was from her father that she inherited a deep love of all creatures wild and tame. Fox cubs and caged birds, dappled fawns and white rabbits all found themselves under the mothering wing of the sensitive child.

Fifi's deepest affections were reserved for her mother, whom she loved intensely. Her idolization, however, was perpetually thwarted throughout her childhood, as her mother showed her little love in return. But as happens with children determined to pursue the unattainable, this only made the young child try harder. Fifi felt she could only win her love by striving for perfection and became driven at school in Troppau, the *Oberrealschule*, where she was over-conscientious about her work, diligent in her music lessons and controlled in her manner. She never questioned a forgotten promise or outing and never showed her mother how much she yearned for her when constantly left in the care of nannies and governesses.

By showing such 'tolerance' towards her mother and by acting in such a self-disciplined manner, Fifi could occasionally seduce her into giving the emotional treats she so craved. Together the two of them would take their paintboxes, brushes and sketchbooks and sit under the giant sycamore trees in the parks of Troppau. Perched on canvas stools, they would indulge in their favourite shared pastime of painting the delicate plants they saw all around them. It was in these intimate few hours that Fifi's frail self-esteem was strengthened. Traute Gessner never gave her daughter lessons in the basics of painting – that was left to Fifi's governess or nanny. This was just a time for sharing, and the two painted until the shadows grew long.

The family also shared a love of music. Fifi was able to sight-read before mastering her alphabet and, aged seven, her piano-playing was remarkably mature for one so young. On balmy evenings when her parents felt in a compatible mood, Fifi and her sister Traute would take a special delight in sitting on the piano bench on either side of their father to sing their favourite melodies. However, such treats were rare. Frau Gessner, despite being kind and gracious to others, harboured a certain coldness towards her offspring and, increasingly, her otherwise friendly disposition became exasperated by her domestic, wifely and maternal duties.

As a young eight-year-old, Fifi often sought comfort from her favourite playmate, an albino rabbit called Hasi. At twilight, as the swallows winged back to their nests, the little girl would run down to the end of the garden where Hasi was kept. As she scooped the white bundle onto her lap she would whisper to him of her dreams and her childish sorrows. The pet became an accepted member of the family, tolerated by Fifi's father, petted by the children and generally ignored by their mother.

During the First World War, luxuries in Austria were scarce and food supplies often short. Living through the tumultuous events which were to change their lives, Traute Gessner's nerves became frayed. Not only was she with child for the third time, but she and Victor were increasingly unhappy together. She was also distinctly bored with the spartan lifestyle the war had forced them to adopt and, in particular, the rituals of epicurism. Gazing out of the kitchen window one afternoon at a large, bushy-tailed squirrel, Traute hit upon an idea. Tonight they would have a special treat. She told no one. Her husband, back on leave from the Russian front, where he was a captain with a motorized unit, was listening to news of the war effort on the wireless in the drawing room, and the children were upstairs with the nanny. Traute listened for meddling footsteps. Hearing none, she took a large knife and stealthily made her way out of the kitchen door and down the garden path.

That night the table was immaculately laid. Heavy silver cutlery smoothed away the starched creases of the damask cloth. Candles flickered and threw violet shadows onto the walls. The two girls were surprised and puzzled by all the trimmings, which usually accompanied a special, festive occasion. Of late, it had been a rare evening when they had sat down with their parents to a sumptuous dinner.

As they waited, the appetizing smell of sage and onions wound its way into the dining room. This was soon followed by Milli the cook, holding a steaming earthenware pot. The children's mouths watered as they watched their mother brandishing a silver ladle over the aromatic mystery. With a flourish she removed the lid to reveal a bubbling stew of potatoes and baby carrots, leeks and yellow parsnips, and what appeared to be portions of tender chicken. Large helpings were put onto their plates. The delicate meat melted on the tongue and every last drop of gravy, spiced with herbs from the garden, was mopped up with bread.

All too soon the meal was over. The girls turned to their mother and congratulated her on its excellence. It had been a long time since they had eaten such a delicious stew. In a voice of silvered steel, she laughingly announced that they had all just eaten Fifi's adored rabbit, Hasi.

During her childhood Fifi repressed any outward manifestation of hurt to her self-esteem for not being loved as a daughter, or at times for apparently not being loved at all. Instead, no doubt as a subconscious way of receiving parental approval, she became a fearless and adventurous tomboy, taking intense pleasure in the outdoor life at Seifenmühle, her great-grandfather's large feudal estate near Troppau.

Seifenmühle was a small, pretty village, popular with the people from Troppau, who spent their Sundays and holidays picnicking and strolling along the river banks. Weisshuhn's continued prosperity at the turn of the century had enabled him to buy two country estates there, on one of which he built a summer house. It was named the 'Villa Friederike' and was a gigantic Swiss chalet set in the midst of a beautiful valley by the River Mohra. Covered in ivy, it was a rambling labyrinth built of birch and pine. Throughout the summer, the walls resounded with the chatter and laughter of the various aunts, uncles and cousins who came to stay. As they were too numerous to stay all at once, members of the Weisshuhn clan arrived in relays for their holiday: young cousins from England, decked out in straw boaters and pinafores; elderly widowed aunts from every corner of Austria, dressed in silk and muslin; and stout, cheerful uncles from Germany, Czechoslovakia, Yugoslavia and Poland, sporting felt hats and tweed britches. There were bound to be a number of strays in such a large family, but the few illegitimate offspring were also taken in and welcomed.

Summer days were crowded with all the adventures which fill the pastel dreams of childhood. Fifi and Traute led their mother and grandmother on long rambles into the woods behind the house to seek out the telltale crimson of ripe strawberries. A barefoot Fifi, accompanied by her closest playmate and cousin, Peter, was always the first to ride one of the pet donkeys which pulled her great-grandmother's small wicker cart out into the fields to forage for mushrooms hidden amongst the ribbons of wild grass. Numerous fancy-dress parties and family celebrations took place. Each evening after dinner, the wooden doors of the drawing room were thrown open to catch the breeze; the scent of hyacinths and roses rested lightly on the night air as the family crowded round the piano.

Fifi spent many weekends at Seifenmühle, deer-hunting with the men in the family. But, for the rest of her life, she recalled her horror when, aged fifteen and out with the family gamekeeper, she shot and killed a young roebuck while it stood completely still in a forest glade, nostrils quivering for signs of danger. The gamekeeper, pleased with her accurate shooting, snapped off a small branch from the nearest pine tree, dipped it in the roebuck's blood and gave it to Fifi as a measure of his approval. Although a photograph of her with the dead animal slung on a pole shows her smiling proudly, she always maintained that the senseless killing made a deep impression on her and she vowed she would never kill again for sport. Throughout her life the memory of the roebuck's death brought about instant tears: 'That night my uncle, who was then head of the family, stood up at the end of the dinner table and said, "Congratulations, Fifi, on bagging your first buck." I was ashamed and shocked but could not talk about it. We were not allowed to talk about those sorts of things – people might think one was neurotic. I certainly do not think I am neurotic.'

2

Betrayal

It had become customary in the summer to employ teachers to tutor the many cousins staying at Seifenmühle. One day, when Fifi and Traute were eleven and twelve, a handsome young tutor from Vienna arrived at the door, carrying a large battered suitcase, a hat to shade him from the midsummer sun and a pile of books under his arm. He was a teacher from the *Volksschule* who, in need of extra money and fond of the beauty of the area, had applied for a holiday job. His name was Hans Hofman. Everybody who came to know Hans immediately fell under his spell. He had large blue eyes, a long nose and a mop of unruly, straw-coloured hair. His manner was easy-going yet polite and he was considered by all to be a perfect charmer. Hans possessed an infectious sense of humour, an intelligent, inquisitive mind and found time to listen attentively to the excited children's tales of their exploits. The most visible flaw to his character, and one which was greatly to affect his later life, was his virulent anti-Semitism. He would stress that Hofman only had one 'f', two being the Jewish spelling.

Hans's presence stirred the already restless Frau Gessner. She and her husband had grown further and further apart, and a final attempt to bear the longed-for son had produced a third daughter, Dorle, in 1919. For years Traute had carefully drawn a veil over her emotions and pretended her life was as calm as a mountain lake. But now the ripples of attraction she felt became obvious. Everyone in the household found Hans's good looks and carefree behaviour appealing; he brought an invigorating vitality into their lives. But the affection Traute felt quickly deepened into a powerful arousal for the first time in her sheltered life. Hans, in turn, found himself drawn to her pretty, vivacious face, her zest and devil-may-care insouciance. They soon discovered their own sympathetic world away from the activities of the others: the intimacies of a shared love of poetry, afternoon walks and lengthy discussions of

Traute's marital discontent. Within a short time they had fallen deeply in love.

The Weisshuhn family, used to marital disappointment and friction in their ranks, at first took little notice of the lovers. As the summer wore on, however, the love affair took a more serious turn, and Fifi and her elder sister became aware of the growing distance between their parents. Victor Gessner spent more and more time by himself in Troppau, burying himself in his work and considering the implications of a separation. His only comfort was the occasional visit of Dorle, now an affectionate and adventurous two-year-old. Within a year, unconcerned by the stigma of scandal, Traute had left her husband and run off to Vienna to be with Hofman. She was a resolute woman with an independent spirit who had finally found the love of her life.

The break-up of her parents' marriage, the ensuing divorce and her mother's remarriage to Hans Hofman changed Fifi's relationship with her mother for ever. Her heart seemed to crystallize into a small, tight knot. She and her sisters developed a deep hatred for their new stepfather. However delightful he had first appeared, he had stolen their beloved mother, caused great unhappiness to their poor father and themselves, and effectively cut their young lives in half.

This increasing hostility was bound to have an effect on Hans's natural affection for the children and, although he remained friendly towards them, he had no intention of having three sullen youngsters living under his roof. Their mother, completely engrossed in her new-found love, appeared singularly unconcerned as to where her children should live. After an unsuccessful and short-lived stay with their father, who was deeply hurt by the divorce and enveloped in his own private sorrow, it was eventually decided, in 1923, that Traute and Fifi would live in Vienna with their maternal grandmother, known to all as Oma, and her second husband, Wilhelm Pretz. Dorle would stay with her father. Neither parent made much effort to encourage close ties between the sisters after the divorce and Fifi and Traute rarely saw their father and Dorle. Father and youngest daughter became increasingly close. They lived together in a large flat in Troppau and, whenever possible, he took her with him on nostalgic trips around Europe. He never talked or opened his heart to her about the failure of his marriage to her mother and, five years later, he remarried.

The adoration which Fifi had tried in vain to bestow on her mother was now lavished on Oma, who became the rock on which all the girl's hopes and feelings fastened. For the first time Fifi felt she had captured an adult heart that loved her for herself. Oma was a fine woman. She possessed all the virtues of superior grandmothers who manage to bridge the gap of misunderstanding so often found in the relationship between mother and daughter. Fifi adored her. Oma's intelligence and warm nature comforted and encouraged her in ways her mother had never been able to. Oma weathered Fifi's moods, surly impudence and anger at her mother with equanimity and good humour. When she grew up, Fifi was convinced that the presence of any fine, upstanding qualities she had were all due to the loving care of her grandmother.

Oma placed total trust in her two grandchildren and never set limits on their freedom. Such benevolence only served to strengthen the close bond between them. Slowly Fifi's formidable strength of character began to manifest itself. The sense of lonely isolation which had previously engulfed her now gave way to a determination to prove herself. At the school she attended for three years she became highly competitive. Yet she remained shy and reserved with those outside her immediate circle. Few of the girls she knew at school were ever invited home in the holidays. Consequently, she had few friends in Vienna, preferring her own company; she reserved her affections mostly for her grandmother and, to a far lesser extent, her elder sister.

Fifi continued to pay occasional visits to her father and younger sister in Troppau, but the visits were strained and unproductive. Her loyalty to her father was tenuous and only resulted from the raw desperation she felt at her mother's betrayal. Dorle recalls that her sister, at the age of thirteen, had grown into a wilful adolescent who was frequently rude to their father: 'Fifi was cheeky but she could be very charming. One could fall in love with her, even as a child. But I think my sister was ashamed of our parents, and particularly our father, because they were not that high up on the social scale.' Her insolence did not anger Victor Gessner; it only deepened his sadness.

By the age of fifteen, Fifi had become bored with the restrictions placed on her strong personality at school and felt that her ambitions were not being encouraged by her teachers. With her grandmother's approval, she left to devote all her energies for the next few years to a musical career. By now she had grown into an attractive young girl, brimming with energy and with definite ideas about what she wanted out of life. There was no doubt that she had inherited her mother's zest and enthusiasm. She had grown tall and strong-limbed and had straight blonde hair which was cropped short so that it fell in a slight curl below her ears. She possessed a pair of wide, cornflower-blue eyes, which, like her mother, she used to disarming effect, and she had her mother's high, rounded cheeks, determined chin and pert, turned-up nose. Hers was a face which, though full of character and expression, just missed being remarkably pretty on account of her mouth, which was straight and thin-lipped. The beauty of the family was her sister, Traute, who had the serene face of a Madonna.

But what Fifi's face may have lacked in conventional beauty was more than made up for by her stunning figure. Though her bosom was not as large as Traute's and her countenance not as lovely, hers was the body that men stared at when the two girls walked down the street. Mary Pottersch, a cousin to whom Fifi was particularly close, recalls her joking, 'Just think, if we swapped faces how marvellous I'd be !' She also remembers Fifi's pantherine grace as they walked along the main shopping street of Vienna, arm-in-arm, one fine spring day. The trailing cars slowed down as they passed the two girls. A young man rushed after them. When he was abreast of the blonde with the amazing figure he exclaimed : 'I wondered what you looked like from the front and just had to see you. Every man who has passed you has turned round.' Mary says : 'At the time Fifi was only sixteen but she had great sex appeal even though she was totally unconscious of this and did nothing to encourage it. She looked just like a Ziegfeld Follies girl. She should have gone on stage and had an audience of thousands. She'd have loved it.'

The two spent their spare time rushing round the weathered, grey-stone city, exploring the art galleries and visiting the museums. In one they came across frescoes dating from the days of Nebuchadnezzar, King of ancient Babylon. Fifi was intrigued by one particular painting. Around the necks of the painted lions and leopards, which were tied to the steps of the palace, were elaborate collars. Excitedly, she turned to Mary and begged her to look, for she was curious as to how this ancient civilization had tamed such wild creatures.

Music and other artistic pursuits took up most of Fifi's day. She was never idle for a moment. She practised the works of Beethoven and Bach daily on the piano. If she was not polishing her scales and studying the history of music as well as composition and the intricacies of harmony and counterpoint for her State Piano Certificate, she could be found painting and sketching. Otherwise she spent her time crocheting, threading beads or making a dress on her grandmother's sewing machine. To each she applied the same seriousness and determination, and while it was a happy time for her, she always wanted more out of life and was forever pursuing rainbows and searching for answers. Fifi was determined to succeed. But it was not to be in the musical field. During the two years' hard work towards her final exam, she strained both her hands, the span of which had turned out to be too small for those of a concert pianist. Although she passed, her handicap would never allow her to reach the top and so Fifi, who never wanted to be second best in anything, renounced the idea of a life in the musical world. Left with no firm plans for a satisfying career, she embarked on a two-year course in dressmaking and, at the same time, spent her evenings at life-drawing classes.

In summer, Oma and her two granddaughters still made the yearly pilgrimage to Seifenmühle. Traute Gessner occasionally came to stay – a special memory for Dorle: 'I missed my mother and longed to be with her in the summer. I can remember when I was twelve having to leave Seifenmühle and go back to Troppau to my stepmother. She stayed on with my two sisters. I nearly died for crying.'

At eighteen, Fifi was a combination of sophistication and vibrant girlishness. But however much she loved her childhood home and its pleasures, her quicksilver spirit was no longer content with days of sport. Instead, she took lessons with a neighbouring sculptor, Herr Kapps, a friend who had made the family tomb in Troppau. Delighted to be tutoring such an attractive young pupil, he spent many hours teaching Fifi how to release a pleasing figure from a lumpen piece of wood. In the process, he began to find her own figure distinctly pleasing. Fifi, caught up in a new artistic passion, affected total ignorance and continued with her sculptures. But Kapps was unable to control his ardour and fell madly in love. The Weisshuhn family were unamused and, while he was still completing his sculptural ode to his new-found muse, portraying Fifi as the Virgin Mary, Oma came swiftly into the studio one day and removed her granddaughter. By now Fifi was well aware of her attractiveness, and this episode heralded her sexual awakening.

3

Butterfly Days

Back in Vienna, Fifi continued to pursue her interest in sculpture, but she also flitted from one new artistic endeavour to another. There was a certain frantic edge to her days as she dabbled in dancing classes and photography and travelled to Italy with her Uncle Karl and his mistress. Life with Oma and Traute was no longer the peaceful haven it had been for so many years. The two girls had always been treated as beloved daughters by their grandmother but recently Heinz, her son by Wilhelm Pretz, and his wife Gretel had moved into the flat. Within a short time Heinz became obsessively jealous of his nieces. Apart from minding his mother's continual outpourings of care and love, he begrudged every penny she spent on them.

Fifi's contact with her parents continued to be sporadic and unsatisfactory. She rarely saw her father and, however hard her mother tried to get her to accept her stepfather, Fifi still harboured a passionate loathing for him and only visited her mother when she knew Hans was away from the house.

On a cold day in the winter of 1929, while Fifi was working in a photographer's studio, the phone rang. It was her mother. Unused to such consideration from her, Fifi immediately knew something out of the ordinary had happened and her spirits sank. In an offhand voice, her mother informed her quickly that her father had died of leukaemia and that his spleen would be exhibited in the Prague Medical Museum. Then the line went dead. Once again Fifi was devastated by the insensitivity of the woman who had given birth to her.

The shock of her father's untimely death, her guilt at not having tried harder to become close to him as she grew older, combined with deep offence at her mother's cold-hearted announcement, resulted in a breaking point in the relationship between daughter and mother. Fifi refused to spend Christmas with her mother and stepfather and from then on saw little of either of them. Instead, she plunged into a series of unsatisfactory affairs with fellow students, which may have taught her the basics of being 'good in bed', as a future lover described her, but only confused her already troubled soul.

In her isolation Fifi also turned to her sculpting. In the year of her father's death, when Fifi was nineteen, she made another lifelong friend, Susanne Peschke-Schmutzer, who was a talented sculptor. They often worked together in Susanne's studio, where Fifi became oblivious to time and spent the whole day engrossed in woodcarving.

'Fifi was an extremely talented sculptor. She preferred making sculptures of animals to people, and her very first was of Plinkus, a dachshund her grandmother had given her in order for her to have something of her own to love. Often Fifi would work the whole day beside me in my studio, and then, poof, she would leave quite suddenly. She was very attractive to men and she could be extremely friendly, especially if she wanted something.'

The two kept up a correspondence, Fifi once writing many years later of her humble admiration for Susanne's achievements. Rarely one to defer to a female contemporary, it was highly unusual for her to declare that her respect was such that it left her feeling inadequate and prepared to surrender to her friend's superior qualities.

Fifi was also taking private lessons with a sculptor named Professor Frass. He was highly talented, about fifty years old, had wild, white hair and worked in a studio in the Prater, the large Viennese park which had once been the hunting forest of the Imperial family. He instantly became good friends with his young student, teaching her the complicated demands of successful sculpture, from the careful design of the figure to the final execution in whichever medium was used – stone or marble, bronze or wood. From her tutor Fifi learned that patience and dedication were essential and that no short cuts were permissible. She became morbidly preoccupied with expressing, through her sculpture, her attitude and reactions to death.

Yet there was time for amusement and laughter as well. One of the highlights of the season in Vienna was the *Gschnas*, the famous fancy-dress ball which was the favourite of the Bohemian crowd. Here an exclusive circle of people, from archdukes to artists, rubbed shoulders. Professors mingled with aristocrats, actors tangoed with countesses. For three nights running different bands belted out the popular music of the day to couples keen on the foxtrot and the Charleston. The proceeds from each evening went to help painters and sculptors.

Fifi's singularly outrageous costumes always managed to get noticed at the *Gschnas*. They were imaginative, artistic and stylish. She went as a Russian candlestick or a harlequin, and once in a garment made of white linen covered in dramatic red embroidery – the traditional costume of Silesia.

It was at the *Gschnas* ball that Fifi, looking glamorous and excited, was swept into her first serious love affair. As she was dancing with a student friend, a hand touched her lightly on her bare shoulder. She turned round to see the laughing eyes of a masked Apache. With the romantic opening line : 'You are mine,' she was whirled off around the dance floor and into an affair which she later described as, 'arousing emotions sometimes almost beyond what I could bear'. Within an hour the young couple left the ball, went out into the cold night and, suiting Fifi's impetuous nature, ran off to Italy for two weeks.

For the next two years Fifi was involved for the first time with a young man who felt as deeply as she did. Her lover was Jewish, the dark-haired son of a bank president, with a wild, bohemian streak which greatly appealed to Fifi. His Jewish background naturally horrified the stern anti-Semite Hans Hofman, who had become a Nazi sympathizer and refused to meet him. This, in turn, infuriated Fifi, who felt great compassion for the Jewish plight. Hofman's blinkered attitude ensured that Fifi remained hostile to him for the rest of his life.

The couple's relationship strengthened, and then Fifi became pregnant. Her lover was unable to contemplate having a child to look after and they agreed that she should have an abortion. The illegal, back-alley operation nearly killed her, and its tragic result was that Fifi was never able to bear a child. It was to be one of the great sadnesses of her life. Soon after the operation, her lover abandoned her. Fifi felt in danger of the roots of her strong spirit being torn away by continual sadness and pressure. During her young life she had always had her catholic interests and inner strength to fill any gaps of solitude, but as hard as she tried, she was now unable to chase away the silences.

For all Fifi's enthusiasm and varying interests, hers was a paradoxically empty life. She had lost her father, her mother had trampled on her affections, she had been deserted by her married lover and she had been forced to get rid of her child. Always gutsy, she managed to suppress many of her fears and continued to show an ebullient, sparkling personality to the world. Her anguish remained unknown to most of her friends and family, with the exception of her grandmother. Only Oma recognized that she was dwelling too deeply on her growing distress and that she was unable to reconcile herself to her loss. Melancholia constantly followed her.

In the midst of all this soul-searching, Fifi also found it increasingly difficult to confront her inordinate fear of death. One day she came face to face with its reality; as she was being driven through the streets of Vienna by a friend, a drunken man staggered in front of the car and was killed. Fifi was traumatized by the accident and became haunted by the memory of the damaged legs of the corpse splayed across the street. It was the final blow to her fragile psyche. She fell into a deep depression and days of complete immobility turned into months. As she grew nearer to a complete breakdown, she became less able to cope with the calamities and surprises which life continually tossed up for her. The pattern, familiar to those suffering from mental disturbance, of isolation and alienation, slowly spread its claws round her mind. Sensing no purpose to her days, emotionally exhausted and wishing to disappear from the world, Fifi attempted suicide by taking a handful of pills. Her sister Dorle was 'sure that Fifi just wanted to die after the loss of her lover and her baby'.

Oma found her lying unconscious on her bed and took her to hospital to have her stomach pumped. Shocked and frightened by her favourite granddaughter's narrow escape, Oma sought the advice of other members of the family and it was decided that Fifi might be helped by the new science of psychiatry. She was quickly bundled off to a well-known psychoanalyst in Vienna. Her active mind was always suggestible and she should have made a perfect candidate, but her forceful nature made her unwilling to open the Pandora's box of her childhood. Although her father had left her immediate circle when she was twelve and it is doubtful whether dressing and behaving like a boy for a short period caused her any permanent damage, the stubborn denial that the traumas of her youth were responsible for much of her mercurial temperament had been cultivated over such a long period that she could no longer adapt. Fifi dutifully lay on the psychoanalyst's couch each day, trying to explain her complex thoughts and understand her recent actions; but she became increasingly impatient at the analyst's preoccupation with, and questions about, her childhood, which she regarded as irrelevant.

Deriving little comfort from the analyst's Freudian assumptions, Fifi left after a year to find another lifesaver. When the second psychoanalyst also failed to unscramble her complex problems, she abandoned any idea of the practice as a solution: '... the only advice I had been given was to get married. But it made me aware of the danger of attributing deep significance to the most natural reactions.'

Once she persuaded her sister Dorle to accompany her: 'She was extremely depressed and wanted to introduce me to analysis. I went only once, but I was treated like a criminal. I think my sister suffered because she asked too much of people and they did not, or could not, give her what she wanted. You cannot expect everyone to give you what you need. But Fifi did. I would have liked to have told her that, but I could not as it was only in the last few years of her life that we became friendly.'

While she was receiving treatment, Fifi also attended daily lectures on psychiatry, but delving into the abnormalities of mental illness only served to deepen her fear and confusion. She befriended a few students in the medical faculty of the university, who urged her to join them in their studies. Like a shipwrecked sailor clutching on to a rotting piece of driftwood, she began to embrace the idea that she could only be saved by a life in the medical field. She immediately deserted the effort of wresting invisible bones and muscles from pieces of wood in favour of secretly dissecting the tissues and tendons of a frozen corpse on a cold slab. However, the mathematical studies necessary for entrance to university were beyond a woman who became easily bored. To distract herself from the dark forces which threatened to swamp her, she went to the other extreme by starting to search seriously for fun. She was twenty-three years old.

Fifi spent many weekends in the Alps, where she stayed in different chalets with parties of friends. One night in the spring of 1935, a friend of hers, Herbert Tichy, a well-known mountaineer and travel writer, was begged by another man at a party in the mountains to be introduced. 'I am going to have to marry her.'

Laughing, Tichy replied, 'Ah, you may have trouble there. Fifi's the undisputed belle of Vienna.'

The keen suitor's name was Viktor von Klarwill. His casual good looks and laconic style immediately appealed to Fifi. He was eight years older than she but, now aged twenty-five, Fifi was ready for love and marriage. She would admit only to herself that her heart was still carrying the bruises from her first love affair. After skiing each day Viktor and his new girlfriend spent evenings round the blazing fire in the chalet, discussing their love of nature and wilderness, sport and the need each had to escape the rigours of city life. He imbued her with his passionate interest in birds. Throughout the spring they met every day and soon became lovers.

Viktor Isidor Ernst Ritter von Klarwill had been born in Vienna in 1902 to an upper-class, Catholic father and a Jewish mother. Until he was thirty-one he lived with his parents and, typical of many Jewish mamas, his mother Elsa spoilt her son ruinously, fussing round him and preparing his favourite dishes. He was a popular young Viennese eccentric, known to his many friends as Rufus or Ziebel. As a mutual friend of Fifi's and his rememberers: 'He was charming, educated and cultured, the nicest kind of upper-class Jew you could imagine.' He was tall and languidly built, with a shock of red hair. His thin face was not particularly handsome but 'strangely foxy-looking', with a long nose. Still, it was friendly enough and his manner was pleasant. His parents were well-off, his job as an official at the Fiat car factory in Vienna, where he had worked since he was eighteen, paid well and he had managed to accumulate a tidy sum of money. After ten years of working conscientiously at a dull job, the young man became a confidential clerk, which gave him authorization to act and sign on behalf of the firm.

But Rufus was not destined for life in an office, where he appeared singularly unambitious to climb any further rungs of the corporate ladder. Life was meant to be exciting, exacting and fun, and he wanted to lead it outdoors where his moral and physical fibre could be tested. He was a fanatical sportsman, indulging every spare moment in skiing and canoeing. With a group of friends he spent his weekends skiing in the high mountains just as the first snows were falling. Each day the men slalomed at high speed down the mountain, criss-crossing from hut to hut. A few of the girls in the party, most of whom were there as attractive and amusing evening ornaments, dressed elegantly in the latest skiing outfits and not over-concerned with their performance on the piste, begged to accompany the men on their runs. Rufus agreed, but only on the condition that they must not expect the men to slow down for them. As they struggled valiantly to keep up, the sight of skis, poles and various bits of female anatomy buried deep in the powdery snow behind them amused and exasperated the expert male skiers as they sailed over the next horizon.

'Every year the girls always fell out because they just could not manage it. But Fifi was different. She kept up,' Richard Hennings recalls his friend telling him. 'That is why Rufus married her.' Rufus was also amazed by his lover's canoeing skills, which he regarded as near Olympic standard.

A short while after they had first met, Rufus proposed to Fifi, pleading for an immediate wedding and hinting at a possible life overseas. Fifi immediately saw the advantages of a life of affluence and excitement with the adoring Jew, however different their backgrounds. Bored with mathematics and chemistry, she saw marriage as a way out of the monotony of studying and as a chance to break away from the tense, claustrophobic atmosphere surrounding Oma and her jealous son. Spurred on by visions of limitless adventures and not a little practicality, she hastily agreed, well aware that while she appreciated Rufus's protestations of eternal love, she did not feel remotely the same way about him. Her sister Dorle's intuition is that, 'It was not a great love. Her heart had never really recovered from the "masked Apache".'

Rufus's many friends were also highly sceptical about the engagement, convinced the two would prove incompatible. Their popular, gentle friend, who had a wry, mischievous sense of humour and little interest in the arts, was about to marry a bold, artistic and mercurial woman, hell-bent on personal success. A close friend of his, now dead, declared that, 'It came as a tremendous surprise to everyone of his circle in Vienna when he proposed to Fifi, since he had always appeared to have profound reservations against marriage.'

On 28 July 1935, Fifi married Rufus in the registry office of the parish of Ramsau, sixty kilometres from Vienna.

Rufus and his new wife set up home in Spitalgasse in Vienna. Their apartment, though small, was prettily furnished with modern furniture which blended well with the angular shapes of Fifi's wooden sculptures. For a while she was content to play the role of the loving wife ensnared in a cocoon of connubial bliss, but domesticity soon began to pall. To her restless eyes the most enjoyable part of the marriage was the travelling and the skiing, which they undertook together, and time spent painting, visiting galleries, museums and the opera, which she was forced, through Rufus's lack of interest, to do alone. Although Fifi insisted that the least fulfilling part of her life was the endless round of dinner parties and dances her husband enjoyed so much, she in fact took great pleasure in meeting and enthralling people who interested her.

But the couple had made the mistake often discussed by wiser, finger-wagging village crones : they had known each other for too short a time to realize that beneath the veneer of physical attraction and a few shared interests, they had little in common. A highly determined woman, in love with risk and still thirsting for personal achievement, had married a meticulous man who was not only used to being waited on, but who was adamant that he be allowed to lead his life exactly as he had before their marriage. Neither was willing to change for the other. Fifi felt she put a great deal of effort into understanding Rufus and blamed their lack of closeness solely on his behaviour which, she claimed, 'cast a shadow over our marriage'. Perhaps she did not wish to admit that, for all her high-spirited enthusiasm, at times her husband found her demanding, emotional and difficult to please. She admitted that Rufus gave her everything she wanted, but she remained dissatisfied.

Rufus was also uncertain about which career path he ultimately wished to follow. As Mary Pottersch remarked : 'Von Klarwill was difficult to have as a husband because he was not very stable as far as his career was concerned. When he first met her he was constantly changing his mind about what he wanted to do, even though on the surface he gave the impression of someone who was, if anything, too ordered.' The combined ingredients of uncertainty, stubbornness and self-justification did not make a good recipe for a lifetime together.

One of the main subjects of contention between the newlyweds was that of children. While Fifi passionately wanted to become a mother, her husband was appalled by the thought of squalling babies interrupting his organized life at such an early stage in the marriage. The topic induced vicious arguments and the strain of such a fundamental disagreement began to take its toll. Life became a battle of wills, which in the end, through pleading and occasional eruptions into volcanic displays of emotion, Fifi won. She became pregnant and felt, finally, that perhaps she had found a real purpose in life. She would have something of her own to cherish, over which she had total control and from which she would receive unconditional love.

Fifi often pondered upon the responsibilities of motherhood. Perhaps, by producing a child, she could finally revive the dormant love for her own mother, which had been twisted into anger. Like many other women, Fifi also acknowledged a hidden fear that, by becoming a mother, she would burden her child with her own awesome personality, just as her mother's equivocal character had affected her. Yet, in the early part of her pregnancy, on days when she was not feeling nauseous, she clutched her clandestine happiness to herself. Rufus could do nothing but accept the situation and try to appear pleased for her sake.

A few months later, Fifi had a miscarriage. She was devastated and sought comfort in the solitude of sculpting, feverishly creating small figures out of wood. Her husband tried to lighten her depression and console her in her sorrow, but Fifi turned away from him, having lost all enthusiasm for any of the light-hearted entertainment with which he tried to distract her.

Rufus, in turn, had his own, additional worries. As a Jew, he was becoming increasingly concerned that his homeland was no longer a safe place in which to live. Fifi talks little in her letters and papers about her feelings on the Jewish situation before the Second World War. Although she fell in love with one Jew and married another, she never referred to their backgrounds, preferring to call her husband 'a Protestant'. Before the war she seems to have befriended members of the Nazi party as she would anyone else, her sculpture teacher, Professor Frass being one. But following the injustices of the war and the devastation wrought on Troppau, Fifi retained a deep hatred of everything German and refused to speak the language unless forced to.

19

It became increasingly clear to the von Klarwills that, in order to find the seeds of a happy life, they must find their future far away from a country divided by political instability, and one which reminded Fifi of so many unhappy times. It did not really matter where in the world they emigrated – Tahiti, California, Tasmania – as long as it held the promise of adventure.

They told none of their Viennese friends. The secrecy and excitement of the gamble was cathartic in lifting the cloud surrounding Fifi's miscarriage. It brought the couple closer than they had been since the beginning of their marriage and created a mutual dependence. As they planned their covert departure, they pored over maps like schoolchildren deciding which country each will rule when crowned king.

Since they had been corresponding with a Swiss farmer who extolled the beauty and vitality of the country, the couple eventually chose Kenya. Being more radical than her husband, Fifi wished to leave immediately, but Rufus realized that if either of them took an instant dislike to this unseen country it might be embarrassing to have to return to Austria with their tails between their legs and no fixed job. However, the greatest threat to returning, which they both silently acknowledged, was that the prevailing attitude of Germany towards the Jewish population could only worsen. Although von Klarwill did not belong to the Jewish church, he had been born to a Jewish mother – reason enough to be pursued and discriminated against. The couple decided that Fifi would travel alone to Kenya to size up the possibilities of a life there. If all proved satisfactory, her husband would pack in his job and join her as soon as possible.

Superstitious and nervous about her future, Fifi consulted a fortune-teller. As the old gypsy stared into her crystal ball, her voice lifted then fell. She told Fifi that she would live in the tropics, and that she would have no children.

On 12 May 1936 Rufus stood on the quay, waving to his wife as the liner steamed out of the bustling harbour of Genoa towards Fifi's final destiny. The two had struck a fatal bargain.

4

Sea Change

By the time Fifi arrived at Kilindini Harbour, where passengers stepped from the liner into a rickety rowing boat to reach the island of Mombasa, she had already fallen under the spell of Africa. Unfortunately for the husband she had left behind, she had also fallen passionately in love with a fellow traveller.

Only three weeks before, the cold clear air of her first African dawn had caught Fifi's breath. Her senses became alert to each new sensation as random washes of purple and red streaked the sky, as if an artist's palette had been left out in the rain. Out of the mirage, date palms waved their ghostly fronds. Shallow saltpans, carved out of the sandy landscape, fringed the entrance to the deserts of Egypt, land of Pharaohs and fakirs, pyramids and friezes. The unfamiliar birdcall of white egrets echoed above her. Fifi, filled with anticipation, watched as the liner slowly sailed, like a venerable dowager, into Port Said.

The haunting, distant sound of the *muezzin* calling the faithful to prayer was drowned by the cry of eager young boys scrambling up ropes lashed to the side of the ship. With liquid-topaz eyes and large grins, they forced their pistachio nuts, fruit and small amber beads into the hands of the travellers with entreaties such as, 'I give you best price, morning price, just for you, just for you, nice person. Please.' They were impossible to resist and Fifi soon found both hands full of warm, sticky dates, the staple diet of the desert. She also bought a string of smooth, rounded amber beads for herself, fascinated by the lights reflected in the yellow resin.

Fifi stepped onto African soil for the first time with feelings of intense excitement. Port Said's harbour was a noisy, ramshackle place. The air was filled with the pungent aroma of spices and burnt coffee beans, mingled with the stench of rotting fruit and vegetables. In this town at the entrance of Suez, simple whitewashed buildings, topped by flat roofs, huddled close to each other. Women, gazing out of kohl-rimmed eyes above their black burnouses, idled in darkened doorways or drifted like silent vestals through the narrow streets. Merchants in long, colourful robes talked business. Their rough hands looked clumsy as they clutched minute porcelain cups of bitter coffee or smoked their opium pipes in the bazaar.

On leaving Port Said the ship sailed down through the narrow confines of the Suez Canal. Dusty palm trees fringed the banks and oxen pulling ancient ploughs sweated as they tilled the baked earth. After a brief stop at Port Sudan to pick up a few passengers, the vessel steamed towards the Red Sea, passing through the Gulf of Aden and finally out into the indigo waters of the Indian Ocean. From there it would follow the concave curve of Africa down to its destination.

In the languid days of sea travel, when journeys to remote parts of the world took many weeks, shipboard romance was an all-too-common part of the voyage. The combination of a holiday at sea with nothing more pressing to do than enjoy oneself, and being packed together like sun-tanned sardines with members of the opposite sex for four weeks, was bound to lead to a number of affairs, illicit or not. Days of deck tennis and quoits, swimming races and, particularly amongst the English, amusing games which customarily involved the men dressing up as women, preceded dinner in first class at the captain's table and dancing to the ship's small band.

A few hours after leaving Port Sudan, Fifi noticed a passenger who had boarded the vessel at the last stop. The newcomer stood by the rails, gazing far out to sea at the birds as they wheeled and plunged into the blue-green water. He was of medium height with brown, wavy hair receding at the temples. An equivocal smile hovered round his well-formed mouth, and he was dressed casually in a beige bush shirt and pale, well-pressed trousers. In his left eye he wore a monocle. Fifi became intrigued by his quiet good looks and reserved manner and determined to find a way to introduce herself. The next day she walked up to him on the deck tennis area, dressed in the briefest pair of shorts and a pale blue top, knotted under her bosom, which showed off her smooth, tanned midriff to advantage. With laughter in her large blue eyes, she smiled engagingly at him and said, 'Hello, welcome aboard. I'm Friederike von Klarwill.'

He turned to face this unknown woman with the strong German accent. He first noticed a sweep of short, thick hair bleached to silver-blonde by the sun. Frank, flirtatious eyes filled a face obviously a good deal younger than his own. He introduced himself as Peter Bally.

Within hours of competing in a light-hearted game of deck tennis against two other travellers, an instant attraction had been sparked between the two. Fifi would later remark, 'When I first met Peter, I felt a sharp tug at my heart and had an immediate impression that we belonged to each other. He seemed such a sympathetic person. There are some forces in us which we cannot control. I was fighting my feelings for Bally, especially as Rufus had been extremely kind and generous to me.'

Fifi's new companion was a Swiss botanist on his way to South Africa after first stopping off in Kenya to study the botanical collection in the Coryndon Museum in Nairobi. His deep knowledge of the plant world had resulted in a book on the subject, which had recently been published in his homeland. The offer of further study in Africa had excited his imagination and the distance involved would also help to separate him from the pain of an unhappy marriage to a wife he had left back in Zurich.

Over the next two weeks the couple shared their secrets and their marital problems. She listened, fascinated, to his story. A new world opened up to her as he told her of his gruelling months in India, researching the medicinal properties of herbs. He explained how he painted the flowers and plants he came across in his travels for future reference. She, in turn, excited him with her enthusiasm and dynamic approach to life, wanting to explore everything that captured her imagination. With her extraordinary verve, nothing seemed impossible.

To Fifi, Peter appeared a compassionate and sensitive man who seemed to understand both her need to excel and her continual search for fulfilment. One balmy evening after dinner, as they sat in deck chairs, the breeze from the east sweeping gently over the ship's prow, she told him of her unhappiness with her life in Vienna. She described the sorrow of her miscarriage and the frustrations of living with a man with whom she was not in love and who had, in her eyes, none of the sensibilities of the artist. She did not need to exaggerate the fears her husband held of a future in Austria. Already, rumours of proposed pogroms against his people had reached the ears of his contemporaries.

For the next few weeks each continually sought out the other. Able to spend so much time in each other's company, both by day and night, their courtship was swift and intense. The spontaneity with which they embarked upon their affair and the empathy they experienced in each other's company led Fifi to believe again in the possibility of happiness. The total ease they felt together gave the illusion they had known each other all their lives.

But facts could not be overlooked. Fifi was a married woman. She had also been entrusted by her husband with finding a new life and home for them. She felt she could not let him down. The anguish of previous love having gone sour, and the feelings of guilt that both she and Peter began

23

to suffer, were lessened by days of laughter and romance far from home as they were pulled into the spiral of new love. But however irresponsible life on the ocean could be, they both knew the path ahead was strewn with unavoidable boulders. Still, there would be time later to think about ways to solve their problems. Fifi became increasingly aware that she would never find happiness with her husband. By the time the ship reached Mombasa, however hard they tried to deny it, they knew there was no turning back.

Through the centuries Mombasa had managed to retain the raffish charm of its past. The old town of narrow, winding streets grew out under the massive shadow of Fort Jesus and down along the cliffs to the sea. The impregnable fort with its grey walls stood on an uneven mound of coral facing the sea breeze, and its brooding presence dominated the island. It had been built in the fifteenth century by the invading Portuguese and was to witness many sieges and bloody skirmishes. In the first half of the nineteenth century, at the height of the slave trade, more than 30,000 terrified Africans were captured yearly in the country's interior and whisked onto galleons moored off the reef in front of the fort. Nearby, small groves of coconut palms fringed the shore and the silver filigree branches of the baobabs guarded the secrets of the island's mysterious past.

Legends about this strange tree are passed on from the elders in the villages and it has been the subject of speculation for centuries, ever since the fruits were found in Egyptian tombs. In the dry areas of Kenya, the Lord of the Rain, Rasa, is believed to live in the large tree which holds up the sky. In Botswana the bushmen assert that the great spirit Gaua gave a tree to the first man and his descendants. But he refused to give one to the most evil of creatures, the hyena. The hyena complained that it was no wonder he behaved badly when he was treated so differently from others. To placate the beast, Gaua finally gave him the last plant. The hyena, out of spite, promptly planted it upside down, leaving the roots in the air.

In the western countries of Africa two centuries ago, the tree was used as a tomb. Poets, musicians, drummers and buffoons were buried in hollow trunks. There was even a baobab tree in southern Africa that was fitted out with a flush toilet by a Major Trollip during the Second World War.

Fifi and Peter explored the maze of Arab shops and houses in Mombasa's narrow streets. The smell of fish and the open gutters, which ran down beside the buildings, hung in the hot sultry air. Each hour offered different smells : fresh and rotting fruit, sweat, incense. The walls of the whitewashed houses, like all Swahili homes in the small town, were cut coral. Their thickness kept out the heat of noon and they were cool to the touch. The couple peered through elaborate doorways, carved on the nearby islands of Lamu and Zanzibar; into courtyards filled with chickens and barefoot children with rings in their noses. Against a background of brightly patterned carpets and clothes hung out to dry, the scarlet flowers and dangling pods of coastal acacia trees moved in the breeze. The newness of it all enthralled Fifi. Beside the road she saw for the first time the dark, rounded leaves of the mango trees pulled down by the weight of their fruit, like fattened raindrops falling from the tips of a giant umbrella. The shady foliage protected the natives from the sun as they sat on their haunches on the ground beneath, playing *bau*, an ancient African game using plump seeds or pebbles on a wooden board.

In the cool of the early evening, at the time of day when the noise of the crows became most persistent, the couple watched Indian families in silks and saris stroll along the seafront. Out to sea a thin line of white horses rippled along the edge of the reef. The graceful lateen sails of the ancient dhows, which plied the waters between Persia and Zanzibar, cut through the horizon. Along the dusty road, bare-breasted Giryama *bibis* (women) with short, full skirts made out of sisal, balanced tin *debbies* of water on their heads as they hurried to reach their villages before nightfall. It would be the couple's last night together for many months. Fifi was to stay with the Swiss farmer in the highlands and Peter would be stopping off in Nairobi. They were booked on the Mombasa train, which would travel slowly through the night before reaching the capital next morning.

The single platform at the station was enveloped in good-humoured confusion. Turbanned Sikhs with flowing beards leaned out of the carriage windows and shouted instructions to their vast families to 'Come this way, hurry, hurry', while Africans, burdened with bundles of belongings tied up with rope, struggled towards third-class carriages. Europeans had a much easier time of it. They were shown by porters eager to make a few shillings to their comfortable compartments in the first-class section of the train.

As the train pulled slowly out of the station, a crescendo of farewells and frantic hand-waving filled the platform. A sea of heads, white, brown and black, strained out of the windows, until their adieus were consumed by the clackety-clack of the wheels reverberating along the track. As the tropical lowlands disappeared from view, curving palm trees, coral buildings and mangrove swamps gave way to tattered banana groves and thatched mud huts surrounded by clumps of mango trees. Tall grasses with blades as sharp as razors hid the smallest animals. The grey, scarred trunks of giant baobab trees, serene in their solitude, stood out like rooted elephants at dusk.

Night falls abruptly on the equator. One moment the sun is on fire, like a large molten orange sitting on the edge of the world. Flames of gold and crimson warm the sky before the night claims it. Within minutes the sun's curiosity has got the better of it. It slips over the horizon to see what lies beyond and melts swiftly into the night.

The railway line from Mombasa to Nairobi had once been a coolie's nightmare and was known as the 'Lunatic Express'. In 1895 cheap labour had been imported from India to help construct the tracks. As soon as the building of the line reached Tsavo, famous for its man-eating lions, all hell broke loose. Coolies were dragged off into the bushes, where the animals would first lick off the skin of their unfortunate victims in order to taste the fresh blood, before cracking their limbs and eating their flesh.

However, train journeys in Kenya just before the Second World War were an easy-going undertaking. Trains were stopped at the slightest pretext, to let passengers shoot or photograph animals. One famous story, told in Elspeth Huxley's *White Man's Country*, concerned Lord Delamere, who arrived at a station with his bull terrier bitch and a litter of four puppies, which he was taking to Nairobi. In getting them comfortably settled he forgot to purchase tickets for either himself or the dogs. When the train had gone, the station master telegraphed a warning to Nairobi: 'The Lord is on the train with one bitch and four sons of bitches. No tickets. Please collect.'

Fifi and Peter's sleeper compartment was neat and clean. As soon as it was dark, the bedrolls were prepared by a porter, who took great pride in turning down the corners of the crisp white sheets with infinite precision. At 7 p.m. precisely, the first call for dinner came. From the corridor the sound of a hypnotic tune on a gong reached the couple long before its bearer. Soon a splendid steward appeared, immaculately dressed in a white *kanzu* (kaftan), with a red cummerbund round his rotund stomach and a smart red fez. After beaming at the occupants he continued swaying along the pitching corridor with his music.

Over dinner, the couple made their plans. Fifi would go back to her husband in Vienna and discuss the situation. Peter would remain in Africa and wait for her to join him. Back in their compartment, Peter held Fifi close. She was tearful at the thought of leaving her lover and confused about what to tell her husband. They made love with all the tenderness that fills the hearts of torn lovers and slept fitfully as the rattling train repeatedly jerked to a halt throughout the night.

Dawn had hardly broken when Fifi and Peter woke next morning to the customary call of 'Jambo Bwana, jambo Memsahib. Chai.' The waiter brought them early-morning tea, which in Kenya could mean as early as five-thirty. They drank it, grateful for its warmth as they had reached the cold air of the higher altitude. A feeling of awe overcame them both as they looked out of the carriage window and saw for the first time the splendours of the Athi plains. Miles of tawny grass, stretching away to the purple of distant hills, were filled with animals. Herds of tail-flicking Thompson's gazelle nervously skitted away at the approach of the train. In a straight line, fat zebras slowly walked with bowed heads, as though they were following the hypnotic tune of a black-and-white Pied Piper. Two giraffes on dancer's legs stretched their graceful necks to graze on the thorny branches of the tallest acacia trees. Wildebeests, the ugly clowns of Africa, took fright at some imagined threat and careered over the undulating landscape like dark, horned demons.

As the train pulled into the dusty station of Nairobi the same chaotic conditions prevailed as at their journey's beginning. Everywhere there was shouting and bustle. Delighted cries of recognition came from nowhere. The Swiss farmer and his family, with whom Fifi was to stay, were there to meet her. For the sake of respectability, a formal and hurried goodbye was necessary in front of them – Fifi had said her intimate farewell to Peter while they were still in their carriage. They promised to write to each other. As she climbed into the family's battered old Ford, her last glance was of Peter surrounded by a number of garrulous taxi drivers haggling over the cheapest price they could offer to the Norfolk Hotel, where he would be staying.

Unknown to Fifi, Peter, although undoubtedly in love, was already wondering about the rightness of his new romantic involvement. Recognizing in Fifi a deep well of unhappiness, in addition to a possible streak of instability, he had become unsure of his commitment. Would she be a suitable partner for life? Under the pretext of helping her resolve her deep-rooted problems with Rufus, he made her agree to visit his older brother in Europe. Besides being a man of wisdom, Gustav was a prominent psychiatrist. Peter needed his brother's opinion before finally making up his mind.

Within three months of leaving, Fifi had returned to Vienna to discuss her predicament with Rufus. He had already guessed that something was wrong from reading between the lines of his wife's letters. The excitement and commitment to a future together was lacking in her prose. Instead, she had written rather too breezily of the fun she was having on the boat, of the interesting people aboard, and of the new sights and sensations of the dark continent. Nowhere in her short, hurried notes did she talk of her love for Rufus or her allegiance to their marriage; she was neither concerned about his welfare nor seemed in any great hurry to see him. He knew her well enough to realize that she was hiding something.

When she finally plucked up the courage to tell him of her new-found love for Peter Bally, Rufus was at first deeply hurt and then filled with anger at the duplicity of his wife. For the next three days he was unable to speak to her, so acute was his pain and confusion. Then he decided on a course of action. He begged Fifi to give their marriage another chance for three months. If, after that time, she was unable to find any harmony in a life together, she would be free to leave. Fifi grudgingly complied. She made an urgent appointment to see Gustav Bally, knowing privately that the arrangement with Rufus was highly unlikely to succeed. She then left to stay with friends in Zurich, where she joined students who were excavating the medieval fortifications in the Lindenhof. Since her husband was in Vienna and Zurich was some distance away, it appeared an odd way to patch up a torn relationship.

It was soon apparent, after her reluctant return from Zurich, that a reconciliation was impossible. As Fifi told a friend: 'Rufus's biggest mistake was he was always so full of self-pity. His whining complaints were endless. Because of that he lost me, as well as quite a few friends.' Whenever they were together their arguments became more heated as the different approach to life of one continued to exasperate the other. Any compassion Rufus or his wife felt for each other was lost in the emotional scenes that recurred in those few months, when the frequent slamming of doors could be heard as one or the other stormed out of the small apartment. They began to talk to each other only when absolutely necessary. In the end, Rufus capitulated. He did not have Fifi's ferocious strength and determination and, like many men married to emotional women, all he now wished for was peace and quiet. He agreed to a divorce.

According to the decree absolute, the grounds were insurmountable dislike between the two parties. Rufus declared that he was a passionate sportsman. He had dedicated all his spare time to sport before his marriage and it was a necessity which he could not do without. He also admitted that his parents, especially his mother, had pampered him and he had never had to worry about day-to-day things such as clothes or laundry. Finally, he confirmed that he was not at all interested in the arts, especially music, as he was completely unmusical.

In turn, Fifi stated that she had been brought up to be independent and was unaccustomed to accepting the duties expected of a wife. Although her husband demanded that she try to become a competent housekeeper, she had no intention of cooking, washing and ironing. Her overriding interest lay in the arts, especially music, opera and concerts, with which she could occupy herself all day long.

The two declared that such differences between them meant that their marriage could not have lasted long. Above all, however, it was their opposing attitudes to children that had made it impossible for them to live together.

On 18 December 1937 the couple were duly divorced. Just three months later, on 12 March 1938, Fifi sailed for Kenya and her longed-for reunion with Peter Bally.

5

Kenya

Kenya, in 1938, was thought of by many as the promised land. Under a larkspur sky, which gave the impression of being the largest on earth, lay a landscape of great natural beauty and variety. The country was overflowing with wild animals, which roamed the plains and forests, hunted for centuries by exotic tribes; it was also blessed with fertile grazing and farming soil for crops of coffee, pyrethrum, tea, timber, sisal and maize.

Thirty years previously, the first wave of white settlers had moved like a small, determined column of safari ants onto the land. Few places on earth promised so much to the senses – cerebral, physical or sensual. A generosity of spirit permeated the land. Excitement and sexual tension hung in air like a tropical thunderstorm. Perhaps the aura of mystery that seemed to enfold the country had slowly evolved over the years from a sense of balance between the vitality of the people and the haunting majesty of the landscape; between the alien customs and mythology of the tribes and the danger from animals in the wild. Bonuses were added: the steady rhythm of Africa, of sunshine and sultry nights and rain on corrugated iron roofs; the sense of limitless freedom and adventure.

Until the arrival of the white population, tribal life continued as it had for centuries; dignified, often hard, and steeped in traditional values. The Land Act dramatically changed the status quo. Millions of acres of prime highland soil were sold for minuscule amounts to eager European buyers. In return, these early pioneers struggled for years, often unsuccessfully, to tame the land to produce bountiful harvests and to rid their livestock and crops of disease and pestilence.

The capital, Nairobi, was a small, bustling town. In 1899 its roads and alleyways had been haphazardly snatched from a windswept papyrus swamp, inhabited by lions and mosquitoes and named *Engore Nayrobe* – Place of Cold Water – by the Maasai. The Wild West atmosphere of this frontier town was augmented by a broad main street, which ran in a straight line from the station to the best hotel, the Norfolk. It was from here that the man who became the leader and political guru of the settlers, the diminutive, eccentric Lord Delamere, his long titian hair cascading down to his shoulders, developed a penchant for galloping on his horse from one end of town to the other, shooting out as many street lights as possible. The Norfolk had a certain cachet as a watering hole and playground for licentious members of the aristocracy. It was also renowned as the departure point for the first hunting safaris, when wealthy sportsmen, complete with a large retinue of native porters, set forth into the untamed land that they knew was teeming with trophies.

Everywhere in the capital there was movement and colour, noise and confusion. Although the sassy hooting of box-body Fords could be heard, very occasionally young Africans were still seen pulling their rickshaw passengers down Delamere Avenue, the main thoroughfare, the rhythm of their anklet bells mixing with the sounds and putrid smells of the sprawling Indian bazaar. Wooden bungalows and offices with corrugated tin roofs, shaded by the sea-grey leaves of eucalyptus trees, sprang up beside the road as rapidly as wild dandelions. In the sidestreets of the town, which were either a dusty ochre powder in the dry season or a slippery quagmire during the rains, a proliferation of flowers grew. Claret-coloured bougainvillea cascaded from rooftops, morning glory twined round barbed-wire fences, and a halo of dark green leaves protected the pale, fleshy petals of the frangipani.

Slim, turbanned Somalis, with thin blankets slung over their ebony shoulders, stood like sentinels on street corners, often on one long leg with the other tucked up behind, as was their custom. Women in colourful *kangas* (sarongs), with baskets of mangoes and maize cobs balanced on their heads, greeted each other as they weaved their way through the throng to the native market. Commercially oriented Indian merchants, assiduously chewing betelnut, counted the shillings from the takings of their straggling *dukas* (shops). Fine-boned Maasai youths, naked except for a loose red *shuka* (cloth falling from one shoulder) and a smattering of beads around their necks and wrists, paraded amongst farmers, civil servants, Boers and restless adventurers.

Nairobi possessed a certain charm. The highlights of the year were race weeks, when an air of excitement rippled through the town's dusty streets. Europeans, hungry for amusement, descended like locusts for days and nights of frivolity, where schoolboy antics and boisterous behaviour were not only forgiven, but encouraged. Many who arrived were accompanied by servants smartly dressed in starched white *kanzus*, green embroidered waistcoats and cummerbunds. Each proud head sported a red fez, and together they moved as would a group of silent but obedient Ottoman pashas. Outside the perimeters of the town, the herds of zebra and wildebeest, giraffe and gazelle, kept a silent vigil in the dark.

Nairobi's most famous landmark was the Ngong Hills, which lay south-west of the town. Four uneven, rounded peaks rippled across the top of the grassy ridge, looking like knuckles of soapstone worn smooth by the forces of time. In the changing light of day, there was a mysterious quality to the blue of the hills, drawing the eye down to the dark creases of forest below the peaks, where the buffalo and antelope hid. On the far side, where the roots of the hills grew deep into the Rift Valley, the winds of a thousand years blew gently over the earth.

When Fifi arrived to settle in Kenya, she was well aware that the country had acquired a certain risqué reputation for bacchanalian pleasures and that there were a number of people living there who wanted nothing better than amusement and a good time. The legend of sybaritic days in Happy Valley had lived on since the 1920s. The question was repeated in dark, suggestive tones over countless dinner tables: 'Are you married or do you live in Kenya?' It was taken for granted that whether they looked like Garbo, Gable or the back end of a Mombasa bus, anyone from Kenya was insatiable enough to dispense with all formalities when it came to seduction. They were ripe for sex, would be willing to fling all their clothes off in the middle of the Muthaiga Club or Piccadilly Circus and be swiftly propelled towards the nearest horizontal surface.

There were those both in Nairobi and the White Highlands who did, indeed, succumb to every temptation offered by 'the three A' s' – altitude, alcohol and adultery. In the 1920s, a small number of English aristocrats had bought land along the Wanjohi river in the Aberdare Mountains. Through the reputation of the lotus eaters, which spread far and wide, the area came to be known as Happy Valley. Their notorious antics took place in settlements around the mountain of Kipipiri, which loomed at the head of the river, and the infamous Muthaiga Club in Nairobi.

One by one, privileged young men and women, often beautiful and rich, arrived to settle in an exotic land far from home. With the speed of amorous lizards they also settled on each other. Relieved to escape the drabness of postwar Britain, they shed their clothes, morals and inhibitions with equal alacrity and abandoned themselves in droves to the pursuit of the sensual – willing flesh, however transient; novel experiences, however banal. Worldly pleasures and erotic passions were considered passports to happiness. Cocaine and morphine were taken as lightly as a glass of chilled champagne. Some played at farming and politics but, accustomed to the durable rites of privilege, most reserved any energy they had left from nights of debauchery for polo, backgammon, horse racing and pink gins at the Muthaiga Club. Despite their considerable charm and breeding, they were a rum bunch. In their hedonistic pursuit of pleasure not a few turned out to be adulterers, liars, alcoholics, murderers, sadists, wastrels, suicides and of course, remittance men.

For most of the year the majority of Europeans were hard-working individuals. It was not that they did not appreciate a rousing good party, pretty women or a few too many whiskies at the club; it was simply that most settlers were far too occupied supervising their farms, ensuring the health of their cattle and crops and worrying about market prices, to spend much time trying to lure their neighbour's wife into the chicken shed. Officials in the field were often swamped with work. Besides producing endless reports to appease the bureaucrats in Nairobi, provincial and district commissioners spent their days travelling throughout their prescribed territories; attending *barazas* (public meetings), where they listened to the needs and complaints of the tribal chiefs and elders; quelling disturbances between warring factions of the tribes, and generally seeing that law and order reigned. In persistently difficult areas, there was always the threat of a spear performing a neat lobotomy on the prevailing DC unless great tact was employed.

The Aberdares lay in the heart of the White Highlands. The pungent smell of cedar enfolded the dark, sweeping forest. Mist hung heavy in the early morning. Scattered on the slopes of the dew-laden mountains stood the *mugumo* trees, the huge wild fig sacred to the Kikuyu god and revered by his people. The paler green olive trees struggled to escape the giant shadow of the cedars in a bid for a patch of sunlight of their own. Wisps of woodsmoke from huts deep in the forest circled upwards, seeking a path through the dense foliage. With the rising of the sun, the crisp air of the Highlands smarted in the nostrils. The nights were cold and the people warmed themselves around fires of pine and cedar. To the west, the escarpment fell away to the pastures and billowing brooks of the Wanjohi valley. The landscape and the light which surrounded it were breathtakingly beautiful, a mixture of bucolic gentleness and primeval wilderness. Vast stretches of grassland were interrupted by steep cliffs and mountains, which soared from the centre of the earth. To the east lay the bamboo groves and glaciers of Mount Kenya and on the other side of the valley stood the high slopes of the Kinangop. Beyond that, like the angry wound of a giant's axe severing the country in two, ran the massive trough of the Rift Valley.

The first to buy land in the Highlands had been Hugh Cholmondeley, the arrogantly confident third Baron Delamere. Some years later, another aristocrat, Lord Francis Scott, second son of the Duke of Buccleuch, followed his example. Both proved to be remarkable men who toiled hard to shape Kenya's future, eventually becoming the white backbone of the fledgling colony.

The Baron was also a passionate champion of the Maasai and had been initiated as a blood brother. These Nilotic people were immensely courageous, often single-handedly killing a lion with their long spears and taking enormous risks in battle. While their women bore their children and the brunt of the heavy work, the vain young warriors of the tribe, the Moran, grew strong and healthy on a limited diet of milk and blood drawn from their cattle. The Maasai stole Lord Delamere's cattle and he continually forgave them. One by one those who lived near him filed up to his verandah each morning, their superb, painted bodies nearly naked. As the Baron chomped his way through a full English breakfast, the Maasai looked on with anticipatory giggles of delight. To start the day off he always wound up his old phonograph and, with unusual care, placed his only record on the turntable. Every day of the week the extraordinary sounds of 'All Aboard For Margate' rippled through the Highland air.

By 1938 Kenya was a thriving colony. Its status had been changed on 23 June 1920, and a good deal of development had taken place. It was a fairly light-hearted country, tough for some settlers, but for the well-heeled and flighty, an excellent playground with an intoxicating climate. The only remaining part of the protectorate was the coastal strip plus a radius of ten sea miles, which was still owned by the Sultan of Zanzibar and rented to the British. The population of Nairobi was now approximately 50,000, 7,000 of whom were European.

Kenya had always been regarded by the white community from Britain as a place for the upper-middle class and above, in that idiosyncratic class system so seldom understood by other nationalities. After the 1914–18 War, a Soldier Settlement scheme was introduced, encouraging ex-servicemen and women to live in Kenya. Those who cared about such matters claimed that the officers went to Kenya and the enlisted ranks to Rhodesia. There was some truth in this, even though much of the claim was fostered by people in Kenya who wished for grander origins.

Education for Europeans was modelled on the strict lines of the British public school and there was plenty of adventure for those who continually wanted to be challenged. A new influx of settlers arrived and areas hitherto hardly mentioned, such as Kitale and Nanyuki, were opened up. However, disease took its toll. Severe malaria, if not treated in time, turned into black water fever, for which there was no cure, and deaths were not uncommon. In many parts of the country, it was essential to be tucked securely under mosquito nets at night.

Although the vast majority of residents in Nairobi and up-country were British, other nationalities were represented and often made successful settlers, especially the Scandinavians. A clear hierarchy existed among the Europeans. They were said to fall, like Gaul, into three parts – the government officials, the settlers and the missionaries.

The settlers suffered the normal social system that they had imported with them from Europe. By now they had long had their own parliament, the Legislative Council, and fought many a tense battle with the government and the governor, who answered only to London. The officials and the settlers regarded each other as necessary evils that had to be tolerated.

The officials, aware that they were bringing Western progress and civilization to a backwater of the Empire, ruled with a firm fist and a stiff upper lip. Amongst themselves they clung stubbornly to the comforting illusion of heightened class superiority. The community of officials, the colonial officers and their entourages, had a tight social hierarchy based on the rank of the officer, which was, in turn, mirrored in their wives. The administration was founded on a network of provincial and district officers, whose influence was absolute in their respective provinces and districts. As adjuncts to these mighty men there were prison, forestry, veterinary, medical, education, livestock, game and other officers, according to the district, all of whom had to work together and many of whom had to live together. Because of the wild nature of most of up-country Kenya, it was deemed safest and most convenient if all government officers lived in a tight village community known as the *boma*, a Kiswahili word meaning, literally 'a fenced-off area'. The grandest house naturally went to the PC, the provincial commissioner, and the others, in order of rank, accepted what was allotted them.

Social life was rigidly maintained along the same hierarchical lines. The wife of the PC was the leading lady and not a few of them were guilty of over-acting the part of fattest duck in the pond. If the local PC happened to be a relaxed fellow, then life could be lived with a certain insouciance. But, in general, this was not the case, as he was there to maintain discipline, law and order and could not afford to slacken his social position. However much this tight-knit hierarchy rankled, by and large, the unspoken rules were understood and adhered to.

The only other group of Europeans in Kenya were the missionaries, who were outside any social system. These pilgrims of the faith were regarded by both settlers and officials as slightly suspicious characters who went around 'spoiling' the Africans. With a few exceptions they kept to themselves, well fortified with Bible and belief against the social scene.

Such was the milieu that awaited Fifi, who was more than impatient to reach the seductive atmosphere of the country in which she had left her lover. Peter Bally was there to meet her at the quay in Mombasa. It was a humid day, the sky pale above the sapphire depths of the water. Peter, tanned and fit, stood among a knot of other men, all dressed in khaki bush shirts and shorts. Looking up, he anxiously scanned the faces on board. As soon as he saw Fifi he began frantically waving his wide-brimmed hat, any doubts about the future temporarily swept aside. She flew down the gangplank and fell into his arms. He laughingly swept her off her feet and whirled her round. The couple had much to tell each other. They left immediately to drive the 300 miles to Nairobi. It would take them all day to navigate the tortuous, corrugated road and both knew by the journey's end they would be exhausted and the Land Rover filled with dead flies and ripples of fine dust. As they left the old seaport behind them, the lushness of the lowlands gave way to the harsh confines of the Taru desert. Caked red earth, covered with a cobweb of parched bushes, lay either side of the road. Impatient clouds galloped across the sky as if late for a rendezvous.

As they drove, Peter and Fifi learned more of each other's lives and discussed their future. This quiet Swiss, naturally reticent and shy with women, revealed long-hidden stories of his childhood. He had inherited the blue eyes, fair, reddish curled hair and unusual pointed nose of his mother, Martha Bally-Forcart. His had been a delicate beginning and he had not learnt to walk until the age of three. Although he was a gay child, he was often ill and, when indisposed, would lie upon his bed and play with an angel of ivory. His favourite toy, and one he kept for many years, was a stuffed camel made of deerskin. He would spend hours watching a beetle, or studying the structure of a flower. When his mother's friends came to tea, he took great delight in scaring them by quietly letting a snake slither out from his sleeve or a small frog jump out of his unclenched fist.

All his life Peter Bally remained afraid of his severe, strict father, Oscar, who had been born into the upper-class Bally family which had acquired a fortune from the manufacture of shoes and leather goods. The family business held no interest for Oscar Bally's enquiring mind; he was more interested in the sciences, particularly chemistry and after graduating from university he took up a well-paid appointment as a chemist at BASF.

Within three years of marriage, his wife Martha gave birth to her second son, Peter, on 9 May 1895 in Schonwerd, Switzerland. Two more boys arrived in quick succession and Oscar, the nearest in age to Peter, became his favourite brother. All the boys spent an obedient, uneventful youth in Mannheim in southern Germany. One of the small irritations which affected Peter's confidence was his turning out to be the runt of the litter, a good few inches shorter than his three brothers.

From the beginning, Peter set his heart on studying zoology, but his wish was denied him by his austere father, who forbade him to study any subject which did not meet with parental approval. Besides, Oscar considered his son to be something of an upstart who was apt to shirk most family responsibilities. Morals of Swiss society were rigidly Calvinistic and failing to fulfil family obligations was high on the list of unacceptable transgressions.

In 1914, in the footsteps of his father, Peter studied chemistry at the University of Zurich. Much to his relief, this was interrupted for a period towards the end of the First World War when he was obliged to take up military service. Bored rigid by chemistry and the confines of life in Zurich, Peter dropped out of university, much to his father's disappointment. Eventually, in an effort to remain as far away from Bally senior as possible, he accepted, as his first paid job, the post of a secretary in Geneva at the League of Nations.

In the meantime, his father had taken on a partnership in a pharmaceutical business which had produced a new medicine against malaria. In 1924 he asked Peter to head a mission to introduce the vaccines wherever they were needed. It was the beginning of a life of travel. Through the kind auspices of his brother Oscar, who had just married and was then living in Bombay, Peter was invited there to spread the word of the new anti-malarial products. He stayed with his brother and sister-in-law in a baronial manor built in the English Tudor style in a suburb of Bombay. Never without a topee to guard him from the harsh Indian sun, he travelled around the area extolling the virtues of his father's medicines.

But the new treatment was a failure and Peter, feeling listless and unwell, was recalled to Switzerland. Storming out of his father's office after one of their typical rows, Peter found himself, at the age of thirty-one, without a job. His ill health continued and, after numerous tests at a clinic which specialized in tropical diseases, it was discovered that he was suffering from a virus contracted in India. It would take him many months to recover fully.

By 1929 Peter was fidgety and becoming increasingly anxious to find suitable employment which would fulfil his deep interest in botany. He managed to set up a visit to Tanganyika for the company of Hoffman-La Roche, in order to search for new medicinal plants – a trip that sparked off a special interest in African herbal remedies. Oscar Bally was livid when, in April 1930, his son abandoned any further thought of a life in the claustrophobic pharmaceutical world of Zurich and left for Africa as an agent for Mobil Oil in Mombasa. At last he was free to continue his research into medicinal and poisonous plants and, soon after his arrival, he published several articles about his findings. The seeds for his greatest achievements were to germinate from his dedicated botanical work in Kenya. Just before meeting Fifi, Peter had published a critically acclaimed book on some of his work in the field of African herbal remedies, *Native Medicinal and Poisonous Plants of Tanganyika*.

Fifi listened attentively to every word of her lover's story. As their Land Rover pulled them upwards towards Nairobi, there was a distinct change in the landscape. Arid terrain gave way to the subtle tapestry of sunlit foliage on the hills. Secret hideaways of riverbeds were revealed by ribbons of verdant green that followed their course. The yellow bark of tall fever trees glinted in the sun, their feathery leaves and long barbs spreading out horizontally like layers of a dancer's pale green tutu. Out of the doorways of the dung and mud huts inhabited by the Maasai, small naked children, accompanied by mangy dogs, ran laughing to the side of the road. The sight of a passing car was still a novelty and one which captivated African children.

As they reached the outskirts of Nairobi, Peter suddenly said : 'Darling, your Christian names are too much of a mouthful and your nickname is too frivolous. You make me so happy that from now on I am going to call you Joy.' She was delighted with it and the name stuck. He then went on to surprise her further : 'While you have been in Europe, I have made friends with the Director of the Coryndon Museum in Nairobi, Dr Van Someren. He has offered me the post of botanist.' Joy was thrilled. Their future in Kenya was now assured.

6

Botanist and Artist

Whatever reservations Peter Bally had about marrying Joy, he now kept them strictly to himself. His brother Gustav had written to him giving his approval and stating that, although he perceived her to be a highly strung and emotional woman, Joy was also a person of great courage, determination and vitality. It was obvious to Gustav that she was very much in love with Peter as she had explained to him that, despite their differing temperaments, she instinctively sensed they belonged together. The psychiatrist felt that Joy would make his brother a capable partner, sharing, as they did, many of the same interests and a love of the outdoor life.

It was obvious the couple were strongly physically attracted to each other and Peter, quieter and more reserved than Joy, became caught up in her enthusiasm for life. By the end of April 1938 they were married. It was the second registry office wedding for Joy, attended by two witnesses who were acquaintances of the bridegroom. Their honeymoon was to be a safari, the Swahili word meaning 'the journey of a day', which never failed to excite Joy.

Peter Bally's great interest was succulent plants, specifically the euphorbias and aloes. This interest was to become his life's work and over the years he became one of the world's greatest experts, collecting over 16,000 plant specimens during his time in East Africa. As a newly arrived botanist he had been included in a team from the museum who were researching the unexplored region of the Chyulu Hills, an arid, volcanic range lying between the main Mombasa road and Mount Kilimanjaro. Understandably, he had no intention of leaving his new wife in a strange town and the team of researchers had deemed it tactful to invite Joy to join them on the three-month safari.

Until now, Joy had zigzagged through life and, despite her many artistic interests, had never completed any formal, professional training. She was

39

determined to prove herself in some field, to find some lasting interest. In some subconscious way it was as if the importance of her husband's work would rub off on her; as if she was personally involved in its success.

The country instantly captivated Joy because of the sense of freedom it gave her, the sense of space and the promise of unexplored places. She was filled with nervous excitement as she was introduced to the specialists who were going to accompany them on the trip. Apart from Dr Van Someren, the director of the museum and a respected ornithologist, the party included a zoologist, a palaeontologist, an entomologist and a geologist. For the first time in her life Joy would taste the seductive tang of bush life. She would experience the cold dawn of Africa, when the mists shroud the roof of the world and the sounds of distant animals drift on the winds to camp; the quiet, early morning voices of the Africans as they awake the sleeping camp and start the business of the day; the smell of fried eggs, bacon, baked beans and fresh coffee sizzling over a newly laid fire; heart-stopping nights, protected by only the thin canvas of a tent from unknown animals padding softly a few feet away; the excitement of piling into a lorry and trekking off to unknown adventure. What animals will be seen, what extraordinary landscape will sear the soul, which unknown plant will be discovered?

As they arrived at Kibwezi railway station, en route to the Chyulu Hills, over one hundred porters were waiting at the base to carry their baggage, equipment and supplies. A great deal of thought, money and organization went into a field trip of such duration. Enough tents for the researchers, staff and porters had to be purchased, as well as all the equipment for a field laboratory. Drinking water and quantities of tinned food were carried by the porters, who travelled ahead of the party of whites to set up camp.

The comparatively short, twenty-eight-mile stretch encompassed every terrain, from waterless badlands with sparse humus to the umbrella of dense forests. A carpet of burnt almond covered the near-barren end of the volcanic range. There the lava and the lapilli-covered slopes of the craters received, on occasions, the mists of the morning, but the full fury of the rain clouds remained unknown to them. At midday, the wind was still and the sun beat down on a land without life. Few tribesmen, always on the lookout for that most precious commodity, water, bothered to wander into the arid area. Towards the southeastern end of the range, the pendulum swung dramatically. After the short rains the slopes were coated in a fragile mantle of green and, where the hills arched their narrow back, thick rainforests, inhabited by fauna and woodland flowers, crept down the grassy banks.

Joy's initiation into the secrets of this exhilarating new world filled her with wonderment. For the first time she could witness her husband's single-minded passion and remarkable knowledge of botany. Each morning she awoke, eager to begin the day's search, wanting to take part in every experiment. Whenever possible, she accompanied Peter, exploring the craters and helping him collect the sparse vegetation from the slopes. She learned to shoot down flowers from the tops of the forest trees with a bow and arrow, and discern which liquid from plants was edible.

There were times, however, when it was easier for the botanist to go off alone on his collecting forays. Having no knowledge of the particular types and classes of plants her husband was looking for, and knowing she could be of little help, Joy stayed behind, frustrated. As Peter's work took him further afield in search for rare and elusive plants, she accompanied him less and less. But Joy was a woman who needed a great deal of attention. Her emotions continually rose to the surface when Peter, sometimes lost in a world into which his wife could never fully enter, appeared distracted. Although he was a man who enjoyed the company of others, and especially that of his bride, he was equally content to be alone. Her female intuition told her that even though he loved her, he would never be happier than when involved in his absorbing work. A friend who undertook a botanical safari with Peter recalls : 'No one knows how hard a life collecting plants can be. I was younger than Peter and I could not do anything when we came down from the mountainside. I could not even stand.'

Bally rapidly came to realize that, if peace was to reign in camp, he would have to find something for his wife to do on the days when he was unable, or unwilling, to take her with him. Being a renowned botanical painter himself, he presented Joy one day with a gloriosa lily, now the national emblem of Kenya, saying, 'Joy, why don't you settle down and try and paint this flower while I'm away?' The thought intrigued Joy. But, dissatisfied and disappointed with her first attempt at a watercolour, Joy ripped the sketch in two, lamenting, 'I cannot paint like Peter. This is completely useless.' When he returned, her husband calmly took the two pieces and looked at the work. It was enough to help him reach a decision that was to change her life. 'This is not bad. Why don't I seriously teach you to paint flowers?' he said.

Peter was a man of his word and a patient tutor. He taught Joy the precision needed in botanical illustration : the exact measurements of each part of the flower and leaf should be shown, scientific discipline must be maintained and the colour must be accurate. His flower paintings were always painted for future reference and scientific accuracy ; the details of each tuber, each leaf, each stamen and pistil, were depicted with infinite precision. The fledgling artist later gave a lover the first torn attempt at a gloriosa lily but then, in a fit of pique, demanded it back from him. It remained in her possession until her death.

After her initial disillusionment Joy responded to the challenge in a more characteristic way – with enthusiasm, deep concentration and the spirit to express herself without a trace of self-consciousness. It was just as well. Her days in her newly adopted country were still few and she, as yet, did not understand its ways. Like a chameleon who leaves the dazzling sun for the dark of a forest where no flicker of sunlight penetrates, she was slowly finding her way, changing and camouflaging to suit the terrain. She was unaccustomed to the physical stresses of life in the bush and understandably nervous when confronted by wild, dangerous animals for the first time in her life.

She was also a woman who needed men. In her quest to find love and the perfect match, Joy attached herself to men whose lives and work she admired. In the early days of each involvement she would throw herself into her new love's way of life, taking on his interests and causes. In the case of von Klarwill this meant socializing, skiing and mountaineering with him; with Peter Bally, although she had no particular appreciation of botanical plants, again she wanted to show an interest in what he was doing. She took up painting, but in his style, trying to replicate his way of capturing the essence of the flower or plant. Her own, individual style would take some time to develop. As Peter Bally's friend René Haller, a botanist and agronomist, said: 'With Peter she jumped into painting. Then later with George, who was this wild man of the bush, she plunged right into the excitement of his untamed way of life. So actually, for a man, she should have been the ideal woman, because if you could handle her, she could adapt to any situation.' The trouble was that few men could handle her.

After two months on safari, on a walk one morning with Peter, Joy's legs felt strangely leaden as she followed his footsteps along a path hacked out of the undergrowth. She suddenly staggered when a tremendous pain in the pit of her stomach raged through her body. She cried out and Peter, until then absorbed in a plant he had found, rushed back to help his wife. He loosened the leather belt which was fastened round her shorts and leant her against a tree. It soon occurred to Joy that she had suffered these severe pains once before. They stayed there in the quiet of the woods for a while, with Peter constantly mopping his wife's brow, until Joy found the strength to walk back to camp. A few hours later, amid tears and great pain, she suffered her second miscarriage. She was, once again, distraught.

Perhaps the Austrian fortune-teller was going to be proved right after all.

Their 'honeymoon' safari over, Joy and Peter returned to Nairobi. Indian traders dominated the town and beggars, often deliberately crippled by their parents to make them more pitiable, vied with each other for the most profitable corner on which to acquire a few meagre cents. Shops were spurting up all over town. The sole proprietor of a Persian laundry in Government Road advertised 'Gold mines for Sale'. Wardles, the chemist, was patronized by every European who came into town from the bush to do their monthly, or yearly, shopping. Choitram's prided themselves on being the 'Premier Silk Store' of East Africa, having been established in Zanzibar in 1880. Musical instruments and gramophone records could be purchased at Shankar Dass. The two main grocery shops, R. B. Duncan and Erskine and Duncan were owned by Europeans. They made a small fortune through their efficient service and first-rate produce.

Despite the many different nationalities, Nairobi was a European town. Although the black population far outnumbered the white, they seemed to slip into the shadows of the pavement during the day. The newcomers' importance as administrators and farmers overshadowed the lowly position of the African in a land that had once belonged to him and his forefathers. But it was the Asians who brought most colour into the streets. Soft saris, like bright, flowing jewels, and white *dhotis* (trousers) competed with the traditional dress of the native population. Colourful rings of beads decorated the necks and shaved heads of the Kikuyu, and from long loops of skin in their earlobes fell beaded and metal earrings.

For their first year in Nairobi, Peter and Joy lived in a boarding house close to the museum. Having been given a substantial amount of money by Peter's mother, they built themselves a house at the end of Riverside Drive, an area which was still relatively wild. The house was of medium size, Moorish in style and built out of the heavy, yellow-grey stone so prevalent in Nairobi. Homes were now more elaborate than the wooden shacks thrown up by the early settlers and officials. On the whole, though, they were fairly unimaginative bungalows, once described by a visiting journalist as 'Equatorial Ealing'. Rich settlers designed ornate stone houses for themselves, the stone hand-trimmed on site by African labourers, but less elaborate wooden houses, built on stilts to avoid the voracious white ants, were regularly built for the less well off. Those possessed of a more innovative mind, particularly up-country, built houses made of mud and wattle, thatched in the African fashion, which often had great charm. Almost all houses had verandahs, both at the front and back of the building. The back verandah was the place where the Memsahib took her daily sick parade of African staff, dressed their wounds, dosed them with Epsom salts, molasses and other simple, but effective, medicines.

What saved the uniformity of these homes was their surroundings. Houses in Nairobi and the Highlands had become famous for the beauty of their gardens. Exotic trees had been imported and thrived in the rich soil and benign climate. Persian lilac and jacaranda blended well with the local flowering trees; indigenous Nandi flames blazed with huge scarlet flowers that frilled at the petals' edge; pale pink clusters of the Cape chestnut blossom soared into the sky. Trim lawns, bathed each morning by the dew, were edged in rows of colour. Beds of cannalilies and aga-panthus, roses, zinnias and plumbago were fanned by the wings of sunbirds as they flitted between the scented plants.

The Ballys' garden was particularly beautiful. Dorian Rocco, who knew the couple when he was eleven, remembers: 'What was special about the place was the spectacular garden, which went right down to the river at the bottom of the valley. It was full of rare and exotic plants which he [Peter] had collected on his safaris. I was not at all keen on botany but Peter Bally managed to interest me in it. I had a great deal of time for him. He was very kind to me as a child, not outgoing, relatively silent; he made much more of an impression on me than his wife. She made absolutely no impact at all. Peter was a knowledgeable, typically scientific type, he must have been a bit of a bore to live with, not exactly a ball of fire. But I found Joy was terribly silent, rather a sheepish little blonde, not at all what one found in her later.' Joy was then thirty-one years old.

Joy made much more of an impact with girls. Two of the Ballys' neighbours were Sir Derek and Lady Erskine and their children, Petal and Francis. Derek Erskine, owner of a string of polo ponies as well as a thriving grocery business, was known to all as the 'Galloping Grocer'. He was famous for his lisp and for his habit of wearing red, embroidered velvet slippers to hunt balls. Petal was also eleven years old when she first encountered Joy, and Joy made an indelible impression. Petal became fascinated by the striking Austrian who had painted a flower in her autograph book: 'Joy would come riding with my father and myself over our land, through the coffee *shambas* [plantations] and out onto the plains. She was always impeccably turned out. Her breeches and boots were beautifully cut and showed off her marvellous figure. Her hair was very 1930s, swept up with combs at the back with lots of blonde curls on top. I thought she was madly glamorous, especially when she came to dinner with my parents, dressed in some elegant outfit, looking so European with her blue sparkling eyes and immaculate make-up. She always wore a slash of crimson lipstick and had bright varnish on her nails.'

The Austrian's natural sense of dress stood out in Nairobi. European clothing for the day had become increasingly casual. Fewer 'Bombay bowlers' and double terrais were worn; instead men, women and children wore wide-brimmed, soft, felt hats. Women were to be seen in what were mostly ill-cut trousers and the shapeless dresses covered in dreary flower patterns so loved by the colonial English. Men wore long, baggy shorts which stopped just above the knee and were jokingly known as 'Empire Builders'. Their long khaki stockings were pulled up to the knee, with the peculiar result that the only part of the man's leg to receive any sun at all might be his patella. Senior administration officers wore ceremonial dress for special occasions. The traditional outfit included helmet and sword and the governor outdid the finery of his subordinates by displaying an exotic cluster of plumes in his helmet.

It did not take Joy long to realize that she was an outsider in Kenya simply by being foreign. She was proud of her own background, safely within the higher echelons of Austrian society, but anyone born and reared away from the then pink parts of the world map was automatically treated with deep suspicion by the British. Joy was a foreigner married to another foreigner. As an Austrian, she found the deeply imbedded self-control of the British profoundly tedious. Peter Bally, as a highly respected botanist at the museum's herbarium, was forgiven his foreign birth by virtue of his qualifications and expertise. But Joy had her own battle for acceptance to fight. With the exception of a few friends, like Dr Jex-Blake and his wife, Lady Muriel, who admired Joy's flower paintings, she was an outsider. As she said herself, 'Being regarded as a foreigner led to a deep sense of isolation.'

As soon as Joy had finished a number of flower paintings she showed them to Dr Jex-Blake and his wife. So impressed were they that Joy was asked to illustrate the second edition of *Gardening in East Africa*, of which Jex-Blake was editor. This erudite couple were passionate horticulturists who had, like many others in Kenya, a remarkable garden teeming with indigenous plants. Lady Muriel had also founded the Horticultural Society of Kenya. According to a friend of the Jex-Blakes, the newcomer's popularity was not noticeable among the settlers: 'Dr Jex-Blake reckoned Joy was "man mad". She was good-looking and she would "use" any man. But Joy was pleasant enough to those who were no threat to her.'

Joy's liking of the opposite sex had now become apparent to Kenyans. In her thick Austrian accent, she pronounced to anyone who listened: 'Men in Kenya are so sveet, but ze women, zey are cabbages.'

Joy, having begun to paint seriously, was understandably nervous about accepting Dr Jex-Blake's commission, which entailed depicting hundreds of plants in watercolour. The paintings were to be grouped by plant type ; coastal, arid and semi-arid, unusual plants, those from the Highlands and mountains, Nairobi and Lake Victoria regions. It was the start of many months of satisfying work. Joy soon found her own individual style, which was not as botanically accurate and detailed as her husband's, but which had more artistic panache. The weakest part of her work was in the rendering of leaves, which lacked the expressive confidence of the flower petals. Of all her paintings, her flower portrayals are by far her best work. So immersed and determined did Joy become in her flower painting that she illustrated five books on the flora of the country, including a couple on trees and shrubs, receiving the Grenfell Gold Medal in London for her achievement.

As Joy worked, Peter discovered that one of the less likeable aspects of his wife's character was her intolerance of any rivalry. On one of his rare discussions about her with a friend, he said : 'To begin with, she was going to help me paint flowers for reference in my work. We painted together, which was most enjoyable. But after a while, Joy had to prove she was better than I was, that she was the more accomplished artist.'

As soon as word had spread that Joy was putting together a collection of paintings of indigenous flowers, people arrived each week at the museum with rare plants for her. Many weeks were spent in the wilds on safari with Peter, either collecting specimens for his work or searching for unusual flowers for her illustrations.

Aware that his wife, who loved animals, needed something small to pet and cherish, Peter had given her a Cairn terrier puppy, which she called Pippin. The dog never left her side and she loved him dearly, treating him like the child she was unable to have. Bumping along in the lorry on safari, sitting happily between the couple, Pippin joined in when Joy sang, 'accompanying' her in duets. At night, on trips to infected areas, the small animal slept, with all the presumption of a queen's favourite, under the dome of a mosquito net so that it would be protected from the dreaded tsetse fly.

Joy's first safari to the summit of Mount Kilimanjaro, the highest mountain in Africa, remained long in her memory. Kilimanjaro was the most magical and romantic of mountains, and she could hardly wait to tackle it. As day broke over the small village at its base, Joy suppressed a tight-chested gasp as, standing beside Peter, she breathed in the cold air. It would take them three days to reach the top. The ethereal grandeur of the mountain, shaped as it was like the curved back of some vast whale, filled the sky. Thin wisps of clouds drifted and coiled like the seven veils below the snowline, as if teasing the plum-pudding crown into covering its modesty.

The group soon found itself in dense forest, where arum lilies paraded their cowled heads along the banks of the small mountain streams and where the ground was covered with red seeds from 'Lucky Bean' trees. Thick groves of bamboo rustled in the breeze ; birds fluttered and darted everywhere. The snap of a branch, caused by some prowling animal deep in the forest, occasionally broke the silence. Unaccustomed to the altitude, the party paced themselves for the upper reaches, which they knew caused mountain sickness. At 8,000 feet they reached the landmark of the Bismarck hut, which the Germans had built before the First World War, and stopped for their first night on the frost-bitten mountain. All of them lay, exhausted, on wooden benches. The spareness of the hut and the uncomfortable cold afforded them little sleep.

At dawn the following day grassy tussocks covering the moorlands slowed their progress. Giant heather dwarfed them ; beautiful lobelia, with their mass of creamy white flowers, towered into the air. Joy collected the mites which lived deep inside, placing them in her killing bottle to take back to the entomologist at the Nairobi museum. On the third day they crossed the saddle between the slopes of the main mountain and Mawenzi, the smaller craggy dome which lies like a benevolent mole on its side. In spite of short, sleepless nights and tiring days, adrenaline kept up their spirits.

That midnight, as the crater glistened under the silver reflection of the moon, they began their final ascent. Joy, although used to climbing among breathtaking scenery in Europe, was nevertheless trembling with excitement, awed by the outline which loomed straight above. She savoured the moment. Many hours later, after struggling across the loose lava, they reached the ice-capped crater. As the sun came up to greet them, bone-weary but exhilarated, they stepped onto the firm ice at Kaiser Wilhelm Spitze, signed their names on a piece of paper and placed it in the bottle kept there.

7

Internment

Through her work at the museum, Joy met a number of interesting people. Among these were Dr Louis Leakey, later to become its director, and his wife Mary. Leakey's office was filled with artefacts, books and papers heaped in a chaotic jumble. He received visitors in his habitual dress of blue shirt and khaki trousers, and invariably bushbabies would appear from under his collar or a snake would slither out from under the clutter of books and papers on the floor.

It is not certain quite what friendship originally existed between Joy and Louis Leakey. Apart from being a celebrated and controversial anthropologist, famous for his excavations of hominid fossils in Olduvai Gorge, he was a passionate admirer of good-looking, intelligent women. He was especially drawn to those who were energetic and who strove to be successful in their own field.

It was while Joy was helping the Leakeys piece together fragments of bone from an excavation in the Rift Valley that they heard the announcement of the outbreak of the Second World War. Aware of what this meant for her family home in Austria, Joy collapsed in a heap of tears.

In the early days of the war Joy, being Austrian, was naturally regarded with some suspicion by the British. She had made plans to visit the Congo with two women friends but, on crossing the border into Uganda, the three foreigners were detained, questioned and searched for several hours, stripped, and treated as spies. Joy, livid, was convinced this was a practical joke played on them by Leakey. Fairly early on, Leakey was involved in Kenyan security, having been recruited by the intelligence services. He had, Joy noticed, taken unusual interest in their travel arrangements. On the other hand, she felt he knew perfectly well that her loyalties during the war lay with the British.

The women were eventually allowed to continue their journey, but later, on returning to Nairobi, Joy discovered that her troubles did indeed lie at the great man's feet. Leakey, suspicious about Joy's Austrian connections, had telephoned the police at the frontier and had arranged for her to be searched. According to his wife, Dr Mary Leakey, Louis hated Joy and was convinced she was a spy, although he had no evidence. Although Joy stated that, when she accused him, Leakey apologized and the affair did not mar either their friendship or Joy's respect for him, the truth is that, after the incident, Louis Leakey became, for a period, the recipient of Joy's intense dislike.

By mid-1940 the war made it difficult to travel outside Kenya. Her flanks were being threatened by Mussolini's forces, then occupying Abyssinia. Unable to compete with the might of the enemy, which numbered 300,000 fighting men, Kenya was nevertheless determined to defend herself. Six battalions of the King's African Rifles were stationed on the borders, supported by one mounted Indian battery – in all, 7,000 men were drafted. In addition, a small defence force, the Reconnaissance Regiment, was formed by the farmers, whose blood was up. They were known as the Reckies.

By August, British Somaliland was occupied by the Italians. They had captured the border outposts of Moyale and El Wak in the barren deserts of the Northern Frontier Province, later called the NFD (Northern Frontier District), an area of 120,000 square miles. The British retaliated by bombing Assab and Diredawa in Abyssinia, as well as the Libyan ports. Then, with typical British efficiency and verve, the Kenyan forces quickly retook El Wak. The initial thrust of the Fascists was curtailed, but the war against them in the plains and mountains of the north was to continue until the end of 1941. A song composed by British officers of the Kenya African Rifles stationed in the lonely, isolated outpost, Wajir, summed up the mixed feelings of the troops :

> Somali, Somali, we're here for your sake
> But what the hell difference does the NFP make?
> Mussolini can have it with a great rousing cheer,
> Moyale, Mandera, El Wak and Wajir.
>
> They say that the Ities are ready for war,
> They want Abyssinia, but God knows what for.
> But if they want somewhere, why not NFP?
> They can have every acre, it's okay by me.

The British were becoming increasingly nervous, following Il Duce's advance into Ethiopia and Somaliland, that there were too many foreigners in Kenya, perhaps with pro-Nazi leanings. One morning, as Joy was busy painting a flower for the collections, there was a knock at the door. In walked a policewoman, followed swiftly by a stern-looking escort. They told the Austrian curtly that she was under arrest and would be detained in a POW camp for the duration of the war. Joy burst into tears. She pleaded in vain that a serious mistake had been made. Stunned, she was ordered to pack a minimum of clothing and personal belongings. Since she was vehemently anti-Nazi, the thought that she might be treated in this way had never once crossed her mind. However, there was no evidence until war broke out in Europe that Joy felt so strongly about the Nazis; indeed, she numbered a few Nazis among her close friends. On the other hand, she was also extremely pro-Jewish.

In due course, Joy and her fellow prisoners were removed from the makeshift camp in Nairobi and taken by train to Molo, a small farming town in the Highlands. Here, at an altitude of 8,000 feet, a more permanent camp had been erected to house a number of women of various nationalities. Joy, joined by other depressed and shocked women, was soon settled in a farmhouse. A high, barbed-wire fence enclosed the area and sentry boxes were posted at the four corners. Living conditions were primitive: each woman was allotted a wooden chair, a camp bed, a mug, a plate and cutlery. Joy was first furious and then deeply upset by the quick transition from respectable painter married to trustworthy botanist to the degradation of being treated as a prisoner of war. Full of anguish about being in captivity, she allayed her unhappiness by sketching the flora around the camp, 'taking me into a world where no human being could hurt me'.

Back in Nairobi, Peter was frantically trying to obtain his wife's release. He had managed to discover why she had been arrested. The CID, aware of her friendship with the Jex-Blakes, had questioned them about the Ballys' other friends. When told that Joy and Peter were often visited by German-speaking people, the police had moved swiftly. The fact that some of the visitors were Swiss, whose native language happened to be German, apparently did not occur to them. Archie Ritchie, the well-loved chief game warden, considered it ridiculous that Joy Bally had been interned. It was only through his and the Jex-Blakes' herculean efforts in immediately tackling the governor, that Joy was allowed her freedom.

Peter immediately set out to collect her and, to help calm her nerves, he thoughtfully arranged a flower-collecting safari. They decided to go north into British Somaliland, the capital of which was Hargeisa. After the fall of the Italians, the British had set about restoring some sort of administrative order to the area; but their efforts came close to resembling

Joy with her mother

1920. Joy aged ten, with Traute, ready for a fancy-dress ball

Collecting mushrooms in Seifenmühle. Joy is on the donkey pulling her great-grand-mother's cart. Her mother and Traute stand in the background

1922. Victor and Traute Gessner with their three daughters, Joy, aged twelve, Dorle and Traute

1924. Joy and Traute

Joy having killed her first roebuck, aged 15

Joy dressed as a 'Russian candlestick' wooden doll for the Gschnas Ball in Vienna

Oma, Joy's adored maternal grandmother

Joy. Summer, 1931

Viktor von Klarwill

Joy on board ship travelling to Kenya,
1937

Joy and Peter Bally

Joy and Pampo, her orphaned baby elephant, at Isiolo

1936. George Adamson on top of Marop

May 1946. George and Joy on safari

Joy bottle-feeding Elsa at Isiolo

Elsa and Makedde

Elsa out hunting with George and Makedde

Joy and Elsa, close companions

June 1960. Siesta – Joy and Elsa on the banks of the Ura river

a comic opera. As the war was still in progress, the administration came under a civil affairs department of the army and the unfortunate governor, who had previously been in the civil service in India, suddenly found himself turned into an army personage and given the rank of brigadier. The country was run by a handful of ex-civilians-now-army, who had to follow totally unfamiliar army regulations. Everyone appeared to be running around playing a role for which they were highly unsuited – the miracle was that it worked at all. The war was causing huge difficulties in bringing supplies to the area and living was stressful. Only three decent houses remained standing, the biggest of which was occupied by the governor/brigadier.

Katherine Challis and her husband, a member of the administration, lived with the rest of the officials in a tented encampment, which was a large area surrounded by a thorn *zariba*, a cut-thorn bounding hedge. She recalls one particular day: 'Into this farcical situation appeared a motor car with two Europeans, a demanding wife and an extremely embarrassed, quiet husband. The wife demanded petrol to enable them to carry on their journey.

"What journey, there's a war on. What *are* you doing here?"

"I'm painting flowers and I *must* have petrol immediately," was the unexpected reply.'

The administration/army personnel were incensed. Petrol was in short supply and should not be wasted on two oddballs who had, apparently, come from Kenya for the ridiculous purpose of painting flowers. No petrol could be provided, but that meant that these strangers had to stay somewhere. The beleaguered governor was obliged to offer them the only accommodation available – his own guest cottage.

The Ballys' stay did not last long. After two days the exasperated governor instructed: 'For God's sake get the blasted woman out of the place at any price. Send her anywhere but get her out of here.' Joy was given her petrol and they left. Other people who badly needed petrol were not amused. It had been apparent to all that, though Peter Bally felt highly uncomfortable throughout, his wife was not the least bit fazed. But then Joy was a woman who never took 'no' for an answer. She had managed to get out of Kenya into the Congo and nothing would stop her from travelling in Somaliland while a war was in progress. She was sublimely indifferent to the existence of any obstacles. In whatever undertaking of the moment, she forged ahead, living under the illusion that other people's rules should not impinge on her own life.

Back in Nairobi three weeks later, Peter, tired, unwell and needing a complete break, made arrangements to travel to South Africa. Joy mentioned casually to a friend that, considering how sick Peter was, she felt most unhappy not to be accompanying him. If the reason for her letting him go alone was her painting safaris, surely she would have been willing to postpone her trips for a few weeks if she was so concerned about him? The real reason was that the marriage had begun to run into serious difficulties. Morna Hale, wife of the Garissa DC, was convinced: 'Peter went to South Africa because he was exhausted by Joy.'

When later asked about her relationship with her husband, Joy guardedly commented: 'Peter was extremely introverted. He was quite the most wonderful partner, and stimulated me in every possible way. He was far more intellectual than I was but there was a big gap in our age, also in our temperament. I loved Peter more than myself but I realized that I was always the stronger and the more extrovert one. Often he fell into a depression which, with all my love for him, I found impossible to watch.' She had deliberately excluded the one area in which her husband failed to stimulate her – in bed. Peter, low-key and gentle, simply could not satisfy his wife's voracious sexual demands. And as Joy was a woman used to getting what she wanted, she did not appreciate her designs being thwarted, least of all in her love life.

One of Joy's strongest character traits, and one she was unable to overcome, was that of extreme impatience with those around her. It was not in her make-up to take the time to understand or unravel the psychological problems of her husband. Her energetic appetite for life left little time for reflection. The more frustrated she became with what she could only view as rejection, and the more she voiced her opinions, the worse the situation grew. This unsatisfactory state of affairs went a long way to causing Peter's depression. His friend Richard Hennings recalls: 'Of Joy's three husbands. I think Peter was the most Germanic in character. He felt that the man should be the boss and the wife should do as she was told.' That clearly was unwise when dealing with a woman as strongminded as Joy. Many years later Joy bumped into Jean Hayes, a neighbour of Bally. 'How is Peter?' she asked. 'Is he still impotent?'

During her husband's absence in South Africa, Joy decided to accept an invitation to visit the Northern Frontier District, the vast, remote wilderness bordered on two sides by Somaliland and Abyssinia. It was a place far away from the trappings of civilization, a place where nomads lived harsh lives, understanding and obeying different laws; a world without boundaries, full of the smell of wild honey and the landmarks of *manyattas* (mud huts) and mountains where, in the dry season, the bare, bleached bones of the land lay silent and still.

Joy was to stay in Marsabit with Alys and Gerald Reece, the officer in charge of the area. On leaving the straggling town of Isiolo, the 'gateway to the north', the road meandered amongst the web of camel tracks to Marsabit and eventually to Abyssinia. It ran along the grassy slopes of the Mathews Range and out into the grey sands of the Kaisut Desert. The lichen-bearded forest of Mount Marsabit rose out of the desert to greet Joy like an old sage addressing his people. Hot and exhausted after the long drive, Joy welcomed its cool shadows. Avoiding the freshly steaming trail of elephant droppings, the driver passed the thatched roofs of the mud and wattle huts which guarded the maize *shambas*. They soon arrived in the primitive town of Marsabit, which comprised a small square, complete with flagstaff, and a few scattered houses nestling into the side of the mountain. The small oasis in the middle of the scrub was also the proud possessor of two *dukas*.

Alys Reece welcomed Joy to their whitewashed cottage. Luckily she had no idea that Joy intended to stay six months. Although she later stated that she had gone to Marsabit with the intention of helping with the children, Alys, now a gentle old lady living in Scotland, cannot recall that she ever had. 'She was restless and had no rapport with my children. One day, she became impatient with my son because he refused to get dressed. She snatched his toy off him and, in the scuffle, she knocked him to the ground. I remember being rather irritated by that. Joy always did what she wanted to do. She talked incessantly about Peter Bally – for some reason she was extremely cross with him. I don't think they were particularly compatible. She was fairly well aware of her attraction, I don't think physically, but because of her European difference and lively personality and also her painting ability. In fairness to her, she had a right to have quite a high opinion of herself.'

The Reeces were keen on riding and owned around twenty hardy Boran ponies. The animals, fast and sure-footed, were bred by the handsome tribe and were excellent in tackling the difficult countryside which was covered with lethal antbear holes. Early each morning, after the ponies had been saddled up by the head syce, the two women trotted off. 'Joy and I rode together because we both loved it. She didn't know much about riding when she first came, but learned quickly. She was very courageous, almost to the point of foolishness, and immensely brave when chasing away wild game.'

Occasionally they came across the greater kudu, which inhabited the hills, or the small klipspringer, which bounded silently through the tall grass. However fearless, Joy's first encounter with an elephant on foot, when she nearly walked slap into it, clearly terrified her and she remained frightened of elephants for the rest of her life.

Sarah Tennant, Alys's daughter, started out life in Marsabit. 'It was a fairly isolated existence. There were Mother and ourselves, Pa walking round his patch, a DC plus or minus a wife, and a policeman. Joy rather looked down on my mother and made her feel inadequate. Whether it was a feminine desire to feel superior, I don't know. She was lucky to have Alys there as tolerant as she was – a lot of people would have thrown Joy out. When she was in a good mood everything was fine; in a bad mood, it definitely wasn't. I remember she cried quite a bit, but I did not get the impression she was unhappy. Pa found Joy very tiring to be around.'

During the war and the early days of the colony, the NFD was a bachelor stronghold. For many it was a spartan and lonely life, with few Europeans for company. Forever having to leap into a lorry and dash off into the wilds, the young men appreciated the appearance of practically any female. Some men, in their need for the companionship of the fairer sex, took beautiful Somali or Boran women as lovers.

To entertain these lonely young men, the Reeces held weekly parties. One Kenyan, then a young officer, recalled those days: 'There was always huge competition as to whom we would dance with. We all made a bee-line for either Alys or Rosemary Whiting, another beautiful girl. Joy wasn't popular, although she was attractive enough; but she was so clingy with men, a real vampire.' Later, back in the mess when the men discussed the evening, the second-in-command joked: 'Oh, I had a dance with the Austrian girl, perhaps she's a spy.' For the duration of the war she was known by them as 'The Austrian Spy' and years later, when Joy got to hear of her nickname, she accused one of the men, Robert Nimmo, of having been the one who reported her to the government. 'Total rubbish,' he reported later. 'We were just having a bit of fun.'

Sarah recalled the sexual rumours surrounding their guest: 'I got the impression that there were one or two young men in the NFD who didn't manage to escape Joy's clutches, for all their efforts. She was determined to have them, no matter how great the danger.' A few years later, Joy's carnal needs were to become legendary.

During the war, those stationed in the NFD were rationed to one bottle of whisky a month. To add a bit of spice to their parties, Alys rapidly became a demon at making home-made ginger beer, always mixing jaggery into the liquor. Learning one day that a battalion from the border was arriving in Marsabit en route to Nairobi, Alys and Joy decided to hold a party which would include a bizarre steeplechase. Alas, there were not enough horses in the area to go round. The two women ran frantically about, rounding up every other four-legged beast capable of carrying a man. An extraordinary scene ensued, of laughing men, high as kites on spiked ginger beer, tearing round the dusty outskirts of Marsabit on a selection of the town's steeds – bewildered donkeys, mules which staggered under the weight, and camels – all of which looked distinctly bored with such unbridled lunacy.

Joy's trip to the NFD sparked a love for the area that was never to leave her. She remembered her stay with the Reeces with great fondness and for many years nostalgically reminisced with Alys about jogging beside the ponies on cold morning rides, trying to balance the children in their saddles with one hand while holding onto the reins with the other. Both remembered the children's determination to go ever faster, and their delight when the two women could no longer keep up.

In Joy's extended trip to the northern stretches of Kenya, she gained an added independence from her husband. It was this time apart that was to herald the end of their marriage.

8

Garissa Christmas

Joy and Peter's reunion after his four months away was not particularly successful. Although she still felt strongly attached to him and enjoyed a modest intellectual rapport, Joy wanted more love, physical contact and devotion than it was possible for any one man to give her. Once again she felt a void in her emotional life. Once again she was disillusioned with the state of marriage. In what she considered to be self-defence against his lack of attention, she continued to taunt her husband about his sexual inadequacies. The beleaguered man who, under intense pressure, was often prone to health disorders, was beginning to wonder how much more unhappiness he could endure. He now understood that, however parallel their minds might run, their personalities and aspirations would never be compatible. He decided to pull away.

While Peter took refuge in working long hours at the museum, Joy threw herself into yet another painting commission. Her extraordinary knack for finding just the right antidote for her immediate emotional ailment would serve her more than once in times of trouble. In quick succession she produced a number of flower paintings which were to be presented to General Smuts. The charismatic South African statesman had acquired a reputation as a political oracle, despite once proclaiming to an audience in 1939 that 'the expectation of war tomorrow or in the near future is sheer nonsense'. Among his wide interests was botany.

Yet, despite their differences, Peter and Joy continued to go on safari together. Peter carried on collecting plant specimens for the herbarium in Nairobi and drug companies in Switzerland. It was while on an expedition near Garissa, while Peter was hunting for a special desert species of *Caralluma*, that fate once again intervened.

Garissa was a small, dusty outpost on the Tana river in the eastern part of the NFD. The hottest town in the country, it hovered, like an undecided kite, between the coast and the desert. A few white, thick-walled,

Arab-style houses were scattered around. At sunset, due to the intense heat, people moved onto the flat roofs to drink sundowners and catch the slightest of breezes, even to sleep. Nearby, crocodiles infested the muddy river, their eyes and snouts lying motionless above the surface, teased by hovering dragonflies. In the heat of the day, the thick undergrowth and spreading acacias protected the elephant and smaller game that lived beside the water, and the continual chatter of birds resounded from the tops of the trees.

Garissa was a diminutive administrative centre, boasting only a handful of Europeans. Nevertheless, it was of great importance to the country's success. The post of district commissioner was held by Willie Hale, a charismatic, intelligent man, as capable of handling a Somali uprising as of throwing an impromptu party to liven things up. For Christmas 1942 he invited the Ballys and a few other friends to join him and his wife. The guests at the Christmas Eve party included the Hales, Peter and Joy Bally, George Low, the local veterinary officer, a police inspector, and George Adamson. Willie Hale promised a special evening, arranging a big *ngoma* (celebratory native dance) and as dusk drew near, the small group of Europeans gathered, full of anticipation and seasonal good spirits.

Joy and Peter, being the first to arrive, had pitched their tent a few hundred yards away from the Hales' house. Joy, always nervous of elephant, insisted that they protect their tent with a few flimsy strands of barbed wire, since hippo and elephant had a habit of wandering up nonchalantly from the river, tripping straight over the tent ropes and bringing down a sea of canvas onto startled occupants.

As Joy washed the dust of the desert out of her pores and dressed for the evening, she thought about the legendary character she was about to meet. Her appetite had already been whetted by descriptions of George Adamson. Her hostess had explained that he led a hard, lonely life in the bush and, as a result, was rather silent. He was a listener rather than a talker and, as he puffed on his pipe, would occasionally grunt one of three replies : 'Oh' ; 'Really' ; or 'How extraordinary'. According to one PC, George would not sit back and read a book at the end of a day's march ; he would spend a couple of hours mending donkey saddles. Then he would have a stiff whisky. Joy learned that he had been appointed by the government to look after the game in a vast area in the north of Kenya, which he administered from Isiolo. He was also, of late, totally woman-proof. The challenge proved irresistible.

George Adamson, who had become something of a romantic figure in the country, was famous for one particularly hair-raising escape. To find solace and to lessen the anguish of being jilted by a French girl with whom he was passionately in love, he had disappeared into the bush. There, one day, he had been badly mauled by a lioness. 'She took me in her jaws and shook me like a rat,' said George. In considerable pain, he was finally rescued many hours later by African rangers who worked for him. Once back in his tent, he became delirious, suffering not only from loss of blood, but also from malaria. Bathing his wounds in Epsom salts and dosing himself with handfuls of sulphanilamide pills every few hours, George waited six days before help arrived.

In the middle of the third night an additional test of George's stamina arrived in the form of a rogue elephant that charged directly at the tent. With great fortitude, George yelled for one of his men to help him. The cook rushed in, dragged George into a sitting position and quickly gave him his gun. Just before both men were flattened, George managed to fire. The huge beast, shot through the brain, fell in a heap in front of the tent. George's fame spread far and wide.

Curious to see if this hero lived up to his reputation of being woman-proof, Joy went to great lengths to look her most sensational. All her charm and not a few feminine wiles would be used tonight. She was well aware that men were initially drawn by her physical magnetism and this evening she was going to make the most of it. Knowing full well that European women in the bush were not known for their sense of style, Joy was determined to outdo the other female guests in the glamour department. She chose a long, slinky, silver dress, which she knew showed off her slim figure to advantage. Her blonde hair was swept up and ended with a bubble of curls on top. Blue eyes sparkled under a smattering of mascara and her carefully applied, bright-red lipstick added a vampish finishing touch. She joined the others on the flat rooftop.

Soon the laughter and clinking of glasses was disturbed by a commotion below the house. Joy looked down. The natives, preparing for their *ngoma*, grew silent as a line of camels appeared out of the desert. Joy maintained that George Adamson was riding at their head, but Willie Hale remembers it slightly differently : 'George did not arrive on a camel, that's absolute nonsense. Camels are vulgar creatures – if you walk ahead they eat you and if you walk behind, they drench you. He was on a donkey.'

Joy saw an attractive, broad-shouldered man of medium height. His strong arms were covered with blond hairs and he looked slim, with rather bony knees peeking out beneath his khaki shorts. His ears stuck out slightly beneath thick, fair hair, which was already receding slightly at the temples, and a beard and moustache covered his rugged face. She liked what she saw.

After a quick wash, George leapt up the outside staircase and joined the others on the roof. The host had gone to great trouble to ensure that there was plenty to drink. Although the tribal troubles had swept away from Garissa by that time, the war was still in progress. The parched whites were reduced to a small ration of beer. Appalled by this unacceptable state of affairs, Hale and the local European policeman would dash down to Kismayu and purchase bottles of booze made by the Italians in Somalia from sugar alcohol flavoured with millefiori. Bottles labelled 'Rhum' and 'Wisky' soon winged their way back to Garissa. All agreed it was potent stuff.

As soon as George appeared on the roof, he was greeted warmly by his friends and introduced to the Ballys. George's immediate impression of Joy was of an animated, uninhibited blonde who spoke extremely odd English. Joy admitted she was immediately attracted by George's blue eyes, suntanned face framed by blond hair, and goatee beard.

Drinks continued to be poured down the throats of the jocular party. George, who had never tasted the lethal Italian brew before, scoffed at the idea that it might inebriate him, professing that he never got tight. Determined to prove George wrong, Morna Hale and Joy laced his entire dinner with brandy. As he later noted with typical understatement: 'My recollections of the evening are blurry.' Even his host admitted: 'We had one hell of a beano.'

While the small colonial party celebrated the festive season in the traditional way, the time arrived for the tribesmen to revel in their own ancient rituals. There was a magic about these dances, as if the song of Africa stretched, quivering, out of the depths of the land and offered itself to pagan gods through the hypnotic chants and primeval ecstasy of its people. As the new moon sliced the sky, the moving bodies of the sleek Somali and Orma snaked their way one by one into a circle and started swaying to the rhythms of the night. The low chanting gathered speed. Rows of blue and red beads and small alabaster-white cowrie shells rose and fell on the necks and wrists of the women as they undulated towards their partners. The young men held their noble heads and warrior spears high, the sweat of their gleaming black torsos caught in the silver light. As ancient rhythms were beaten out on the drums, the dancing became more uninhibited. The taut bodies of the men jumped and reeled into the air and the swirl of feet sent dust billowing into the night. Tension and excitement. Laughter and frank sexuality. Teeth whiter than the moon. The jaunty breasts and agile arms of the ululating girls provoked their partners into a frenzy of showmanship. For many hours, the chorus of voices and the stomping of dancing feet challenged the distant noises of the wild as the animals crashed through the riverine bush.

The abandoned merriment of the dancers excited the Europeans on the roof and some of the men changed into *kikois* and rushed down to join in. The only man to stay on the parapet with the women was George. Joy, sensing her chance, moved in. Lavish quantities of drink continued to drain away the night as the two sang at the top of their voices and quickly got to know each other. With the rapt attention of a hawk eyeing its prey, she alternatively flattered and flirted. Morna Hale said: 'She was a great flirt. To begin with George was most embarrassed that this married woman was making such a play for him.' Willie Hale commented: 'There is no doubt that when Joy set her sights on George, Peter was behind her giving her a kick in the pants to get on with it. But she lacked the one thing every woman must have. She had not an atom of natural charm.' Hale's predecessor, Archie Ritchie, later said: 'George was like a sitting rabbit.'

Memories remain vague as to exactly how the party ended. It was presumed that George, in an inebriated stupor, staggered off to the *banda* (hut) in which he was to sleep. Next morning he found himself still fully dressed down to his boots, which had spent what was left of the night on his pillow. His head was to be found dangling off the other end of the bed. Joy had eventually found her way back to the tent she was sharing with her husband and, in the process, had torn her silver dress. Shreds of fluttering silver were discovered next morning hanging off the barbed wire. The story that George, much to his amazement, awoke the next morning to find Joy lying beside him, appears exaggerated. Perhaps, with Peter Bally having retired long before her, Joy had been angling for a few passionate kisses in the moonlight although, according to Willie Hale: 'Good God no, Joy was not naughty with George that night.' Never the less, Joy had already made up her mind that the wild man from the bush was the way out of her troubles. 'When I met George, he seemed to fit in with my whole confusion.'

Having taken a liking to Peter Bally and his wife, George, in a rash moment over a bottle of 'wisky', and egged on by Joy, had invited the couple to join him on a camel safari. The next morning, having completely forgotten his invitation, he was appalled to discover that they were keen to accept. As George said: 'The last thing I wanted was company, especially that of a frivolous young woman from Vienna.' The die was cast.

A few days after Christmas, George and the Ballys set off to follow the Tana river down to the coast. Camel safaris sounded romantic but were arduous forms of travel. The way would be hot, dusty and painful for Joy who, never having been astride a camel in her life, soon found her back chafed, raw and bleeding. But her physical stamina and immaculate outfit, from solar topee to smart canvas boots, impressed George. Full of admiration, when looking back at the beginning of their life together he reminisced: 'Joy never complained. She proved herself to be incredibly tough and could walk the whole day without turning a hair. She could walk me off my feet and she found a tremendous lot to interest her.'

Starting as soon as day broke, the caravan stopped at midday before the sun became blisteringly hot and the ropes rubbed the hide of the camels too deeply. The animals were hobbled and allowed to graze on the sparse vegetation before being saddled four hours later and ridden until night fell, when camp was pitched. During the night, Joy lay awake under her mosquito net, thinking of George and the new world he had opened up to her. In the distance she heard the roar of lions and the devil laughter of the hyenas. The darkness throbbed with a thousand cicadas.

It became apparent just a few days into the safari that the mutual attraction between Joy and George was deepening. A web of tension surrounded the small group. Peter could hardly have failed to notice his wife's uninhibited coquetry, but George, being an honourable man who respected his guest, felt that to respond to Joy's advances was totally out of the question. The only way to avoid her clutches was to separate before the situation got out of control. He decided that he would continue his safari on his own and the Ballys would join the Hales, who would soon be arriving in Bura. But he had underestimated Joy's determination. Two days before they arrived at their destination, Peter surprised Joy and George in the latter's tent. George, deeply embarrassed and dressed only in a loose *kikoi*, immediately shot out of bed. Being of the old school, he quickly sputtered, 'Sorry old chap, but I love Joy.'

Furious at his wife's flagrant duplicity, Peter faced George and said coldly: 'You can have her,' before stalking off into the night.

Peter Bally, according to a friend, was a man 'who possessed strict Protestant principles'. Once he had been humiliated publicly by Joy, there would be no turning back. Until he had formed a plan for both their futures, they were forced to continue together to Lamu, where he hoped to find new plants. Joy complained bitterly about having to leave the bush to go to the island – she was not at all enthusiastic about travelling so far in order to see nothing but Arabs. The real reason, however, was that she had no wish to be separated from her new romantic target.

The situation was obvious to Willie Hale: 'She wanted to go on safari alone with George but he managed to slip away from us.'

George was also confused. Although he was aware of his growing love for Joy, he understood the complications for all concerned. He also asked himself whether, in spite of his feelings for Joy, he really wanted to marry her. He justified his deepening affection by telling himself that the Ballys' marriage was already in trouble and Joy was seeking some sort of panacea.

After her initial disappointment and bad-tempered behaviour, the Hales remember that Joy calmed down and behaved herself in Lamu, a sleepy town on a palm-fringed island which lay off the northern part of the coast. Originally inhabited by peoples from Syria, and having seen its heyday with trade from Arabia during the time of slavery, an air of romantic decay now hung over the place. A labyrinth of arched, narrow alleyways linked the whitewashed Arab-style houses to the ancient harbour where dhows arrived on the monsoon wind from Arabia, their wooden holds filled with spices and sweet dates. At one end of the boats, Persian carpets were spread across the deck. Grandees of the town, when welcomed aboard, lay upon them and accepted small offerings of Turkish delight dusted in a powder of fine sugar. A small Arab boy fanned each guest and sprinkled rose-water on his face and arms.

At twilight the women of the town left the dark interiors of their houses. Dressed in black *bui-buis* and looking like a flock of expectant ravens, they gathered with their friends in front of the mosque. Confident of their beauty, these women's looks were only surpassed by the reputation of their skills in the art of love-making.

The smell of jasmine and coconut lay heavily on the evening air. Rats scampered past the open gutters while men, bare to the waist and dressed in *kikois*, bartered their goods as they sat, cross-legged, in their shops. On one of his frequent trips, George once saw a sign in a shop : 'This is hygene house, no spitum or other dirty business permitted.'

By George's account, he tried to avoid any relationship with Mrs Bally. For the next six months, after returning to Isiolo from the coast, he concentrated on capturing poachers and succeeded in putting her out of his mind. But fate intervened on a trip to Nairobi, when he saw Joy in the distance, walking rapidly towards him down the main street. Turning his face away, he quickly changed direction, but it was too late. She had seen him and pursued him all the way to the Norfolk Hotel, where he was staying.

Through mutual friends Joy had found out George was in Nairobi and she invited him for tea the following day. At first he refused, but accepted after receiving the same invitation from Peter Bally a few hours later. And, as George has put it many times, 'that was that.' When he got to the house in Riverside Drive, there was no sign of Peter. Joy flung herself at George. Fixing him with her large blue eyes she admitted : 'Immediately I heard the stories of your narrow escape from the lioness and the elephant in Isiolo, I knew you were the kind of man I wanted to live my life with. Our safari together only strengthened my belief.' George, amazed that she still clung to a future with him, insisted on discussing the situation with Peter. When the two men met later, Peter again confirmed her hopes and Joy left home.

Peter had no intention of ever having his wife back. It was largely a matter of self respect. His close friend, Richard Hennings, recalls, 'He wanted to get out of the tangle he'd got himself into.' It would be the solution to all his problems if Joy went off with George, and he was most alarmed at the thought that she might want to come back to him. Her moods were such that he was frightened of being with her.

According to a neighbour : 'If he suspected that Joy might be arriving, Peter would call on a close friend who lived nearby. Or he would ask this friend to come and stay the night ... anything to avoid being alone with Joy.' Bally was less pleased when George appeared to waver and there was a short time of indecision. It was becoming increasingly apparent to George that Bally was trying to offload Joy onto him, thereby forcing him to marry her. Though a man of conscience, George was also practical ; but Joy, sensing his confusion, swamped him with alternate displays of anger and passion. Not only did she want men to fall wildly in love with her, they had to want to marry her immediately.

All three participants were perplexed and unhappy. Thrown into deepening emotional turmoil, Joy decided to cut her losses and endeavoured to return to the safety net she assumed would be provided by Peter. There were other factors that swayed her. However much George satisfied her sexually, he did not appear really to love her. Also, he did not have the superior intellect of her husband, which so stimulated her. Perhaps her married love life would improve. Perhaps, after all, the two could repair what should have been an idyllic life, if only Joy could control her raging emotions.

Bally, appalled at Joy's turnabout, became increasingly nervous that the attachment to George might unravel. Richard Hennings clearly recollects that, 'Joy, having walked out, came back twice, each time late in the day, begging him to take her back.' The first time Peter let her stay overnight, in a separate room, but the second time he refused and dropped her off at a hotel in Nairobi. Hennings had the impression : 'I don't say that he loved her, but he was very annoyed and rather bitter when she had originally gone off with George Adamson. Peter, who was not outwardly emotional, told me this, wanting sympathy and reassurance that he done the right thing. I duly obliged.'

In desperation Joy wrote repeated letters to Peter. She stopped him on the streets of Nairobi, beseeching him to take her back. She even went so far as to throw herself prostrate at his feet. It was all to no avail. Other friends add that during this time of indecision Peter actually locked the house to avoid seeing his wife. One day Joy, completely hysterical, managed to break in and barricade herself inside. After returning from work, Peter had to sedate her with a massive amount of tranquillizers in order to get her out of the house.

Fed up with Joy's 'carrying-on', George allowed his confused emotions to get the better of him. One night he simply walked into the Ballys' house, punched Peter in the face for being so clinical about the disintegration of his marriage, threw Joy over his shoulder and dragged her out into the night. Peter admitted later to the Hales that if Joy had not gone, he would have had a nervous breakdown.

George was convinced that Joy had deliberately taken him by surprise. After a few months of passionate involvement and the best sex he had ever had, he realized what he was letting himself in for. One night, apparently while somewhat in his cups, George let it slip that he 'did not want to marry anyone, and he most *definitely*, of all women, did not want to marry Joy'. In any case, she was still married. Kenya might be known for the loose morals of the Happy Valley set but this behaviour was *not* expected of government officers. He had tried to tell Joy before that there was to be nothing more, but as soon as Peter and Joy began to see separate solicitors, he gave in to the realization that he was a captured man. As he has said : 'It was only when the Ballys were divorcing that I surrendered to the attraction Joy held for me and fell madly in love.'

Perhaps the bitterness of her experience with Peter Bally pulled a cloud over Joy's burgeoning affair with George. Although to everyone involved at its beginning, it was Joy who did the running, she blamed George for leading her down the path of temptation, which resulted in the break-up of her marriage. For many years she would tell anyone who listened how she had begged her husband's forgiveness : 'Oh, if only I could have Peter back, I would go down on my knees.' This was once swiftly answered by one NFD wag : 'Forget about your knees, Joy. You've been down on your back for so many people since that he'll never return to you.'

Joy was just into her thirties and had now been married twice. Surely she, more than George, knew what she was doing ? Could her desire to seduce George have been pure design on her part ? Here was a man who could give her an absolute stake in the country ; he was British and a government officer. Here was a man who lived an exciting life as a game warden in one of the most romantic parts of Kenya.

1943 saw a period full of anxiety. George felt it was the most stressful

64

year he had ever known. Up until then, of his own volition, he had led a simple and somewhat monastic existence. His was the life of the bush, with large but straightforward decisions of how best to capture ivory poachers; how to find and destroy man-eating lions. Now, suddenly, his emotions were in turmoil and even the smallest decision was difficult to make. Joy had no money, nowhere to live and felt bitter that, despite all her pleading, Peter Bally had refused to take her back. She had to make the most of a botched job. George was practically penniless and there was certainly not enough money to pay for a divorce.

Peter Bally came to the rescue by announcing that he would see to all the legal expenses. However, not only was the new couple's behaviour disapproved of by some of their more inflexible friends and acquaintances but George, aware that divorce was still a dirty word, was worried that he might be sacked for such a flagrant breach of government ethics. Once again their friends Archie Ritchie and the Jex-Blakes intervened with the mandarins. George was much relieved to hear from the chief secretary that, if all matters were handled discreetly, with a quick divorce and a quiet wedding, he was in no danger of losing his job.

As a game warden in the NFD, George was based in Isiolo. Joy naturally wanted to be near her new protector and lover and saw no reason why she should not camp near his house, where she planned to carry on collecting and painting wild flowers. But this plan was thwarted by George's superior, who regarded the proposed arrangement as highly improper. Shunned by many people and uncertain of her exact feelings for George, she decided to withdraw, like a wounded animal, to the sanctuary of Mount Kenya, roughly fifty miles away, where she would continue her record of mountain flora. George arranged to accompany her for a few days to help her set up camp. He was full of apprehension about Joy's lonely vigil, but she insisted on solitude. This period spent alone would produce paintings and sketches of over seventy different flowers.

The first thing she did to organize her stay was visit an old farmer at Timau, on the slopes of the mountain, with a view to borrowing his oxen and wagon to haul her camping equipment up the Sirimon track to the moorlands. But his one set of work oxen were busy on the farm and the army and essential services had taken the rest. Undeterred, Joy persevered with other farmers in the area to help her with her project. She arranged for two men to bring weekly supplies on horseback to her camp and eventually, after much persuasion, she found pack mules to transport herself, George and her staff of two. In those days the primitive Sirimon track was impossible to traverse in the rains. But with her usual determination Joy, accompanied by George, a gun bearer in case of encounters with elephant or buffalo, a cook and Pippin, loaded up the wagon with tents, cooking apparatus and provisions and set off up the mountain.

They pitched camp at 14,000 feet on the edge of the forest beside the open moorlands, a good three hours' walk from the nearest help. It was a haven for an artist. High above rose the craggy peaks of the mountain, sliced by the equator and creased with folds which concertinaed around the summit. Chasms, mantled in darkness, yawned on either side. At Joy's feet, like an intricate patchwork quilt, lay a mass of small alpine flowers. Along the banks of the streams, delicate wild flowers waved in the restless wind and giant lobelias, red-hot pokers, delphiniums and tall gladioli grew out of the snow-covered slopes. Large and small animals roamed around her camp : eland and antelope, rhino and baboons. Once George was no longer around to protect her, the only threat to Joy's peace and safety were the buffalo which menaced the camp each night.

Each day, the moorlands were covered with fresh morning snow. By lunchtime, as soon as the mists had cleared, Joy set off in search of a suitable site for painting. Holding her sketchbook and a hot-water bottle to keep her warm, she was followed by Pippin and the gun bearer, who carried her canvas painting stool. Totally absorbed, she sat for hours, her feet warmed by her small dog.

Raymond Hook was one of the farmers who helped Joy. A keen naturalist and classical scholar, he had gained a reputation for eccentricity and had pioneered the crossing of a horse with a Grevy's zebra, producing the odd-looking zebroid. The dun-coloured animal, with the head of a zebra, bore dark stripes which faded gradually away towards the tail. Hook, used to training cheetahs for Indian maharajahs, had tried to race zebroids against greyhounds in England. Greatly impressed with the young woman's attempts to live alone on the cold mountainside, Hook was determined to give her as much assistance as possible. He told her to pitch her tent beneath a tree she could easily climb if a buffalo charged ; he explained where she could find the most unusual and beautiful flowers. Joy, fond of men who proved useful to her, felt Raymond was one of the few she could always rely on.

Whenever George could leave his patrols and foot safaris, he rushed off up the mountain to see his lover. Distance and the promise of sexual fulfilment lent a certain urgency to his need for her, and by now he was besotted by Joy. Although she had doubts about the future of their relationship, she enjoyed the presence of his strong personality. Together they searched the moorlands for plants and talked over the golden flames of the fire each night. They fell asleep early, wrapped in each other's arms in Joy's small tent.

However, the couple's peace was not always undisturbed. A solitary bull buffalo had also decided to pitch camp near Joy's camp. It troubled her and she begged George to kill it. Not unreasonably, she harboured a real fear of this grey-black hulk, whose horns resembled a massive, curved helmet. The bull buffalo is the most unpredictable of all African animals and Joy knew a lone bull was prepared to attack without the least provocation. Carrying a light rifle, George silently followed the animal's tracks through the grass, being careful not to alert it by stepping on fallen branches or dry twigs. As the animal stood grazing, a shot rang out, scattering the birds and echoing down the valley. George hit him in the shoulder but, in a cloud of dust and torn grass, the enraged bull turned and charged. There was no time to escape. As George stood there, his heart pounding and prepared for the worst, the bull collapsed a few feet from him, the bullet having passed through the heart. Joy and George lived off the tender meat for over a week.

Unbeknown to Joy, her first husband, Rufus von Klarwill, was also in the area. He was looking for suitable land from which to start safaris up the mountain, and had just completed a ten-day walk round the peak with his friends Raymond Hook and Richard Hennings, mapping certain areas, exploring the flora and birdlife. He eventually found land along the Naro Moru river and built a few small cottages, which he used as a base for his safaris, and for many years a hut on the mountain was known as 'Klarwill's Hut'.

Richard Hennings recalls that, after their initial safari, they came down off the mountain. 'We needed a drink and went straight to Nanyuki, into the famous bar on the equator run by one of the Hook brothers. I had a sore backside from the walk, and desperately needed a bath.' While the two men were in their cabin they heard a female voice calling her dog. Rufus immediately recognized the voice as that of his former wife and came to the door with his friend. 'Sure enough there was Joy, fair and attractive, talking nineteen to the dozen. She and Rufus talked together quite amicably. I "wondered if George would stand the test".' Rufus later confessed to a friend : 'If I was still married to that woman, I would be pushing up daisies now.' Hennings described him : 'If you want to sum Rufus up in a few words, he was a genuine mountain man. And, like all mountain people, he was philosophical.'

There is no doubt that, if each husband led Joy into something unusual that culminated in her fame as a conservationist, then she in return had a deep effect on each husband. Perhaps by the very force of her own personality this was inevitable. Being 'touched by Joy' was an experience that was not to be forgotten and there could be no apathy in the response : she caused great admiration, or respect, or intense loathing, but never indifference.

For Joy's part, however, by the time her stay on Mount Kenya was over and her divorce had come through, she was experiencing severe doubts about marrying George. Perhaps she was nervous of making a third mistake. Perhaps her love was not strong enough. Her withdrawal not only caused George acute mental anguish but also made him feel that he had been well and truly duped, comparing his situation to the preliminary courtship of lions : 'The message had gone out from the female and had produced a response from the male, which was then rebuffed.' He was also furious. After putting his foot down and mobilizing the support of his friends to help convince Joy of his love, she capitulated and they arranged to be married on 17 January 1944. The day before, Joy, who was again wracked by a well of doubt and brooding melancholy, decided she could not go through with the ceremony. In her despair she swallowed a bottle of sulphanilamide tablets. Although she later stressed that she wanted to commit suicide rather than marry George, hers was undoubtedly a plea for help.

At any rate, the pills did not have the desired affect and produced nothing more severe than an acute attack of vomiting. Having survived, Joy confessed her suicide attempt to George, who immediately drove her over to Dr Jex-Blake. He knew his friend would be discreet. While the doctor's wife, Muriel, comforted Joy and tried to discuss her real motive for taking such drastic action, Dr Jex-Blake talked things over with her shaken fiancé and suggested that it would be best to leave Joy alone for a month so that she could get over the trauma and finally make up her mind about marrying him. George reluctantly agreed.

A few hours later the couple thanked the Jex-Blakes for all their help and drove off. Before they reached the end of the drive, according to Joy, George had reneged on his promise to the doctor and given her an ultimatum. As they drove back to town he threatened to blow his brains out if she refused to marry him by lunchtime. In graphic detail he assured her that she would never be able to erase the picture and would live with her remorse for the rest of her life. Over a calming ice cream, Joy's favourite food, she finally gave in.

Within the hour, a frantic George had found a wedding ring, two witnesses, a registrar, and had dragged Joy off to the district commissioner's office. By lunchtime they were married. In George's words :

'It was a simple wedding, on African soil, of an Irishman born in India to an Austrian who was leaving a Swiss.'

It was not an auspicious beginning and an even more uncomfortable few days followed. George had arranged to spend the first part of their honeymoon with friends of his who lived in Limuru, near Nairobi. Apparently the couple had not expected them and were taken by surprise when the newlyweds turned up on their doorstep. Joy felt that it was plain they were considered an inconvenience. Had her husband forgotten to warn his friends beforehand? Joy had never felt at ease with their hostess, whom she described as a highly sophisticated, insincere socialite. The woman obviously had no liking for the Austrian either. Immediately sensing Joy's discomfort, she suggested bitterly that Joy could always leave George and go back to Europe, pretending that she had picked up some tropical bug. The remark was not destined to make the couple any happier.

Many years later Joy admitted that she had discovered that her 'honeymoon' hostess and George had enjoyed a sexual liaison before their marriage. According to Joy, the husband was unaware of the affair and continued to trust George implicitly. Convinced that George never slept with his previous lover during their marriage, Joy nevertheless remained nervous of her. For months she insisted to close friends that the woman enjoyed scheming between herself and George, cutting her dead when there was no one else around, but gushing all over her when they were in George's company. George accused Joy of imagining things whenever she complained about the woman.

In a discussion at the beginning of their marriage, according to Joy, George told her that he believed in using fear to enforce cooperation from others. She told her cousin Mary that George believed that nobody would act for another person unless they were afraid or pressured. She maintained she had the opposite philosophy, and that what she could not get done voluntarily, she didn't want. Alas, Joy was mistaken in her assessment of her own character. As for her husband, George later admitted to a close female friend: 'If I hadn't been so drunk, I would never have married Joy.'

9

Isiolo

Joy had married an exceptional character. George was one of two sons born to an Irishman and his Scottish wife in Etawah, India. Terence was born a year later than his brother, in 1907. Harry Adamson, an able and adventurous man, had joined the Royal Navy, travelled round the Horn in a sailing ship, and later went out to India to plant indigo.

Like many British families during the Raj whose lives were intricately woven into the fabric of the country, Harry Adamson's wife's family had been in the country for three generations. Katherine Adamson was a highly-strung, tidy-minded creature who adored her family and was an expert gardener. George had inherited the calm, easy-going nature of his father, while Terence, observant and introverted, took after his perceptive mother. As children, their favourite toy was a large stuffed elephant on wheels, given to them by their parents. For the rest of his life Terence, during the few arguments he had with his brother, reminded him: 'You always sat on the back and I always had to pull the bloody elephant.' It was a good indicator of their relationship.

Three years after Terence's birth, Harry Adamson moved his family to Dholpur, one of the princely states. There he spent his days organizing the Rajah's army and, having taught himself engineering, helped to build the railway system.

George was no different from other small boys in India and he revelled in the bloodthirsty excitement of boyish adventures: pig-sticking alongside Rajput soldiers in the hot savannah of Dholpur; firing his mother's gun; dreaming of hunting big game. When the temperature in the plains reached 120°, the children were sent off with their mother to the cooler heights of Simla, as was the custom.

Following in the footsteps of other British boys in the colonies, George was packed off to England at the age of eight. He attended Dean Close School, Cheltenham, a school for clergymen's children, and intensely disliked every day of his life there. Terence seems to have been the more academically successful of the two brothers, carrying off the French, Latin and maths prizes. George's talents leant towards the sports field, where he won his football and hockey colours. The year he left, the school magazine announced that George, among others, had been congratulated on passing his certificate 'A' in the Officers Training Corps. The day he left, with his brother, was one of the happiest of his life.

When Harry Adamson retired, his restless nature took him to Kenya, where he bought a small coffee farm in Limuru. As soon as he had finished school, George joined him. He was eighteen years old and the year was 1924. It did not take him long, however, to realize that the life of a coffee planter was not for him and, much to his father's chagrin, he left. Many jobs came the way of the young man. He worked on a sisal plantation, built roads, went into the transport business, traded in goats and beeswax; none of which appealed or were successful. George soon hit on an idea which he was convinced was going to make him rich. Together with his close friend Nevil Baxendale, he set out for Kakamega to look for gold. They staked their claim, adopted a lethal rhinoceros horn viper, which they named Cuthbert Gandhi (he shared a propensity with his namesake for 'fasting unto death'), to guard their expected haul, but failed to find enough of the precious metal to make one gold filling. After many long, hot months of back-breaking work, they returned empty-handed to Nairobi.

George was now as poor as a church mouse and life was made much harder by the Depression, which had found its debilitating way to Kenya. Terence, his brother, was faring no better. On arriving in Kenya a year after George, he built his parents a stone house in Limuru to replace the *banda* in which they were then living. From this home, the eye could gaze on both mountains, Kenya and Kilimanjaro.

Harry Adamson died in 1927 and Terence began to run the farm. Instead of coffee bushes, which grew unsuccessfully at that altitude, he planted the land with wattle trees and a small amount of money was derived from the tanning extract from the bark. His mother, living with her son, continued to take the greatest pleasure in her peach and plum trees.

After Harry's death, Joy asserted in a letter to a friend, Katherine Adamson took to drink and, towards the end of her life, her precarious mental health deteriorated further. She had the reputation of being 'slightly batty' and behind her back her neighbours called her the 'Duchess of Kildare'. Although it is not substantiated, Joy insisted in letters that her mother-in-law spent a short time in Mathari asylum in Nairobi before her death in 1948. On marrying into the family, Joy announced that although she could understand how deeply shocked George was by having an insane mother, she was astounded by his negligence of the matter. It was beyond her comprehension why George almost never visited his mother or sent her any small present to brighten up her drab life. Terence, closer and more like her in character, was the son who looked after and fed his mother during her illness, a fact he was apt to remind George of later: 'Why was it me who always had to stay with Mother?' George would give a wry smile and shrug his shoulders.

Life was tough. Neither George nor Terence had any money to spend on the essentials of life – tobacco, alcohol or girls. The only pastime which the two brothers could afford to indulge was hunting. They tore round the animal-rich countryside on a dilapidated motorbike with a sidecar, armed with only one antiquated rifle. Owing to their poverty, they had a limited number of bullets, none of which could be wasted; each one had to find its mark. After bagging their prey, they propped it unceremoniously in the sidecar and headed for home.

It was only in the natural environment of the bush that George felt at ease. From Masondu, a Dorobo tracker whom he had befriended, George learned the valuable lessons needed by all fine hunters – the ancient arts of survival and tracking which were to become so much part of his life. From the agile old native, George learned how to stand downwind from an animal; to listen and understand each sound in the bush; to tell from the scent and spoor what animal had passed by and how recently; to know from the tracks if the animal was healthy or wounded or even dying. George learned the secrets of the bush.

For the next four years, from 1934 to 1938, George lived a rootless existence, trying his hand at various jobs and participating in the epic adventure of crossing Lake Rudolph with Nevil Baxendale. He became a professional hunter and took parties of tourists on photographic safaris. Finally, in July 1938, George landed a job as a temporary game warden. He was thirty-two years old and earned £30 a month. This job would change the course of his life as he came to realize with increasing certainty that animals had as much right to a place on earth as man. The desire to protect them became the main force in his life.

Soon after their short, unsuccessful stay in Limuru in January 1944, George, impatient to show his new wife his life in the Northern Frontier District, set off with her for the north. Their home was to be Isiolo, where George had spent the past five years as assistant game warden, responsible for policing an area of more than 100,000 square miles of mainly semi-arid thornbush.

Endeavouring to preserve wildlife, which often led to direct conflict with tribes and their ways of life, was demanding work. A large and frustrating part of his job was to curtail the ivory poaching. No sooner had one gang been apprehended than the wasted carcasses of the elephant and rhino they slaughtered so casually would be found elsewhere. It was ludicrous to imagine that George's force of thirty rangers and one clapped-out truck was sufficient to patrol this vast area. But patrolling the NFD was considered by all government officials to be the *crème de la crème* of jobs in the bush. The area was wild and beautiful; the life adventurous, exciting and far away from the centre of government; the animals were plentiful and the tribes exotic, if troublesome.

Isiolo was the dusty heart of the Northern Frontier administration. For most of the year it was dry and windy and the land around was the colour of shifting grasses – amber and topaz, burnt yellow and ochre. The winds swept down over the small township for months before the arrival of the small rains, and dust-devils arose out of the land like capricious dervishes. Beyond lay the boundless semi-desert, a forbidden landscape of volcanoes and scrub, doum palms and sand, where no white man could tread without a permit, where vultures drifted on the wind over the limitless plains.

Outside the small, straggling town two roads stretched away towards the horizon until they were just pale blue ribbons fluttering between the earth and sky. One led to Abyssinia, where wandering tribes told tales of an emperor who was followed wherever he went by tamed cheetahs on chains and holy men who built their churches deep in the ground at Lalibela. The other road led to Somalia, where the beauty and grace of the women was much admired, the area whence the troublesome *shifta* (poachers) would roam south of the border.

The town of Isiolo itself consisted of one wide dusty main road and a couple of flimsy *dukas* made out of mud and wattle, where Indian merchants sold sugar, salt, tea, tobacco and tins of assorted fruit. Enos Fruit Salts, Ovaltine and ginger biscuits were considered essentials. The natives, intrigued by the white man's tastes, imitated them by purchasing bottles of Enos. The more sophisticated and knowing they became of the Europeans' habits, the more they turned their allegiance to sugar and to one-pound packets of tea and coffee. Each week tribesmen arrived in town after a journey of many miles from distant villages, took their donkey into the heart of the darkened shops, loaded the patient beast with one hundred pounds of tea and returned, triumphant, to their families.

Isiolo also boasted a bar, a simple, square bank, a mosque and a fine

Somali butcher, who slaughtered the animals in accordance with Moslem law. The whites in the *boma* grew their own vegetables and had no intention of doing without the few luxuries which made life in the harsh outpost a little more relaxing. Sir Richard Turnbull, a man described as the finest of all provincial commissioners in the country, remarked : 'There was no shortage of alcohol. We had as much as we liked. I used to get mine shipped from London and wine arrived by the crate-load from Nairobi. Charles Markham [the titular head of a well-known Kenya family] had an ear to the ground. You could always count on him to put one on to the good stuff.' Turnbull would later become the last Governor of Tanganyika and later of Aden, before the colonial sun set for the final time.

The open market was noisy, colourful and chaotic. Travellers came from far away and from many tribes – Somali, Boran, Turkana, Samburu. Under a burning sun tribesmen in red *shukas* carrying spears and *rungus* (a stick with knob on one end) bargained with shrewd, rounded-bottomed *bibis* (women) squatting over their produce for cobs of maize and a handful of ripe bananas. Flies buzzed everywhere. Large bluebottles settled on heaps of dung that the cattle and goats deposited as they passed by and their smaller cousins kept constant vigil in the corners of the children's eyes. Used to insects, the children took little notice and seldom bothered to flick them away while, unconcerned, they played in the dirt with the chickens and chased the scrawny dogs.

Like all small towns, Isiolo harboured a number of local characters. Mohammed Moti, a bearded Sikh trader, owned the mail contract. The entire bonnet of his decrepit Ford 4, which could go no faster than twenty miles an hour, was decorated in garish stickers and ribbons. Across the front a proud label proclaimed 'The Frontier Royal Mail'. Three times a week, bursting with people, chickens and goods, and with a beaming, white-turbanned Mr Moti waving out of the window, the Royal Mail arrived from Nanyuki to a hail of excited shouts.

Another oddball, according to Turnbull, was a 'scruffy little Hindi whom we nicknamed "Gandhi" because he so resembled the great man. He was always hanging round, looking as if he never had enough to eat, as though he was on a permanent fast. We were all rather fond of Gandhi but he was murdered for a few shillings by a Turkana tribesman.' Life was cheap in the NFD.

Isiolo was not as romantic as either Wajir or Moyale to the north. Apart from the usual European official contingent, Isiolo was the provincial headquarters for the police and veterinary departments. In those days game came low down on the scale, but such was the power of the provincial commissioner at Isiolo that he was the only one in the country allowed to pass a death sentence.

Of the officials sent to the outposts, one or two met their end on the tip of a spear and a few were unsuitable and replaced. Some could not stand the loneliness of the outposts where other Europeans went unseen for weeks, while others pined for women and the land of their birth. But most were a tough, adventurous lot, brought up with British gusto to explore new territories and subdue fresh natives. They were willing to put up with hardship and loneliness for the excitement and romance of the country. The women who married these men were, out of necessity, a hardy breed. Loyal and hardworking, practical and resilient, many of them fell in love with the north.

One of the main tasks of the administrative outposts was the controlling of waterholes. The seasonal wanderings of the different tribes, especially the aggressive Somalis, were born out of a perpetual quest for fresh pastures and water and it was essential to be within one day of water for their grazing herds. Provided one tribe did not encroach upon the land and waterholes of another, trouble never arose. If they did, all hell broke loose. Antiquated rifles and spears at the ready, seething tribes were quite prepared to go to war with each other over the rain which collected, often as small puddles, in holes dug deep into the baked earth. If caught at a forbidden waterhole by officials, they would either be shot or fined by having part of their livestock taken and auctioned off by the vet officer.

The home to which George introduced his bride was a few miles away from the cluster of government houses in the *boma*. His small dwelling was suitable for a man who seldom stayed there, and when he did, lived in a spartan fashion. Joy was appalled. She remarked that he only possessed two books: Arthur Newmann's *Elephant Hunter* and a book by a client he had taken out during his days as a white hunter. She lamented that there were only two camp beds, an ugly table whose legs were rammed into the floor to keep it from wobbling and one filthy, torn, old easy chair. The rest of George's belongings consisted of his safari kit, some thirty donkeys and six mules to carry his loads.

With the help of an Italian prisoner of war, Joy set about giving her new home a semblance of civility, eventually transforming it from a caveman's dwelling into a comfortable, attractive home. One of her first decisions was to insist on her own bedroom. She had recently decided she had no intention of making love to George more than was absolutely necessary. George, horrified by his wife's decision to sleep alone, ruefully commented to a close friend, 'Joy and I never slept in the same bedroom from the day we were married.' She set about furnishing her own with one iron bedstead, one idiosyncratic Kenya-type washstand and one upright chair.

Some of George's trophies were kept. A buffalo skull with huge horns hung in the middle of the rush wall in the sitting room, flanked on either side by the smaller horns of two buck. Gone were the camp beds, table and chair. Instead a wooden sofa and two chairs covered in lion skin, a normal custom up-country, surrounded a circular table, and on the floor lay a sisal carpet. Drawings of prehistoric animals hung on the walls and a number of large animal skins were scattered around.

Sometime later George managed to cajole the town council into letting him use a few acres of land on Veterinary Hill, three miles from the town. His brother Terence was coerced into designing and building a new house, which filled him with little enthusiasm for he had scant regard for Joy and the feeling was mutual. Materials were ordered from the Public Works Department in Nairobi, who were paying for the building. A certain vital piece of equipment was needed for the bathroom and George applied to the PWD to have a modern, inside, low-level cistern installed, instead of the usual long-drop hole dug outside.

The chief stores officer replied in a letter to George : 'When ordering you should state whether a closet pan with "P" or "S" trap is required.'

George, slightly confused, wrote back :

Dear Sir,

I enclose requisition form for the 'whole bag of tricks', but must confess that I am a little puzzled by your reference to 'P' and 'S' traps. If the letters 'P' and 'S' stand for what I imagine they do, then by all means let me have the 'S' trap. Although, for the life of me, I cannot imagine why it should be desirable to trap 'it'. I should have thought the quicker one got rid of 'it', the better.

P.S. Perhaps I had better leave this matter of the 'traps' to your discretion, in case conjecture is incorrect.

To which the amused stores officer thought fit to reply :

Dear Sir,

I am sending you a pan with an 'S' trap. This is not what you think 'it' is, but I trust it will prove suitable, the 'S' merely refers to the shape. I can assure you that a trap is very essential ; not for the purpose of trapping 'it' in but to trap 'it' from returning, some things have a habit of turning up when not wanted and least expected, I trust the type being sent will prevent any such possibility.

The few Europeans scattered around Isiolo and the NFD did not find Joy an easy or comfortable addition to their social circle. Divorce and carnal behaviour were still under censure in the 1940s and this feeling was to linger on well into the 1950s. In addition, Joy was viewed by the small circle as 'extraordinary' because of the difficulty she had with English. Her speech was virtually incomprehensible and although it improved as time went on, she spoke rapidly, almost gabbling, in such a thick Viennese accent that she might have been speaking Farsi as far as they were concerned. Conversation became so awkward that few took pains to address her and others avoided her entirely. Nobody in the tight community at Isiolo felt they had much in common with the blonde Austrian, who, in spite of her undisputed talent, was thought egotistical and not one of them. However, Joy did not let this affect her – perhaps she was oblivious to the fact that people failed to understand her. There was more to this place than a handful of uptight Brits as far as she was concerned. She had first been drawn to George out of an immediate attraction to his exotic lifestyle as a game warden and she soon found herself captivated by the space and timelessness of the NFD. It was the most beautiful place she had ever seen and for the first time she had found a place in which she felt truly at home.

According to Lois Low, wife of the veterinary officer, who was later befriended by Joy and who helped her type her books: 'When Joy arrived in Isiolo she thought the wives were useless appendages and ignored us totally.' Lois, a spry old lady now living at Vipingo on the coast, had already been surprised by Joy's opening gambit the first time they met: 'You have a very charming husband, he must be very passionate.'

Lois Low had the singular distinction of being the only woman in the NFD allowed to accompany her husband on safari into dangerous territory. This infuriated Joy who, naturally independent, insisted on being allowed to travel wherever she liked. One day, hearing that George Low was travelling north, she marched into his office: 'George, I hear you are going to Mandera. I'm going with you.' She took no notice when he replied, 'Joy, you know you need the PC's permission to go up there', saying, 'I'm coming anyway.' Low stubbornly refused, but admitted that Lois was going. Joy was beside herself. Lois ruefully remarked, 'It's no wonder Joy hated me so much in the beginning.'

George may have tried to explain to his wife the normal practice in government circles; but given his phlegmatic character, he may have realized that it would be a waste of time and hoped that, as they lived outside the government *boma*, Joy would be out of the way of trouble. Although their marriage got off to a stormy start, from both George and

Joy's point of view their best times together were on safari when Joy, indefatigable and seldom complaining of any discomfort, was a peerless companion. Rather than sapping her strength, the bush acted as a stimulant.

Unbeknown to Joy, George began to correspond with her sister, Dorle, who had settled in England. At times he felt compelled to unburden himself of the difficulties of having a wife who was not always easy to live with. He drew Dorle into his confidence, divulging details about his marriage which he would never have told others. It is clear from the letters that, at the start of the marriage, he was passionately in love with Fifi, who in some respects was everything he could have wanted. Not only did he find her wildly attractive, he admired her intelligence and companionable qualities and was only too thankful that she appreciated their rough, adventurous life together in the bush.

Joy's keen eye never failed to find the unusual fossil, the beautiful plant, the strange rock-engraving. They safaried all over the northern part of Kenya, George dealing with poachers, shooting rogue elephant and dealing with other game control matters; Joy painting plants and collecting fossils, insects, small reptiles and rodents for the Coryndon Museum.

Once they had pitched camp George was invariably out at sunrise, arriving back in camp at ten o'clock. Joy was off with a ranger and Pippin to sit and paint in the shade of a wind-twisted tree. They met briefly for a drink and lunch, followed by a siesta in the heat of the day. In the afternoon both carried on with their respective work, relaxing only at twilight. Even then Joy's restless spirit was in overdrive. All George wanted to do was to sit with his pipe and a whisky, but Joy would hear none of it. She would insist that he accompany her while she hunted for yet another flower to paint. By now he was beginning to plumb the depths of his wife's mercurial nature. He was well aware that, like many women who appeared content with the freedom that bush life offered, she hankered equally after civilized city life. Moreover, she wanted a husband who felt as much at ease in a buzzing metropolis as he did in the wild. It also distressed Joy enormously that George showed no appreciation of classical music or fully understood her passion for painting.

Perhaps by way of compensation for a lack of close friends, Joy adopted numerous small animals. Like most others who lived in the bush, looking after the young of the wild was a natural part of life. George often came across an orphaned zebra, a wounded buck, or an abandoned baby giraffe. These he brought home to Isiolo and handed over to Joy to mother and protect. Besides her closest companion, Pippin, who rode on the front of her donkey's saddle like a visiting statesman, she found a new friend in Maeterlinck, an inquisitive mongoose with teeth as sharp as toothpicks, who accompanied the bizarre assortment of animals on their trips.

George and Joy, with pets poking out of her pocket or climbing round her neck, headed each caravan out of Isiolo on donkeys or mules. Behind them their camels slowly loped, followed by an essential milk cow. To round up the travelling party, George's rangers and any poachers captured along the way walked silently behind the animals. Safaris lasted three to four weeks. During these sojourns they came across the NFD's vast variety of animals: lion and reticulated giraffe, rhino, Grevy's zebra and the blue-legged ostrich. The area was rich in oryx and elusive gerenuk, which stood on their back legs and stretched long necks to nibble on the highest leaves. On certain early mornings or late afternoons the couple watched a lioness stalk an impala or a Thompson's gazelle, then swiftly despatch her prey by gripping its neck and strangling it. Panting, her mouth covered in blood, she remained passive as her mate bounded up and insisted on having his fill. Joy soon came to understand that the lion in the desert differed from his cousin found in the land of the Maasai. The *Felis Somaliense*, named after the nomadic people of the region, was smaller and lacked the full, dark mane. They needed little water, surviving for moisture on the blood of their prey and the juice of the grasses.

Each evening, once free from disturbance and with a whisky by his side, George filled his notebook and drafted his reports from his diary. It was the custom in the colonial service for officers in the bush to send in annual reports. George had a natural gift for telling a story and his amusing reports were much in demand, for they were always full of interesting material to which he did more than justice in his clear, descriptive style. This, in one DC's opinion, 'rendered them readable and understandable to the sort of clots that cluttered up the various department headquarters'.

In those early days Joy showed little sympathy for the plight of game – a situation which would change as soon as she became involved with larger animals. Despite insisting that she hated shooting game, and did so only to help George, she managed to become a fairly decent shot, killing an elephant which had raided a *shamba*, as well as other game for food. A photograph in her album showed her beside the huge pachyderm, gun in hand and a wide smile on her face, with the inscription: 'My Elephant'.

However much the couple enjoyed their meandering safaris, the tensions which plagued them in Isiolo spilt over into their travels. During the first year Joy, still smarting over Peter Bally's marital dismissal, seldom embraced the idea of sexual intimacy with George, preferring to seek satisfaction elsewhere. An added point of contention was the fact that Joy was bored with domesticity and took little interest in their home in Isiolo, longing only for the times they could spend together in the bush, exploring and excavating, collecting and painting. George, upset and bewildered by his wife's selfishness, repeatedly mentioned to Dorle that he desperately missed the domestic aspect of married life. In this unhappy period, he longed for some small recognition of love from Fifi, a sign that she truly wanted to be part of his life, look after him and take an interest in their home in Isiolo.

Even in his sleep he was to find no peace. One of the things Joy could not abide, on the few occasions they shared the same bed, was the fact that he snored. She insisted that he tie a cork between his shoulderblades to prevent him lying on his back. George hoped that things would improve with time. However, he explained to Dorle that he was convinced that if Joy came across a man whom she deemed to possess all the qualities she needed, she would abandon her husband instantly. George, less of an idealist, knew that it was highly unlikely that any man could ever make Joy happy. Yet, despite the insecurity and frustration, it would take quite a few years more before George gave up hope that his wife would love him.

George had two other habits which caused Joy extreme annoyance and which she tried to stop from the moment they married: his fondness for drinking spirits and his pipe-smoking. To avoid the inevitable rows, George began placing his whisky and water, ready-mixed, in an empty bottle amongst ones marked 'Turpentine', 'Methylated spirits' and 'Strychnine', on a shelf in his workshop. Whenever the urge came upon him, he called out: 'Joy, I'm just off to do a bit of carpentry,' and retired to take a leisurely and necessary swig. All went well until the day he took down the wrong bottle and gasped in agony as he realized he had just swallowed a large amount of rust-remover. His friend Jerry Dalton, a park warden, remarked, 'It's probably just what you needed after all the water Joy's made you drink!'

The stories of their stormy battles over whisky were well known in the *boma*. The men rallied round their friend. Jerry Megson was a particularly close drinking crony. After each session at the club, Jerry piled George into his Land Rover and drove him back to face Joy, who they both knew would be in a towering rage. The form was simple. 'One drove hell for leather up to George's house, giving Joy as little time as possible to prepare a reception for George, then slam on anchors at the gate, pour George out of his seat and drive away in a hail of dust.' Speed was necessary to avoid a hail of pellets from the shotgun that Joy, in her fury, often let fly at George. In fact, Joy probably fired in the air, but George was known to get down on all fours to avoid the flak. This caused much merriment in the *boma*.

In order to deceive Joy, George eventually hit on what he thought was the foolproof plan of charging his drinks to the account of his other drinking crony, Jerry Dalton, repaying him later. Telling Joy, 'I'm just off with Jerry to sit up for a lion,' the pair would quickly nip off for a quiet hour or two. But, totally paranoid by now about his drinking, Joy discovered George's newest ploy, whacked him with a dining-room chair and broke two of his ribs.

In her relationship with George, Joy rapidly became the butt of many jokes and her *affaires* were the subject of much speculation in the incestuous atmosphere of the country. One local put it: 'Joy was just one of those temperamental Continentals. What else could one expect from these excitable foreigners?' The gossip at the club often centred around 'what Joy had done to George *this* time!' All sympathies were for George and people often wondered how he put up with such abuse. There were nods of agreement all round when, at the end of his tether, he was heard to mutter: 'Must get away from Joy for a bit.' Off he would go on safari alone. George knew when he had had his fill of 'undiluted Joy', as he ironically put it.

Although Joy could be difficult, it was fully acknowledged in the *boma* that she was gifted, far more so than any of the other wives. The quality of her botanical paintings, her thirst for knowledge and her musicianship were fully recognized. Not only was she deeply interested in plants, it had to be admitted that she really used her talents. Yet, while she may have had their grudging admiration, Joy had no real friends.

10

Safari Life

Like the elephants which, every evening, drifted down to drink at the furrow outside the PC's office, the small European community gravitated in each town in the NFD towards its favourite watering hole, in the shape of the club. Wajir, in the middle of the desert, boasted the Royal Wajir Yacht Club, though no lake or sea existed for hundreds of miles. On mess nights the men, who were tough administrators by day, pranced around in nothing more than a black bow tie and a colourful *kikoi* knotted round the waist. Marsabit was the proud owner of a Whaling Club – though there was no whale within 1,000 miles. A pool was deemed essential to the Garissa Curling Club. Prison labourers, who had never seen a pool in their lives, were used to dig the hole. When the DC arrived to inspect the progress he overheard one African, who was scratching his head, say to another, 'What do you think the DC is digging this hole for?' The other replied, 'I think he must mean to catch elephants in it.' From then on the swimming pool was known as the Elephant Trap. Men in fancy dress, holding broomsticks, bashed away at their opponents' wooden curling stones which floated on the water.

Isiolo's watering hole was known as the Bath Club and everyone in the town was an honoured member. The real fun centred round the swimming pool, with grown men, who were seasoned administrators, acting like undergraduates. The young women took turns running the bar, right next to the pool, and whoever was in charge wore a black silk topee as a badge of office.

Bunny Allen, a charming retired white hunter, famous for his good looks and devilish ways, now living in Lamu, remembers one occasion well: 'One night, it was Joy's turn to run the bar. She looked perfectly splendid in her topee with her lovely golden hair lapping around it. After I had made some saucy remark to her, she pushed me into the swimming pool. As I went, I grabbed her white skirt, which instantly parted from her body. There she was, standing on the edge of the pool, the hat of office still in place, with a little black blouse and a large, white, bare bottom. She was not in the least put out. "Oh, well," she laughed, and jumped into the pool to join me.'

Although she seldom went to the club, in her own home Joy could be a vivacious and attentive hostess. But practically everyone who was entertained by the Adamsons agreed that the food was execrable. Abysmal stews, dried-up macaroni and sardines on soggy toast were served. On one memorable occasion, Joy had given the Turkana cook vague, hurried instructions to prepare boiled chicken, fried onions and meringue. The meringue pudding was duly produced and looked especially tempting. But when Joy dipped the serving spoon into the middle, she discovered a mass of soft, curling onions. She was livid with the cook's mis-understanding of her very basic Swahili, particularly when the party burst into fits of giggles.

Joy was always on the lookout for a good-looking man to seduce and her dinner parties were as good a time as any to appear provocative. She took great pleasure in dressing up and carefully applying her make-up, things she had little need for in the bush. Being totally uninhibited, she refused to wear corsets or petticoats. Robert Nimmo, then a handsome DC at Isiolo, clearly remembered one evening when Joy's feminine wiles were put to full use. 'When Joy had her "pash" on me, she showed it by asking us to dinner every single night. Once, after dinner, Joy said she wanted to show me something outside. I have to admit I was rather nervous. There was a bright light in front of her and I was standing behind her. And there was the silhouette of her naked body through this thin cotton dress. She didn't do a thing for me. After a while she got fed up when she realized she was not going to get anywhere and went off to chase someone else. George just puffed on his pipe and took no notice.'

Try as he might, there was nothing George could do to please his wife. Slowly, he began to repay her neglect by deliberately pulling himself away and retreating to the peace of his own camp or safari whenever her moods and tantrums became too much for him to bear. It was a pattern he was to follow for the rest of their marriage. By now he was nearing forty and, despite deeply regretting his personal unhappiness, he came to the conclusion that Joy could do what she liked as long as it did not interfere in any way with his way of life.

But Joy was a possessive woman, given to obsessive, sometimes violent fits of jealousy. Never having come to terms with the emotional turmoil of her youth, as an adult she had a compulsion to control and manipulate. She had little conception of her own deep needs beyond a desperate hunger for achievement. Her lack of respect for her husband dictated that he should give in to her demands at all times. But his personality was also strong and determined. All too often George and Joy were at logger-heads.

Within a few months of their marriage, serious disagreements had arisen. George, despondent but still determined to salvage the situation, told Joy that she was free to leave in six months' time if she was still unhappy. But before then he said he would take her to Lake Rudolf, promising her that she would fall so totally in love with the area that all their domestic troubles would fade into the background. Joy agreed to give it a chance. When camping throughout the area, however, Joy told a friend that she had to leave George every three weeks because he drove her to such despair. Apparently, he was selfish and unresponsive; but if that was so, he had in her an equally selfish, physically unresponsive wife. Thus, even on safari, there were now disagreements. On one short trip, Joy claimed that, as they were riding along on their mules, she realized to her horror that George had taken only one camp bed, for himself. When she asked how he could possibly treat her this way he laughed and told her that it would do her no harm to sleep on the ground, or to eat *posho* (maize meal) with the rangers. Speechless with rage, Joy refused to budge another inch until he returned to Isiolo to collect a camp bed and some food for her.

For his part, George became increasingly frustrated with his wife's erratic behaviour and exaggerated or imagined slights. Moreover, being a man of normal appetites, he did not appreciate being starved of his conjugal rights. While they were nearing Mount Kulal at midday on one safari, Joy claimed that George insisted on having sex with her and produced a dirty rubber that he had obviously used before. She adamantly refused, but he apparently grabbed his rifle butt and hit her with it until she almost fainted. She collapsed and lay moaning on the ground while George, unrepentant, marched ahead. His wife was forced to wait for the rangers, mules and donkeys to catch up with her. Finally, two of their servants found her and persuaded her to join the safari as there was no other transport in that remote part of the NFD.

Within hours of arriving back in Isiolo at the end of that trip, Joy went straight to the local police station to lodge a complaint against George. Through her tears she told the superintendent that, apart from hitting her, George had no idea that his part in their marriage meant more than a primitive sexual relationship, whether or not there existed any harmony between them. But her complaint was annulled since she had shared a camp with George since the incident took place. Why did Joy, a highly sensual creature, so detest any form of intimacy with her husband?

Two weeks after this incident the unhappy couple had another savage row. Joy resented the fact that George appeared to have forgotten all about it by the evening and, as usual, insisted on making love. As usual, she refused. She maintained that George then took hold of her and threw her to the floor, banging her head on purpose. All of a sudden he stopped and stared down at her with eyes full of hate. Pressing his fingers around her throat he began to throttle her. She looked up at him helplessly, unable to move. Just as suddenly, he jumped up and walked out.

The following morning a visitor came round to see George. As he was leaving Joy whispered that she needed to go to the police station in Isiolo urgently and asked for a lift. Within minutes of bumping down the dusty road, she was confiding in the police inspector, a friend of both the Adamsons. He answered: 'Joy, you have two choices, you can take your case to court, in which case George will be kicked out of his job and go to prison, or you can keep quiet.' After some deliberation she chose the latter, hoping that her husband would realize how badly he had treated her and improve his behaviour.

It was well known in the *boma* that George was driven to the limits of his endurance by Joy and that theirs was a violent marriage, with Joy on occasion attempting to beat up her husband when her emotions reached fever pitch. One witness of the aftermath of George's exasperation was John MacDonald, a compassionate, sprightly, Scottish vet. One day he visited Joy, who was sketching Pampo, a baby elephant which had been given to her and which she was having great difficulty in rearing. As John approached Joy, who was wearing a khaki sundress and kneeling in Pampo's pen, he noticed that her whole upper torso was black and blue. 'Her arms, her shoulders, her back were all exposed. I kept looking at it and I finally plucked up enough courage to say, "Joy, whatever happened?" Joy replied quietly, "Please don't ask me," and turned away.' Why did Joy wear an outfit which displayed her bruises? Was it a deliberate act to elicit sympathy?

John continued: 'A day or two later, I mentioned the episode to George Low, my predecessor, who said casually: "Oh, George would have taken his rifle butt to her." George was a gentle man most of the time but when he did explode it was bad.'

Robert Nimmo agreed: 'Joy could provoke an angel. Nobody thinks those things about George because he seemed so genial, but a man can be driven crazy by lack of sex. I think that was really what lay at the bottom of it, pure endless frustration.'

In the second year of their marriage, a woman who was staying with the Adamsons witnessed Joy's constant needling of her husband. During dinner one evening George could stand it no longer and lost all control. Their guest looked on in horror. 'He flew at Joy and started to throttle her, beside himself with anger. He would have killed her if I hadn't yelled for the servants, who pulled George off her.'

After a second foot safari with George to Lake Rudolf and a dangerous crossing in a small boat to South Island (forbidden by the government) yet another friend was appalled to see that Joy was beaten and bruised about her eyes and temple. In a highly emotional state she explained to Robert Nimmo that, after a row, 'George had taken all my clothes away and let me walk around naked. Then he had had his way with me.' She cried as she revealed she had been one month pregnant. During their row, George had hit her in the stomach, causing her third miscarriage, but it is possible that George refused to believe that the child was his.

After eighteen months of married life, Joy was near to breaking point. But what was the bond that held the two together? It remains an enigma why Joy returned repeatedly to a man she drove to violence, whom she taunted and ridiculed. And why did he, in turn, tolerate her sexual rebuffs?

Biological urges were still raging within Joy. She was by now frantic to have a child. She had suffered three miscarriages and was convinced that she would never be able to carry a child to full term. But George divulged to Dorle that Joy did not want his child because she was fearful it would inherit his mother's insanity. He considered this a ridiculous assumption. It was beyond his comprehension why, if Fifi was so desperate to conceive, she spurned every advance from the one man who was prepared to give her a child – her husband. Not only would Fifi be too old in a few years' time, but George was equally anxious to bring up a child that he could shower with love – perhaps to make up in a small way for the affection that was missing in his life.

Determined to have a family, Joy pestered every female in the *boma* with questions about children, fertility, miscarriages and gynecologists. After numerous visits and tests, in which nothing dramatically wrong was found with her reproductive organs, Joy returned to the NFD. Whether she was willing to conceive with George at this point is not known, but a number of other men were approached with babies in mind.

An exceptionally good-looking Englishman, who must remain anonymous, was one contender. He and his first wife were entertaining the Adamsons when, at one point in the evening, he found himself with Joy on the verandah, deep in a heated discussion. Joy, always forthright, made it plain that she would like a child by him. He recalled her saying, 'If you don't want it the natural way, can we do it by artificial insemination?' Her quarry felt highly insulted and replied, 'What do you think I am, a stud bull?' It was the end of the discussion.

Exploring, collecting and painting became Joy's overwhelming priorities. But however much she enjoyed safari life, her unhappiness continued to spiral. Robert Nimmo recalled that period: 'She was as restless as a caged leopard, desperately searching for some great work on which to pour out her energies. She seemed to know she had something more to contribute to life but could not find it.'

In January 1946, Joy threw herself into painting a series of tropical fish down on the coast. For a few weeks she stayed with George at Kiunga, a small fishing village near the Somali border. It was the time of year when the monsoons swept up the beaches, making the roads impassable and marooning any visitors. Grey sheets of rain fell in short bursts. For a long time after the storm clouds passed, warm, fat drops of rain continued to drip from banana leaves and small beads of moisture glistened in the throats of the moonflowers. The smell of the earth hung low, clean and fresh as a child's breath. When the sun came out, the sand, white as morning snow, blinded the eye and its heat burnt the soles of the feet.

Each morning, to protect her bare feet, Joy stepped carefully from the shadows of the coconut palms and frangipani trees down the hot path from their simple makuti-roofed dwelling. Where the sands began, casuarina trees were feathered against the sky and the round, grass-green leaves of the Ipomoea creeper snaked their way along the ground. In front of them lay the vast coral gardens of the Indian Ocean. Rippled sand ridges, covered with layers of soft brown seaweed, led them down to the water's turquoise edge and, further out, the native dugout canoes bobbed up and down in the strong breeze.

Joy and George, with snorkels, goggles and harpoon guns, waded into the water and soon found themselves in a silent world of moving colour. Innocent-looking red-and-white striped lion fish, whose feathery quills gave a powerful sting, glided past waving sea anemones. A line of yellow and black angel fish with delicate trailing fins, looking like nervous seahorses, followed each other. As the couple's flippers stroked the water, the scales of the blue and green parrot fish appeared iridescent in the shafts of sunlight which filtered through the waves. Curving mouths of large clams silently opened and closed and stone fish lay camouflaged. Shoals of minute fish, the lapis lazuli colour of a butterfly's wings, shimmered past them.

Joy caught specimens of the most colourfully marked fish and, after swimming to shore, placed them in a pail of salty water. She had to work quickly, before their iridescence was lost. Each fish was captured in a quick colour sketch, which would serve as a model for the detailed watercolour she would later paint. After finishing her sketches, she preserved the fish in salt in order to transport them to the Coryndon Museum where a plaster cast was to be made of each one. Together with her paintings of flowers, Joy's coral fish paintings are amongst her most skilful depictions.

11

Tribes and Lovers

In the summer of 1946, Joy received a letter informing her that her much-loved grandmother, Oma, had died. An added blow was the news that Seifenmühle, the place of her happiest memories, had been drowned by the largest reservoir in Czechoslovakia. Her fragile emotional world finally collapsed again and she found herself sliding into a severe depression. After lengthy discussions with George, in which she questioned every aspect of their life and marriage together, it was decided that Joy should seek treatment for her depressed state in London. Her passage would be paid for as she was married to a government official.

The couple were by no means well off, but Joy was able to finance her stay by selling her flower paintings to the Coryndon Museum. In her understated autobiography Joy admitted simply that she felt ill and went to London for help. She never mentions what the precise nature of her ailment might have been, but at least she recognized that she did, indeed, have a problem. As a parting request, George asked her to bring him back a gift of a rifle and a pair of binoculars. In the ten months Joy stayed away, her money dwindled precariously and she never bought George his present.

While in England, she stayed with her old musical friend from Vienna, Susi Jeans, and her scientist husband, Sir James. Susi, realizing that Joy was in the midst of a personal crisis, asked her own doctor to recommend a psychoanalyst. 'Joy was bitterly unhappy that she had no children. She had a great deal of love to give and this was the tragedy of her life and the reason she had so many lovers.'

Twice a week Joy poured out her troubles to the sympathetic woman doctor in London, with whom she established a close rapport. But a short period of treatment was insufficient to heal her deep psychological distress. It would have taken months, even years, of concentrated treatment to penetrate each scar, to cleanse each wound.

To while away her evenings in England, she concentrated on the chess-men she was carving out of ivory, which would represent the tribespeople in the remoter parts of Kenya. She had brought over ivory chips, which she had commandeered from the game department, and the chess set was to be made up of African boys and girls, with the kings and queens wearing exotic headdresses. The knights would be depicted as giraffes. But the set would be one with a difference. Not only would the castles be phallic totems, but each male chesspiece would be distinctly sexual. Susi Jeans recalls: 'There were all sorts of shapes of sex organs. Each set piece looked identical, but you could tell the difference by the male genitals. It was a strange idea and looked rather odd. She began the carvings in our house and my husband was most amused.'

Joy's nerves were further buffeted when, in the midst of an impromptu musical recital in his house, Sir James collapsed and died. Following so shortly after the sudden death of Oma, this second shock was devastating.

Joy spent much of her time in London at Kew Gardens, searching in vain for Peter Bally, who worked there on his visits to England. She still held a torch, albeit diminished, for her second husband. 'He is the only man I loved who never loved me,' she wailed more than once to her cousin Mary. In between her visits she took life-drawing classes at the Slade, touted her flower paintings around, hoping for an exhibition, and showed the editor of the *Geographical* magazine various sketches of tribesmen she had encountered on her safaris with George.

After eight months, Joy left England after what was an essentially unsuccessful trip and made her way to Vienna to see her mother and sister Traute. Vienna was overrun with Allied forces and Joy was deeply shocked by the bomb damage inflicted on the city she loved. She was appalled at the severe rationing, the drawn, ageing face and old clothes of her once-beautiful mother and the stories her sister told her of the many rapes and beatings the Russian troops had inflicted on the women of Vienna. Joy discovered that her old foe, Hans Hofman, was in prison for two years for his propagandist teachings under the Nazis. She found her mother visiting him daily, taking him different delicacies to eat. Traute had always remained in love with Hans and theirs would be a long and devoted marriage. Her daughter found the situation insufferable.

For the past year, Joy had been convinced that Victor Gessner was not her real father. She had been told by an old sage in Kenya that her father was still alive, though Gessner had long since died. While they were together, Joy, in her sister Dorle's words, 'pestered my mother daily into confessing the name of the man who had fathered her'. Traute Gessner was horrified at such accusations and refused to discuss the matter further.

Joy, who had never forgiven her mother for abandoning her husband and children, told her before she left : 'I have never been able to talk to you about what matters to me. We no longer have anything in common.'

She had a similar problem with her elder sister. Discussing Traute with a friend, Joy declared that they never really understood each other, but wondered why Traute could not be friendly. During the few hours they were together, her sister had wanted to force an affection which neither had ever felt for the other. Joy thought that Traute was too calculating and egocentric. In June 1947, Joy left Vienna, glad to put all the memories behind her. By the time she arrived back in Kenya, she was in a far worse state than when she had left – the trip to Europe had only caused her depression to deepen.

Joy had specifically told George not to meet her boat train in Nairobi ; instead she had asked a friend, Harold Gardner. Much to her chagrin, as soon as she popped her head out of the window, she saw both men standing there. Climbing down from the train, she took her husband aside and quietly told him that she had no intention of living with him again. George was devastated.

During her absence George had promised to look after Pippin, Joy's beloved cairn terrier. According to Joy, George would only release the dog into her care on one condition – she must return to him and continue to live together. 'This is total blackmail, George, and you know it,' she retorted. Since she desperately wanted Pippin back, she agreed to travel with George to the farm at Limuru, which had been left to him and his brother, and where the dog was staying. But when she arrived, she was appalled to find the animal listless and thin. She immediately picked him up, determined to leave George and walk back to Nairobi with her pet. She later claimed that Pippin had been so traumatized that he never again sang duets with her.

Once again, according to Joy, the beatings started. On one occasion, after being particularly frightened, she ran out of the house, hitched a lift to Nairobi and went straight to the magistrate's office, pleading for help. Again, she was given the alternatives of keeping quiet or ruining George's career. Deeply upset, she left, but ran into the Watsons, friends who knew the marriage was in serious difficulties. Sensing her great distress, they invited Joy to stay with them until she decided her next move. After a few days, she calmed down and decided not to go through with a divorce, but to stay away for a time. Meanwhile George, also in deep distress, turned for comfort and advice to his old friend Archie Ritchie and gradually overcame his sorrows. After staying with the Watsons, Joy travelled to Nakuru to stay with other friends. She received desperate letters from

George, begging her to return to him and promising to behave himself. Joy, taking pity on him, capitulated and decided to give him another chance.

Tribal conflict was an accepted part of life in the NFD. Among the feuding tribes which indulged in internecine raiding in the Ilemi Triangle and Turkana were the Topotha, Dongiro, Gellubba, Dodoth and the Turkana themselves. Fewer than six inches of rain fell each year in an area dotted by anthills, many as high as thirty feet, built by ants from their spittle. There were no hardier people on earth than these tribesmen and none that had a tougher existence, for they subsisted on a diet of milk, wild berries and a rare feast of rancid meat. Their stock was their sole possession, their homes flimsy, lean-to structures of thorn, which provided little shade.

All the tribes possessed large numbers of Italian rifles, a legacy from the war, and peace in this frontier area was dependent solely on the efficiency of the Kenya police. Raids were violent and vicious and no quarter was given or expected – old and young, men, women and children, were killed and livestock stolen. So tough were these people that one Turkana, whose hand had been shredded by a bullet, was in such pain that, while making his way back to his *manyatta*, he took a sharp stone and trimmed his hand off at the wrist. Punitive punishment for raids was imposed in the form of heavy fines calculated in terms of cattle, sheep and goats. One old NFD hand commented: 'If the Turkana, a philosophical, uncircumcised people, found themselves under threat of arrest, they would have whipped out a razor and circumcised themselves on the hoof to prove they weren't Turkana!'

One incident involved a party of Dongiro warriors who raided a Topotha *manyatta*, causing many deaths and injuries before driving off a large number of cattle. News of a substantial fine of 600 head of cattle or ten *shoats* (sheep or goats) for each head of cattle was conveyed to Attiliabong, chief of the tribe, and to the tribal elders. A meeting was arranged. As defence advocates, Attiliabong and his six headmen arrived promptly. The latter were naked though superbly coiffured, with each head entirely encased in a red-ochre mudpack implanted with cows' teats displaying an array of ostrich feathers. Each lean, gleaming body exuded the rancid smell of animal fat, well cooked by the sun. In the underlip of each man a hole was punctured for feeding in the event of tetanus and stoppered with an ivory plug. They wore beaded necklaces and on their wrists were fitted circular fighting knives sheathed in leather. Each carried a spear and an identical neck-rest, which also served as a stool, from which hung a small leather snuff box.

Attiliabong, minuscule in stature and only sixty years of age, looked ancient, like a gnarled and stunted thorn tree. He was grandly attired for the occasion in a fancy shirt, dress coat and khaki shorts and carried a topee. While he sat in a canvas chair, his headmen sat on the neck-rest stools, taking great care as they did so not to injure their most prominent physical feature, of which they were justly proud.

Leslie Pridgeon, the Assistant Superintendent, proceeded to express the displeasure of King George, the provincial and district commissioners, as well as himself. It was then the turn of Attiliabong, a splendid actor and orator. In a distressed and deferential tone, he said, 'I, Attiliabong, am Chief of the Nyangatom against whom you wish to impose so severe a punishment. My tribe is poor, there has been no rain and our cattle are dying and have no milk. The women have no food or water and they too are dry, our babies are starving. I, Attiliabong, am old and weak, I have no strength, my arms are withered like the dead branches of a tree.' Pointing directly to the mountain behind, he continued, 'The mountain that you see clearly Attiliabong cannot see. Go and ask this great king across the sea to end this punishment which would destroy us. He will listen to you.' The headmen nodded and sighed their agreement as their chief sat down.

After Pridgeon told his tribal audience firmly that they knew full well the consequences of the raid and that King George would not tolerate any further delay in payment, Attiliabong drew himself up to his full height of just over five feet and presented himself in an entirely different role: 'I, the great Attiliabong, chief of the Nyangatom, the greatest of tribes, that own this land as far as the eye can see and beyond, the mountains and the plains, the water and the grazing, I rule my people and they obey only me. You, you, child hardly dry from your mother's womb, by what right do you come to my land and order me, Attiliabong, to surrender to you 600 head of cattle and speak of a king across the sea who is greater than me? I know of no king. There is only one man to give orders in this land and that is Attiliabong, whose voice alone is heard.' Attiliabong made and repeated each point with great emphasis by stamping his spear into the ground and spitting on the earth with scornful defiance. He was applauded by grunts of approval, spear-stamping and squirts of tobacco juice by the headmen.

Having given the performance of his life, Attiliabong then stomped off, followed by his retinue. Alas, his impressive bravado had been in vain. After being seduced with two sacks of tobacco, the great man ordered his cattle to be herded forty miles from the Tapeisi hills and by nightfall his fine was duly paid.

*   *   *

It became obvious to Joy, during their travels around the north, that the traditional culture of the people was rapidly disappearing. She was one of the lucky few who saw at first hand the complex tribal customs, the ancient rituals of circumcision ceremonies, the powers of the witchdoctors and rain-makers. Having completed a few sketches of tribesmen to use as models for her phallic chess set, she now set her mind to painting portraits of the different tribes. She explained her reasons to her cousin Mary, whose memory remains sharp. 'Joy said, "I want to document the tribes in their authentic costumes and ornaments so that future generations can see them, because in another fifty years they will all be swept away. As soon as they get a pair of second-hand khaki shorts or an old top hat, they throw away their beautiful headdresses."'

Joy then plucked up courage to show her fledgling portraits to various government officials who, realizing the fading interest many tribes had in their traditional customs, agreed to give Joy a contract to paint twenty of Kenya's tribes. She signed on 14 February 1949 and was given £1,000 to cover expenses.

To begin with, George was delighted by Joy's commission, writing to Dorle of his immense pride in his wife. But he was in two minds about the future, knowing that they would be spending little time together because they would be working many miles apart. He was glad that she was currently painting a tribe within an easy day's drive of Isiolo and he intended to spend every spare minute with her. He did not mention that, despite his loneliness, he was finding distinct relief from some of the stresses of the past.

A few weeks before each assignment Joy notified the administrator of the area of her arrival. They, in turn, arranged for African sitters, wearing their tribal regalia, to turn up on the agreed day. Being on a tight schedule, she bargained on two days to paint each model. But life in Africa is not a hurried affair. A walk of many days is undertaken lightly, and there is no compunction to meet a deadline. It is *Shari ya Mungu* (in God's hands) as to when you arrive at your destination. More often than not, Joy was forced to wait.

At each location she was accompanied by an *askari* (police escort), an interpreter and the loyal Pippin. (One neglected aspect of her work was the superb photographs she took of each of her sitters and a few of their elaborate ceremonies which, until then, had never been recorded.) From her models, who included chiefs in long coats of blue monkey fur, dignified elders, warriors in lion's-mane headdresses, and circumcisers wrapped in the skins of leopards, holding sharpened knives, Joy learned the complex, mystical customs of another age. She painted *laibons*, whose rank was paramount. As far as the tribe was concerned, these powerful men made the rain fall from the skies, ensured fertility, sanctioned raids and provided magical protection for the warriors. She watched a Boran soothsayer read a family's future from the intestines of a sacrificed bull. Through their ornaments' symbols she learned to tell the difference between Chuka girls before initiation, young married mothers, widows and those who bore the stigma of remaining barren. She realized the importance to the tribes of cowrie shells, valued as a sexual emblem representing the vagina. Tribes living far from the sea went to great lengths to obtain these small, alabaster-coloured shells, which were used in birth rites, circumcision and marriage ceremonies. Of fundamental importance to her work, Joy learned to distinguish genuine tribal ornaments from fake.

Most delicate and intimate of the rites, and one which needed great tact from a white woman if she was to witness it, was the circumcision ceremony and the seclusion which followed. It took a great deal to convince the chiefs and elders of the tribe of the importance of her work before they allowed her into this most secret aspect of their life. Amazed at her good fortune, she was given permission to photograph infibulation ceremonies of Boni girls. Although the self-control of the initiate was of prime importance to their future, it was the seclusion which was considered vital to the formation of their character. During the isolation period, which can last, depending on the tribe, from weeks to two years, no one may set eyes upon the the young boy or girl other than the one person readying them for the day when they must fulfil their obligations to the tribe.

One afternoon, the wife of Chief Muruatetu of the Embu tribe took Joy to view the circumcision of her niece. As they walked towards the gathering, they saw women noisily running back and forth towards the centre of the crowd, frantically waving green branches. In the midst of the shouting women was a young, naked girl. Since a good marriage depended on the girl betraying no fear, she was determined to control her emotions, however agonizing the cut of the knife. She was clutching a bunch of leaves as instructed by the elderly woman circumciser who, in a hurried cackle, then told her to sit down and spread her legs wide apart. Two female assistants grabbed her arms and legs and pinned them to the earth. The young initiate was rigid with fear.

After washing her hands in brackish water, the circumciser rubbed dry chicken droppings over the genitals of the girl to take the moisture out of the slippery skin. Within a few minutes she produced a blunt instrument out of a banana leaf and, with a couple of swipes, cut off part of the clitoris. The assistants then forced the girl, who had remained silent throughout, to jump three times to ensure there was no bleeding. As the girl was blindly obeying their orders, some of the old women of the tribe had surrounded the circumciser and were probing the severed clitoris. One of the women carefully picked it up and folded banana leaves around it. Another woman then had it placed between her first and second toes. Clutching onto the small parcel, she was led off into the bushes at the edge of the gathering, where, with a firm shake of her foot, she kicked it away.

Each day Joy took picnic lunches out to the area where she painted, wearing pith helmet, no make-up, either brief shorts or Empire Builders and, when she felt in the mood, a loose-fitting bra top. She was in the area when the government decided to move several thousand Turkana tribesmen, who had settled in Isiolo, back to their home district. The job of supervising the move was given to the DO at Isiolo and to George, accompanied by Joy.

By the time they reached Baragoi the DO, George and Joy were travelling in three separate camps and hardly speaking to each other. Joy walked about naked except for a very brief pair of pants, which in the words of the DO, 'was not the sort of behaviour which the Baragoi elders expected of a white woman, whose appearance was fairly rare in those days. I told her to put a shirt on when attending a stock sale and she obviously thought I was rather stuffy.'

The Africans, many of whom were Moslems, were immensely bothered by Joy's scantily clad appearance. After a transfer of administrative staff at Kapenguria, Joy came back to work and the new DC was instructed to arrange for a few Suk models. One sitter arrived for a painting session dressed in a belt of shells and little else, except a cover for his manhood. Joy appeared with her easel and paintbox wearing a pair of minute shorts and a thin, chiffon scarf used as a bra top. Occasionally, while painting, she wore nothing over her breasts at all. That evening the local chief arrived to see the DC with the request that the 'lady who is painting my people should wear more clothes, like other European ladies do'. Joy remained unabashed.

Joy's determination to bend the wills of the officers often met with little enthusiasm. Many a DC, when informed of her impending arrival, conveniently remembered a tribal uprising in the furthest corner of his territory, leapt into his Land Rover and roared off. Others would make a mad dash for the sole loo, saying, 'Let me in, let me in,' whenever they saw her approaching. However, there was one officer in the area who more than appreciated Joy's feminine qualities. At the beginning of her project, she arranged to paint members of the East Suk and Elgeyo people near Kapenguria. The time she spent with her host and hostess was most opportune for Joy as the couple were going through severe marital difficulties. Joy became determined to release the husband and made it clear that she was available. Over the next few weeks the affair crystallized and once again she fell wildly in love. In the beginning, the pair were inseparable. Nights in which all her pent-up sexual tension was released became paramount and she gave no thought to George's pain. The officer's wife was aware of the situation, which only helped to quicken the demise of an already doomed marriage. It has always been thought that Joy was named as a co-respondent in this man's divorce. This was not, in fact, the case.

The 'flutter' between the couple continued sporadically for the next three years. Although Joy never lived with him openly, she used her painting expeditions as an excuse to be with him and spent the best part of a year away from Isiolo. The couple made every effort to go on safaris where they were sure not to meet any other Europeans. Despite his sexual infatuation, the officer was not in love with Joy. As he was between a sad marriage and looking for a suitable partner, he perhaps made use of her availability as an interregnum. A friend, who wishes to remain anonymous, recollects the affair: 'My feeling is that most men, including this serious love of hers, even if she attracted them, never intended to get really interested in her. They would rather she stayed married to George and just had illicit nights out with them.'

George, upset, fully aware of his wife's numerous lovers but not unduly surprised by her latest infidelity, wrote to the man involved at some stage during the affair. The letter started as one might expect, with George suggesting that he should leave Joy alone. George then went on to suggest that the man did not know what Joy could be like and warned him not to take her seriously because she was a bit mad at times and did not know what she was doing.

Eventually, the government officer, having fallen in love with another woman, broke off his affair after a flaming row with Joy. The disappointed artist, heartbroken by his cavalier treatment, crawled back under the safe, tolerant wing of her husband. But only for a short while. George's first impulse was to refuse to take Joy back, but seeing how emotionally disturbed she was, he did not have the heart to divorce her, claiming that it made Joy extremely miserable each time she realized that the man she fell in love with had feet of clay when it came to wanting to make an honest woman of her.

Occasionally George's renowned sense of humour and of the ridiculous got the better of him when it came to his wife's affairs. Once, when Joy was having a quick fling with a visiting scientist who was on safari with the Adamsons, George booby-trapped her tent with rope and tin cans so that her lover aroused the whole camp trying to climb in that night.

But George could also be humiliated. When a handsome young lover of Joy's breezed into Isiolo, Joy took a *kiboko* (a whip made out of rhino or hippo hide) to George and drove him into the guest house while she spent the night with her newest amour. The next day found George drowning his sorrows in a glass of beer in Mohammed Moti's *duka* in Isiolo.

It was well known in the NFD that Joy chased her paramours from camp to camp. A young DO in Meru became so used to her calculated libidinous arrivals that he achieved the fastest record for tent-striking in the north, on one occasion doing so twice in one night. The writer and conservationist, Ian Parker, says: 'As young game wardens, it was crudely said amongst us that you only went in to see Joy three-by-three and at arm's length, or you would be eaten alive!'

One man who clearly remembered his first encounter with Joy, in 1949, was the late Sir John Cumber, then DC in Kabernet, in the Baringo District. The area had been gazetted as a Closed District and, as a safety measure, no one could enter without a pass signed by Cumber or his district officer. A few weeks before Cumber's arrival, trouble had arisen among the Suk tribe who, like all the cattle-owning nomadic tribes, suffered from eye infections caused by the dust raised by the hooves of their cattle. In order to help themselves, they decided to make a pilgrimage to the top of Mount Elgon where, so they believed, their god would cure their eye complaints and blindness. This was allowed by the authorities as long as the pilgrims kept to the clearly marked cattle track, the sole object being to prevent the Suk cattle, not all of which had been inoculated, from spreading their diseases to the European-owned cattle on the farms through which the track passed.

A subversive movement within the tribe demanded a straight passage from Baringo District direct to Mount Elgon, which was forbidden. Realizing that the *moran* were getting out of hand, the DC summoned a *baraza* with the chief and elders to find a solution. Thirty policemen from Nakuru arrived to maintain order. In the middle of negotiations, one hundred spear-carrying *moran* announced they would proceed straight to the mountain with their cattle. Filled with excitement, they started jumping up and down and removed the *duthus* (covers) from the spear blades. Recognizing the signs of *moran* hysteria, the police superindent – an old hand – advised the DC to read out the Riot Act. As this was being done and the *askaris* were lined up ready to fire, the *moran* were lowering their spears for a charge. A young, inexperienced police officer, who had recently arrived from England, then gave the order to fire. The DC countermanded the order and ran out towards the *moran* believing they had no intention of charging. The senior policeman was speared instantly. Seeing they meant business, the DC then ran back to the police line, followed by dozens of wild warriors. Fifteen *moran* were shot before the young inspector, the DO and the tribal police corporal were overwhelmed and speared to death.

In spite of this sort of incident, Joy by now was bent on increasing her artistic output. She wished to record the fifty main tribes of Kenya, as well as many of the sub-tribes. It meant extra money must be expropriated from the government as well as additional, lengthy separations from her husband. Joy claimed that she sought George's blessing for the task ahead and, once it was given, she immediately equipped herself with a suitable car. It is more than likely that she told George she was going off into the bush to paint her tribes and he would have to accept her decision.

George began to resent deeply the separations and his wife's insatiable appetite for her work. Normally reticent, his letters to Dorle were becoming increasingly emotional. He lamented that each time he returned from his solitary safaris, he was convinced that he would find himself deserted by Joy. She was never there to welcome him with a hot dinner or a soothing drink. The feeling of emptiness so preyed on his mind that eventually he began to prolong his trips in order to lessen the pain. He had also reluctantly come to the conclusion that Joy regarded him as a bit of a bore, although she was more than ready to return whenever she was in difficulty.

One week after Sir John Cumber's arrival in Baringo, he had just left his thatched hut on the shores of the lake, Kampi ya Samaki, the camp of the fish, when a plume of dust was seen on the horizon of the flat plains ahead of him. It approached at great speed and, as it got closer, Cumber recognized a Second World War American Jeep with its windscreen lowered onto its bonnet. As it passed without reducing speed on the narrow track but with a cheery toot on its bronchial horn, Cumber noticed that the passenger sitting beside the African driver was a scantily-clad blonde who merely lifted one hand in part salutation before disappearing in a cloud of thick dust in the direction of his camp. He immediately ordered his lorry to turn round and, arriving back at his headquarters, found the woman, now clad in a thin cotton dress over her shorts and bikini top, gazing out over the lake and sipping a cool drink. Her superb figure impressed him. On dismounting, Cumber strolled over to her, wondering what had so unexpectedly hit the most dangerous part of his new district. Joy, turning from the lake, which glistened in the morning sun, smiled cheerfully as she introduced herself. Cumber replied: 'Tell me, did you obtain a permit before journeying through West Suk? Don't you realize there's recently been a massacre?'

Joy appeared genuinely puzzled and said, 'I have been in the area twice before and have never needed one.' Shaken by the news, she produced a permit signed by the chief native commissioner in Nairobi, authorizing her to enter all districts in order to undertake her commission of painting head-and-shoulder portraits of senior chiefs. She turned her blue eyes on Cumber and changed the delicate subject: 'Come and look at my canvases.' They were piled under hessian covers in the back of the Jeep. 'My main concern is to keep the dust from settling on the portraits before the oil paint dries.' Jokingly, Cumber said, 'At the speed you were travelling there was not even time for a shadow to settle on them, let alone dust.' She laughed. 'Yes, that's the purpose of my speed.'

Cumber recalled: 'Joy used all her attributes to good effect in my presence, but there was stern duty to be done. In those far-gone days DCs seldom met ravishing blondes, scantily clad, in the middle of the *bundu* [bush] miles from anywhere. It was almost a fantasy come true and, having an artistic bent myself, her paintings filled me with added admiration. I shall always remember that once-in-a-lifetime surprise – a blonde in the bush who, for my money, was well worth two brunettes in the *boma*.'

Joy's extraordinary outpouring of over 700 paintings of Africans' fast-disappearing tribal culture was a dedicated gift to a land and its people about which she felt deeply. It was a courageous and difficult undertaking by a woman who, for all her faults, had, through her artistic talent, a good deal of poetry in her soul. She travelled vast distances on foot, donkey and car in extreme temperatures, over lava deserts and rain-sodden mountain slopes. She frequently fell sick with malaria; she endured such indignities as falling off her mule after being charged by an angry rhino and her calf; she travelled through bush country known to be the territory of man-eating lions. She had intermittent attacks of severe fever and for months on end lived on a meagre diet of eggs, ripe bananas and local vegetables. Undeterred, she lived for most of the year in isolated places, among simple people who were not always willing to pose as models. But somehow she managed to regard her difficulties as minor obstacles to be brushed aside for a greater cause.

Joy's tribal paintings were important primarily as contributions to both ethnology and anthropology rather than to art. Judged simply as a portrait artist, Joy was almost entirely self-taught and this was evident in her work.

She evolved her own solutions to representational problems, sometimes more successfully than others. As a result, her style is personal and distinctive. She frequently had difficulty with anatomy, often having little understanding of her sitter's torso. Her ability to model in the round was occasionally defective, lapsing into the two-dimensional. Folds of drapery were also crudely rendered. But she developed her own technique for the portrayal of black flesh, which involved strong lighting of the subject's features to increase contrasts. She brought to bear the same meticulousness of observation on her human subjects that she showed as a flower painter. She was, in general, an industrious recorder of fact rather than a lyrical evoker of mood, although in a few of her portraits she successfully penetrated the surface and gave an emotional depth to her sitter.

George eventually came to loathe Joy's painting commission. He dashed off a letter to Dorle in which he stressed how worried he was that Joy was constantly out of touch. He felt increasingly concerned because he knew that, whether she had malaria or was in trouble, nothing would prevent her finishing the project. While he knew he had married an exceptional person and could not help but admire her courage, all he now longed for was the day Joy stopped striving for what he could only view as her ridiculous 'idealism'. Through her selfless commitment to her painting, plus her growing neglect of him, George was now convinced their marriage was heading for disaster.

One of the arguments between the couple concerned the amount of money Joy received from the government. She insisted on passing all her work to the people of Kenya, regardless of how insolvent it left her. Each painting was handed back to the government for £5, including expenses, even though friends were eager to pay four times that amount. Try as he might, George could not persuade her to change her mind.

George was becoming slightly nervous of his increasingly intimate correspondence with Dorle, pleading that she show great discretion in what she wrote. It would be natural for Joy to want to read any letters from her and there would be trouble if George kept making excuses. Besides which, it would distress him greatly to see Joy vent her anger on her sister.

The two women had never been close and little correspondence had passed between them. Dorle recalls: 'George thought perhaps if I let out my feelings to Joy she might have understood my hard life. He said that if we confided in each other more, both of us would benefit. But, because Joy always reproached me for not doing the right thing by not working and staying at home to look after my children, I no longer continued writing to her.' It would be twenty years before they exchanged intimacies.

Dorle was the first to break the silence. Interested in politics, she wrote to ask her sister about the Rhodesian problem. Joy replied that she was taken aback to receive Dorle's letter and declared curtly that, as it was not her practice to commit herself one way or the other over any political problem, she was not prepared to answer the question. Dismissive though it seemed, Joy's reply was enough to start a constant flow of letters between them.

Dorle had travelled to England in 1948, where she later married an Englishman. Today they live in a small house in Lancashire overflowing with a lifetime's possessions. Now, aged seventy-two, she slightly resembles her sister in her later years and has the same strength of personality and passion for writing letters, though Dorle's are far more articulate. However, she shares none of Joy's ambition and, unlike her famous sister, she never fails to be friendly, hospitable and generous. A highly eccentric woman, living in relative poverty, she is given to spending the days nearing the full moon upstairs in bed under a duvet. As she potters around her house, hot-water bottles are strapped onto her back over layers of unkempt sweaters to keep out the English damp. She has instant recall of family history and within minutes can produce photographs and letters from both Joy and George, hidden under piles of newspapers and clothing.

Through their letters, Dorle and George developed a deepening mutual attraction. George felt this was a natural instinct and thought it must be because Dorle seemed down-to-earth, as he was. Joy, on the other hand, always wanted the impossible.

12

Shadows on the Sun

Six years after their marriage Joy again decided she wanted to have a baby, followed the advice of a doctor in Mombasa and had her tubes blown free. She was advised to take a holiday with George as soon as she had recovered as she would most likely be able to conceive immediately after her operation. The couple spent two weeks camping in the Shimba Hills and Joy claimed that George was kind to her and they decided to give their unhappy marriage another try.

One of the conditions laid down by Joy was that George should tactfully wean himself off his friendship with the 'predatory' woman in Limuru. George promised to do so. After the trip, Joy was left pregnant, but for the next four weeks heard nothing from her husband. As she knew he was dealing daily with unpredictable animals in the wild, she became increasingly worried that an accident had befallen him. When he finally wrote he told her that on his way to Isiolo, he has spent the night with the friends in Limuru. Over a bottle of wine they had decided to go for a three-week safari to the NFD, where they had had a very enjoyable time together.

As soon as she heard the news, Joy maintained, she suffered another miscarriage. Frustrated that George never missed an opportunity to meet up with this particular couple, she wrote to the husband that the reason she avoided his wife was because she and George, always so close, had once had an affair. Was he aware of it? Apparently, soon after receiving Joy's letter, the couple left Kenya. On the few occasions they returned, George saw them as often as possible. If it was true that George had had an affair with his best friend's wife, he had obviously been forgiven. In November 1950 Dorle, realizing that her sister was making George deeply unhappy, wrote an intimate letter to him. She offered herself to him, a man she had never met but for whom she felt tremendous sympathy. George was deeply moved by her overture for by then, he must have been sorely in need of love and understanding. But in his reply he admitted that he was still very much in love with Joy and was prepared to wait another twelve months, by which time he hoped matters would have resolved themselves one way or the other.

Over the question of divorce, which the couple had frequently discussed, George had always been quite prepared to shoulder the blame and give his unhappy wife her freedom, but he refused to pay any alimony. Joy, on the other hand, was adamant that, on both moral and legal grounds, she was entitled to such payment. Indeed, as George wrote to Dorle, he felt it was he who had every right to divorce her after her adulterous behaviour – he had ample evidence of two affairs she had had with men in Kenya, which he could produce had he wanted a divorce. He poured out his frustrations of the past seven years in which he complained their sex life had been virtually non-existent. What made him particularly bitter was that Joy had left Peter Bally because he was unable to satisfy her sexually. George had experienced no problems in this area during the period of Joy's initial attraction to him. Considering his normal appetite, he mourned his lack of sexual intimacy, saying that at times life had been a nightmare for him. He then divulged that he had never been unfaithful to his wife.

Apparently, Joy had often told him that she couldn't have cared less if he slept with other women, if that would relieve his frustration. But he was well aware that if he so much as glanced at another woman, Joy was consumed with jealousy.

Having described his deep emotional turmoil, he gently explained to Dorle that he could not possibly ask her to wait for him. All that she could reasonably expect was that if Joy and he separated, then he would love to meet her, and if they thought they could be happy together, then he saw no reason at all why they should not get married. Dorle does not regret her generous offer to George: 'My sister was cruel to George. I think I could have loved him,' she says.

Early in January the following year, on a trip to the coast where George was involved in control work, Joy began painting the local Boran and Swahili. The couple were the guests of the district officer in charge of Kipini, John Brown, a large, red-haired man known to all as 'Marmalade John'. George and Joy's tent was pitched below Brown's house in an eerie place filled with tombs of numerous other DCs who had died of malaria. Their old friend Willie Hale, who had introduced them, was also staying. All three were invited by their host to dinner. Joy described the event as a pleasant evening in camp. As it was hot, she took her eau de cologne and squirted a few drops on everyone, intending to refresh them. But apparently Marmalade took this as an insult, stood up, took a *kiboko* and hit her on the back. Joy was stunned. He then raised his arm for a second blow and, despite her protests, struck her for a second time with all his strength. She left and retired to her tent, expecting George to deal with Brown. But George said nothing, giggled and seemed to regard it all as a big joke. So the next day, she left Kipini without an apology from Brown, or any defending action from George on her behalf.

Willie Hale, however, refutes the story : 'We were all sitting in George's tent having a drink before I went up to have a bath in the house. When they didn't appear for dinner, I strolled down to the Adamsons' tent to see what had happened. George recounted the story. It seems Marmalade was sitting comfortably in his canvas chair when Joy, skittish and full of spirits, jumped up and started to spray him with her scent. Though he protested, she deliberately danced round and kept it up till he gave her a swift backhander and started to stalk off to the house. George sat there for a moment, puffing away at his pipe and said, "Marmalade, you're no gentleman." Marmalade would hardly go around wielding a *kiboko*. Joy just loved to see two men fighting over her. She was trying to get a reaction out of George.'

Joy had recently been given an infant rock hyrax, a small, furry animal and a close relation of the elephant and rhino. She named her Pati Pati and the pair soon became inseparable. Joy spoilt her mercilessly, walking around with Pati sitting on her shoulder, feeding her her favourite titbits of mango and pawpaw from her breakfast plate and letting Pati's passion for alcohol become a daily ritual.

George had recently acquired a young assistant, Denis Zaphiro, who, in his second week in Isiolo, witnessed one of Joy's outbursts when dining at their house. Pati Pati, as usual, was perched on Joy's shoulder and she was busy feeding her bits of bread, which she had dipped in her soup. George, already irritated by the animal's constant presence, eventually said, 'Joy, for heaven's sake, do put that animal down. It's most unhygienic.'

'What does it have to do with you ?' Joy retorted.

'It has quite a lot to do with me. I am head of the household and this table and I am not going to sit here watching you make a fuss of an animal which has just peed down your arm.'

Joy cried, 'You brute,' picked up her plate and hurled the boiling soup straight into her husband's face. Denis leapt up and rushed George to the downstairs bathroom, swiftly followed by Joy in tears. When she finally calmed down she wept, 'You are my darling, George, I am so sorry, I am so sorry.' Wrapped in her arms, George replied, 'Joy, don't be so silly, I'm all right.'

Four days later Joy was engaged in a watercolour painting of a fine-boned Somali chief on the back verandah of the house, opposite the kitchen. Beside her on a table was a small bowl in which she washed her brushes. On the other side, in a similar bowl, lay her tea from which she occasionally sipped. As soon as it became cold, Joy shouted to the small Turkana boy who worked in the kitchen: 'Lete chai moja ingine,' (bring me another cup of tea). After a short while he emerged and handed her a cup. Angry that he had taken so long, Joy flung the tea into the young boy's face. He gave a piercing scream as the hot liquid burnt his skin.

Denis was on the front verandah fixing a puncture when he heard the boy's cry. Rushing over, he arrived just in time to stop the enraged Somali chief from plunging his dagger into the white woman. Using soothing Swahili he calmed the chief down and settled Joy back on her canvas chair. She instantly regretted what she had done and hugged the crying, frail body of the little African to her. When a close friend later remarked, 'Joy, you are completely unbalanced at times,' she replied with a resigned shrug: 'Maybe I am, maybe I am.'

Although fifteen years younger than Joy, Denis became one of her amatory quarries during the five months he was in Isiolo. One particular evening, after a heated argument in which he had been angered by Joy's persistent sexual advances, the usually quiet young man rounded on her, telling her she was 'a Viennese alley cat. You're a stupid bitch and I wouldn't be at all surprised if you were a prostitute.'

A few days later, the Hales, the Adamsons and Zaphiro were sitting round the breakfast table on safari when the wind blew the cornflakes packet onto the ground. Denis saw it fall, but was deep in conversation. Joy, sitting on the other side of him, pulled his sleeve and said, 'Denis, the packet of cereal has fallen down.'

'Just a minute Joy, I am talking to Morna.'

Joy, who hated being ignored by anyone and realizing that she had failed to make a conquest, screamed loudly across the table, 'All you are interested in are other men's wives. You even made a pass at me.'

George, knowing that Zaphiro was well aware of Joy's current affair with a policeman, sat silently, squirming with embarrassment.

Denis eventually could take the persistent pressure from the mature woman of forty-one no longer and asked Willie Hale, his boss, for a transfer. Willie's initial response was, 'If you cannot handle a situation like this, you are going to have far worse in the game department.'

Joy's emotional and belittling tirades against George often took place at dinner when she knew her husband usually remained silent. Ayesha Walters, wife of the Garissa DC, was present one night when, after a slight disagreement, Joy told the assembled guests: 'With my first husband I had beautiful clothes. With my second, I had lots of books.' And then she looked up the table at George and said, 'With this silly little man, I haven't got anything at all. And which husband are you anyway?'

By 1950 the Adamsons were living in a new house, built by Terence. It was a typical, rather modest Kenya dwelling, square with small steel windows and a corrugated iron roof.

There was no love lost between Joy and her brother-in-law. He called her 'that frightful woman'. One of his habits which irritated Joy was his twitching as if he had insects crawling down his neck. Exasperated, she would shout, 'Terence, Terence', as if it was a dog she was talking to. Having none of the social graces, Terence, Joy felt, was not an asset to his brother and she went out of her way never to be seen in his company. If visitors arrived whom Joy wished to impress, Terence took the hint and ambled off, knowing his presence embarrassed her. A friend of both suggested the brothers be named Terence and Tolerance, bearing in mind George's outstanding trait, especially towards his wife.

Terence was a solitary man, intelligent, smaller and not as articulate as George. He was also a fine amateur botanist. Much of his life was spent on his own as a bush engineer, living the life of a hermit in a hut in Marsabit and supervising the building of roads, airstrips and large shallow pans in the baked earth for catching water. Completely fearless, he was known to knock off the odd buffalo when bothered. Not a man who felt comfortable in the presence of women, he nevertheless fathered more than one son by an African woman – he had followed in the steps of his brother, who had lived with a beautiful Somali girl before marrying Joy. John MacDonald, the vet, said of Terence, 'He was the sort of chap you could put under a thorn tree in the middle of Africa with no food or water and he would survive. But put him in front of a female and he was terrified. He was desperately shy and never raised his eyes when talking to a woman.'

At the end of 1951, when Joy was still absorbed in her tribal painting, George was earning £1,000 a year and, for the first time, felt financially secure, knowing he could support Joy – her trips cost far more than the amount the government had allocated. Although he knew that she was reasonably fond of him, he never ceased to want more from her – something she was unable to give. He wrote a long letter to Dorle explaining that Joy seemed to be settling down, having reluctantly come to the conclusion that she was unlikely to find a more suitable mate. Despite her numerous disappointments, however, he was well aware she would subconsciously continue to hope someone might appear. Perhaps she was beginning to realize that time was not on their side and that neither was in the first flush of youth.

Yet, a few months later he told Dorle, perhaps as a result of yet another of Joy's fleeting affairs, that enough was enough. He gave Joy an ultimatum – she must choose between her painting and her marriage.

For a time Joy gave a marginal amount of extra attention to her husband but never failed to find fault with his treatment of her. Later that year Robert Nimmo and George decided to explore the country between Marsabit and Wajir, virtually unknown territory. Nimmo travelled ahead and George was to meet him at a certain waterhole. He arrived two days late. Robert remembered the occasion: 'George apologized profusely, saying, "I've had a bit of trouble with Joy. We had a row because I wouldn't let her come. She told me: 'Well, if you're going alone, I'm going to commit suicide, I'm absolutely finished with you.' She marched into her room, slammed the door shut and locked it." George drove off in his Land Rover when a single shot suddenly echoed round the walls of the house. He slammed on the brakes, rushed into the house and broke the bedroom door down. There he found Joy sitting on the bed, laughing her head off, with her revolver in her hand. She had fired it at the ceiling.'

In March 1953, George, who had not left Kenya for over twenty-nine years, was forced by the government to take home leave. Officers were supposed to break at regular intervals and, because of the fierce equatorial climate, were meant to spend part of their leave abroad. George, deliberately flouting the regulations, had accumulated over two years' holiday. Four months later, after travelling by Land Rover through the land of the pygmies and over the Sahara, past Marrakesh and over the Pyrenees, he and Joy eventually arrived in England.

As soon as they had unpacked, the couple had a pleasant tea in Piccadilly with Toni Ofenheim, a skilled surgeon and friend of George's for over twenty years, followed by dinner at her home. Joy recalled that it did not surprise her that Toni spent most of the evening concentrating on George, since she, Joy, was a stranger to her. They parted friends, but, according to Joy, Miss Ofenheim cut her dead for the rest of Joy's marriage. She complained to a friend that Toni repeatedly gave George advice on how to handle her and had created a severe rift between the married couple. For many years Joy accused George of being in love with Toni whom, she remained convinced, he idolized. Apparently George had wanted to marry Toni after their initial safari but she had backed out.

George was completely overwhelmed by the pace of life in large metropolises, modern conveniences and the crush and brusqueness of people. Joy claimed she was embarrassed by numerous humiliating situations when George seemed unable to order meals in hotels but instead sat mute, clutching the menu until Joy was forced to order their food from the bemused waiter. This bizarre behaviour apparently also happened in banks, where George was tongue-tied until the perplexed cashier became so harassed that Joy had to intervene to change George's money. On one occasion in Paris, when George went off to use a public telephone, Joy waited for ten minutes before locating him inside the box. He was staring at the telephone, doing nothing: Joy asked him why on earth he had not asked her how to use it before he left. George apparently lost his temper and began threatening his wife. Joy maintained George chased her back to their hotel and, once inside their room, he started hitting her.

After a night at the Folies Bergère, the couple once again got into an argument about sex. Joy shouted, 'Stop the car', and stormed off into the night with the money and the name of their hotel, which George could not remember. For five hours George drove round trying to find the familiar street. Shaking off helpful suggestions from friendly ladies of the night, he suffered 'one of the worst experiences of my life'.

George was vastly relieved to be sailing home to Kenya after eight months away, leaving Joy behind to lecture in England and Sweden on tribal customs and to try to drum up interest in a book on the tribes of Kenya. She complained that George left her with no money. He even had the nerve to ask her to pay the taxi to the boat from London from money she had earned from her paintings. She deeply resented George borrowing £100 of her money to stretch their leave, which apparently he never paid back. In addition, there were the bills for drinks and laundry on the boat, which amounted to another £100. He later explained to Joy that he had had to offer fellow passengers whisky otherwise nobody would have cared for his company. She maintained he often used the same excuse at home at Isiolo when she complained about their whisky bills.

Having failed to interest a publisher during her month in England, Joy, too, returned to Kenya. The country was embroiled in the Mau Mau uprising. Aware of simmering discontent and tension among the Africans, in particular among the Kikuyu, the Governor, Sir Evelyn Baring, had been forced to declare a state of emergency in October 1952 and had arrested Jomo Kenyatta, then reputed to be leader of the rebels.

George became involved in training patrols in the Aberdare Highlands. He taught his men how to track silently through the dense forests where brave young whites, such as Francis Erskine, blackened their faces, matted their hair and crouched in old army greatcoats, which were favoured by the Kikuyu, on the edges of gatherings of Mau Mau rebels, listening to planned atrocities. The Royal Inniskillen Fusilliers had commandeered the Adamsons' house as their headquarters to prevent the gangs from reaching Somalia in search of arms and food. The windows of the house had been wired up and many guards were placed outside.

The small town became highly agitated on hearing that a leading Mau Mau gangster and his following had escaped from their hide-out and had slipped into the hills of the wild Mathews Range. Fearful of just how rapidly bush telegraph operates, it was agreed between Noel Kennaway, PC Isiolo, and other officials that instead of sending dozens of *askaris*, George would take a small force of men of his choosing and chase the gang, who would take little notice of the game warden roaming the hills. George promptly went to Isiolo gaol and took out a bunch of rapscallions that he had put inside for poaching. He then armed his band of desperadoes, now in game department uniform, set off and found no hideaways and no gangs. They had got away. Kennaway, however, grateful to George for his good sense and bravery, had a small wooden shield made and painted with crossed rifles to 'Commemorate Adamson Force'. Perhaps proud or amused by owning one of the last of the private armies, George kept this shield for the rest of his life, and for many years it hung in his bedroom.

As most of the violence was confined to the Kikuyu area, Joy was able to continue painting throughout the troubles. She was especially stimulated by capturing on canvas a Mau Mau prisoner with long hair matted in mud and a tattered felt hat, who was executed a few days after his sitting.

When she returned from painting she would often ask for George, only to learn that he had left on safari. He would be gone for several days and, she claimed, had not even left her a revolver or guards to protect her against the Mau Mau who, she maintained, were all around their home. In fact, though Isiolo was relatively safe, there was a belt of forest between there and Nanyuki. The Mau Mau lived by day in the dark of the forests, scheming and issuing oaths and violent curses. They came out each night to hamstring cattle and murder 1,800 hundred Africans loyal to the Crown, as well as nearly 100 whites. Towards the latter part of the emergency their rituals were particularly bestial. They would cut off breasts, bury people alive and kill children or parents piece by piece in front of each other. In return, the security forces killed around 12,000 rebels. Although the Kikuyu lost the fighting, the struggle for freedom and independence continued and the old regime gave way within a few years.

In 1954 negotiations were under way for a suitable site for the filming of *Mogambo*. Terence Gavaghan, the DC at Maralal, was engaged in discussions with the film company and was determined that, as they wished to film on land filled with Samburu tribesmen, the natives must benefit. Over a dinner, which included as guests the stars of the film – Clark Gable, Grace Kelly and Ava Gardner – Gavaghan offered the producer the use of the Uaso Nyiro towards Lololokwe, near Isiolo (*uaso* is the Maasai word for river). Gavaghan struck a hard bargain. In exchange for 1,000 tribesmen to be used as extras in the film, 1,000 spears to be specially fashioned by the tribal spear-maker, 300 head of cattle to feed the men and a specific length of time for filming, Gavaghan insisted on three yards of the best quality red silk cloth per man, plus enough meat to fill him, averaging seven pounds a day. The DC would also retain the skins on the tribesmen's behalf. An added demand was that all the electrical installations used in the film should be left behind for the district hospitals, as well as the station wagon, which could be used as an ambulance. Much to Gavaghan's amazement, they agreed.

Joy, never one to miss an opportunity, told Gavaghan she was coming up to Buffalo Springs to paint the Samburu tribesmen while the film was being made. She asked him if he would supply her with models. Realizing that she was climbing on his particular bandwagon, he told her: 'Joy, Metro are paying me for the tribe to produce warriors, not as a by-product for your purposes. You can come up, but you will do it on your own. I cannot help you.' She duly arrived.

By this time Joy, due to the harsh effects of the sun and her strenuous outdoor life, was beginning to lose her notable physical appeal and appeared slightly weatherbeaten. Gavaghan, still a handsome man with a reputation in those days of 'being fairly extravagant in my sex life', recalled his reaction to Joy: 'The fingertips didn't yearn to touch.' He was careful not to appear available: 'I don't think women understand the experience a man has of not wanting to be accessible to a woman with whom he never wishes to have a relationship. It is quite difficult to walk away from someone who is so determined. There is an assumption on the part of many women, who may feel vaguely interested, that the response will be there. I was only struck by the fact that Joy was really marketing something which was unsaleable.'

Coming to the end of her painting safaris, Joy was still full of plans, ideas and projects, still searching for something in which to devote all her energies and her time. She finally decided that she wished to care for orphaned and wounded animals and approached Robert Nimmo, the DC, for a grant of 30,000 acres of land and financial assistance. Unfortunately for Joy, the land round Isiolo was Crown land held by the government in trust for the African people and it would have required an Act of Parliament to give her any part of it. Nimmo recalled the endless *fitina* (trouble) he had with Joy: 'She thought she was omnipotent and could actually get Parliament to do this for her. She was furious when I said I could not possibly do this and vowed, once again, never to have anything more to do with me. But none of the rows mattered, George was my friend, not her.'

Nimmo subsequently received another visit. 'This time she came to my office with her cook, whom she had brought to be beaten by the *askari*, which I could sanction as a magistrate in a few cases. Apparently her cook had spoiled the soup. I said to Joy, "Don't be a silly ass," and sent them both packing. She lost face in front of her servant and simply refused to speak to me again.'

But within a year Joy was to find her life's work, the legacy which was to bring her worldwide fame and wealth.

13

Elsa

Ken Smith, a sturdy, reliable Scot who joined the game department in 1956, played a major part in the Adamsons' life. He gained valuable experience in lion-hunting with George, which he needed for his post in Garissa, an area plagued by man-eaters that had to be shot. Soon after Ken's arrival, the two men set off to shoot a lion which had killed a Boran tribesman one hundred miles from Isiolo, in an area rife with poaching. It seemed a day like any other, but Joy, staying behind in camp with Pati Pati, was unaware that her whole life was about to take on a new meaning.

While looking for the man-eater, Ken and George came across a large lioness which suddenly sprang at them from behind some rocks hidden by bush. Although both the Adamsons claimed that George killed the lioness, it was actually Ken Smith who 'gave her two virtually fatal shots. As I recall, she sort of stumbled out and fell over. Then George and I both fired shots. It was a bit confusing and although she was finished off, she had more or less died when she got the first shot. The hunt had been long and we were sitting down with a thermos of tea when George noticed that the dead lioness was heavily in milk. Hearing a few mewling cries from a crevice in the rocks, we went over and pulled out three, tiny, three-week-old female cubs. The lioness had been protecting her litter.'

Arriving back in camp, George called for his wife. With a cry of delight she picked up the fluffy bundles and immediately started fussing over them. She was now quite accustomed to the trials, not always successful, of rearing young mongooses, bushbabies, elephants, ostriches and small buck, but this was the first time she had been given lion cubs to look after. Her maternal instinct instantly rekindled, Joy, with infinite patience, soon had the spotted furry creatures accepting watered-down milk through a rubber hose that George had rigged up. The runt of the litter quickly became their favourite and they named her Elsa because, as Joy said, 'She reminded me of someone of that name' – Elsa von Klarwill, her former mother-in-law.

It was in the quiet moments while Elsa sat in Joy's lap, eating small morsels of minced meat, sucking Joy's thumbs and kneading her thighs for milk, that the strong bond between the two developed. When not with Joy or George, Elsa was looked after by their gardener, Nuru, who became her faithful friend. Apart from Nuru and later Makedde, George's game scout, Elsa was greatly suspicious of the natives.

The cubs' arrival was a fortunate event for Joy who, having completed her tribal paintings, had been occupying her time with writing and photography. She needed another 'serious hobby' in which to pour her vast reserves of energy, telling a friend, 'Thank goodness I now have something worthwhile to look after.' Elsa's arrival was the beginning of a friendship which culminated in one of the most remarkable relationships ever recorded between human and animal. Unable to find happiness among her own kind Joy, at last, found fulfilment by lavishing particular devotion on a large, potentially dangerous cat. In later years, while trying to make others understand the depth of her feelings for Elsa, Joy said, 'I cannot explain my relationship with Elsa because it is something I cannot compare. I have never had the deep love in the purest sense of the word with any human being before and I was lucky to have some very fine people in my life, including what I thought true human love means. But with Elsa, it was something quite different. She provided love for me.' In its purest sense hers was a love usually given to a child.

Elsa and her playful sisters Lustica and One spent much of their day romping over the house or swinging on a tyre hung from a tree, followed everywhere by Pati Pati, Joy's pet hyrax, who had become their inseparable companion and self-appointed nanny. At night the cubs slept in a wooden shelter in an enclosure surrounded by chicken wire. As their strength grew, each instinctively took to dragging a tarpaulin sheet along the ground between their increasingly powerful front legs, as if they were practising dragging a kill. In order to discipline the cats, Joy and George carried a small stick with them wherever they went, occasionally administering a sharp smack.

As soon as the three became too large to handle and had been banned from the house, Willie Hale insisted they be sent away. Elsa had already knocked down a ranger and, with three grown lions running around the Adamsons' compound, sooner or later there would be another accident. One night at dinner Willie made his point : 'Now George, it's not fair on the Africans. Besides, they are not being employed to look after your lions. I'm afraid you're under strict orders not to use the game scouts.

Follow my leader – Joy and Elsa

A crocodile killed by George on a trip to South Island

Joy with Sir William (Billy) Collins, her publisher

Virginia McKenna with 'Elsa' in *Born Free*

1964. Joy during the filming of *Born Free*

Her Majesty the Queen and Joy wearing identical dresses at the royal command performance of *Born Free*, London, 1966

Pippa, with a broken leg, at the animal orphanage in Nairobi

Elsamere on Lake Naivasha. It is now a museum and memorial to Joy

Joy at Elsamere in front of her painting of her cook whom she had asked as a joke to dress up in all the finery he could find

976. Joy's favourite companions at samere, her family of colobus onkeys

Joy aged 66

George aged 71

George's assistant Tony Fitzjohn with two young lions at Kora

Joy's assistant Pieter Mawson at Shaba

Joy's kitchen at Shaba

George at Joy's funeral in Nairobi

Joy's cairn at Shaba

'People used to think Elsa was a dear little thing. She wasn't anything of the sort, except for those she knew well.'

Joy, sensing that her plan for raising one or all of the cubs was in danger of being thwarted, and furious that Hale was ticking off her husband, shouted, 'If we keep Elsa she will not interfere with George's job and I will take all responsibility for her.'

Willie, instantly embroiled in a heated argument, stuck to his guns. Eventually Joy rose from the table and, hurling the words 'Willie, you're no friend of mine,' marched out of the room. She did not speak to the chief game warden again for fifteen years.

In order to placate his boss and keep some harmony in the *boma*, George agreed to part of Hale's request by hastily despatching Elsa's two sisters to Rotterdam zoo. Willie, well aware of Joy's ferocious determination, says now: 'I have not the slightest doubt that Joy, I won't say wrecked George's career as a game warden, but certainly George only went on safari as directed by Joy.'

The arrival of Elsa had a significant effect on the Adamsons' relationship. Joy stated: 'It was due to her that we shared as much as we ever could share together. She brought us closer than we had ever been.' George added, 'Just as a child might have done.' But once again Joy even managed to find fault with the way George, who was equally attached to Elsa, treated the big cat. She complained to a close friend that she was horrified to see George hitting Elsa with a stick over her nose, the most sensitive and frail part of her face, whenever he was annoyed by the lioness. Joy also maintained that whenever a situation arose where either of them might be clawed by Elsa George always let Joy do the job, telling her that he had no intention of being scratched. She remained convinced that as George kept insisting he was not a glorified zookeeper, he would have given Elsa away after two weeks if she had not intervened.

Elsa's greatest fans were the children of the European officials who lived in Isiolo or Meru, a town a few hours' drive away. Sunday visits to the Adamsons became a regular event. Cars loaded with children, all of whom wanted to stroke, cuddle and help feed Elsa, chugged along the short bumpy distance. Roughly the size of an Alsatian dog, Elsa would stand on her hind legs, with forepaws on the child's shoulders, and lick the youngster's face from chin to forehead in a gesture of great friendliness. The older children could bear the young lioness's weight, but the smaller ones were often knocked flat on their backs. John Cumber, then DC in Meru, remembered: 'Joy and George could not have been kinder or more attentive hosts and loved having the kids there.' Joy went out of her way to encourage the youngest children to play with Elsa but never left them alone while the cub was at large. As a treat, she gave the children hens' eggs and biscuits for tea.

Although in her books Joy claimed that Elsa never attacked or hurt anybody, this was not strictly true. However remarkable and gentle an animal she was with those she trusted and depended upon, Elsa's natural instincts were bound to surface. Besides Joy herself being covered on her back and arms with scratches inflicted by Elsa's sharp claws, the lioness had entered a professional hunter's camp in the area and had badly bitten a young warden through his arm. He regarded this as an added insult to an already difficult situation. For the past few months Joy had found him irresistible, despite the fact he was twenty years younger than she. The more she pursued him, the more venomous was his reaction.

But there were also amusing episodes with Elsa. One evening soon after Desmond O'Hagan had taken over as acting PC from Dick Turnbull in Isiolo, they were at a dinner party at George and Lois Low's when Joy came up to the house, desperately worried and upset. Going up to her husband she cried, 'George, come at once, Elsa's lying on top of the mountain. She can't move; she's dying.' George, totally unruffled, said, 'There's a stretcher on the verandah, take that, get some game scouts and go and get Elsa.' Joy reprimanded him, 'Oh, you are beastly, George, you don't understand at all.' George, in the middle of dinner, said, 'Oh, go on, Joy,' and returned to his food.

One and a half hours went by before the weary scouts staggered down the hill. Exhausted, they put down the stretcher carrying Elsa on the Lows' verandah and were quickly surrounded by the diners, who were slightly concerned that Joy had not returned. George took one look at Elsa and went off to find an enema for her, to placate Joy before her arrival. As soon as he left, Elsa gave a large yawn, lazily got up from the stretcher and trotted off down to the Adamsons' camp, not waiting for such an indignity. According to O'Hagan: 'As soon as Joy returned she went up to George, who was always rather slow, got him by his goatee and said "George, you are so stupid," before rushing off after her lioness. We all thought the whole episode highly entertaining.'

From the inception, Joy talked to Elsa as one might to an intelligent dog. A few sentimental words were obviously used when she fondled Elsa, but no more than many people do with loved and trusted pets. Elsa soon learned to recognize Joy's voice from others. With her acute hearing, she could pick up her 'Ou hoo, Ou hoo' from a considerable distance in areas of thick bush.

When the time came for Elsa to have a collar, instead of measuring her neck, Joy bundled her newest orphan into the back of the Land Rover, newly covered with chicken wire round the sides, and drove down to Nairobi. Six hours later she arrived at the leather and saddlery shop Raper and Pringle, run by Kate Challis. 'God, it's Joy,' said Kate's husband, who instantly ducked out the back door, leaving his wife to cope. Joy plonked Elsa on the counter and made a tremendous show of her. Kate rummaged round for the biggest dog collar in stock but nothing fitted. In the end, in the midst of what she called 'a typical emotional display from Joy', it was agreed that a suitable one was to be made. Half-carrying, half-dragging Elsa, Joy left the shop.

14

Born Free

For much of the next two years, from 1956 to 1958, the Adamsons took Elsa on safari, often to their camp on the banks of the Uaso Nyiro, an area rich in baboon-laden doum palms, fig trees and scrawny acacia bush. In the hot, dry season, the water meandered in a trickle down to the Lorian swamp. There were large outcrops of rock for Elsa to pad over, and foaming rapids which fell into velvet blue pools, filled with fish, in which she could gambol. In the cool of each evening the far-off rumbling of elephant were heard, ambling down to the river where they took long, slow draughts of water to slake their thirst and hose the dust off their backs.

Going on safari was paradise for Elsa. During walks, her body tense with excitement, she stalked giraffe, rolled in fresh elephant droppings, chased mongoose through the bush and retrieved guinea fowl shot by George. She knew instinctively how far she could tease wild animals. Although she remained close to Joy, Elsa slept in George's tent at night, often with a paw out to make sure he was still beside her and, being somewhat coddled, would never sleep on the ground if a camp bed was handy. Her greatest pleasure when travelling through the reserves was to lie, like a serene golden sphinx, on top of the Land Rover. Here the breeze raced through her fur and her keen eyes spotted distant game.

To prevent any accidents while on the move from one camp to the next, Elsa was kept away from the tantalizing donkeys which accompanied them and restrained on a thick chain when in sight of the tribal camels drinking from the well. In order to stop her from giving chase and eventually killing livestock, the Adamsons cut up her meat, to disassociate her meal from a goat or camel on the hoof. George remained sensitive in later years over the criticism he and his wife endured for shooting animals to support Elsa, explaining that they only killed what was necessary.

During these lengthy stays in the bush the Adamsons' marriage, despite being strengthened by the shared love for Elsa, was still as tempestuous as ever. Violent rows were frequent, and Joy continued her list of complaints. After one particularly vicious argument, Joy ran from the camp to escape further beatings from George which, she claimed, their staff often witnessed. Tears pouring down her face, she began to cross the Ura River. Her plan was to make it to the neighbouring Tharaka district, where she might find someone kind enough to give her a lift to the nearest police station. After a couple of hours, she glanced back to see George following her. Apparently, he caught up with her, blocked her path, boxed her ears, beat her and then, holding her by the wrists, forced her to return to the camp. Rather sadly Joy claimed it was only for her beloved Elsa's sake that she remained with her husband.

On a safari with Elsa to the Indian Ocean, Pati Pati, Joy's constant companion for the last six years, died, in George's words, 'of old age'. Joy was inconsolable. She had become deeply attached to the small hyrax, which nestled round her neck like a fur and ground her teeth when happy. Joy immediately blamed George for her death. Pati was getting on in years when they went on holiday to the coast. The heat between Garissa and Lamu was unbearable. Joy took Elsa in the lorry, while George and Pati travelled by car. The convoy separated before Garissa, where George went to chat to the DC, and the couple planned to meet up at a camping site further down the road. But Joy lost her way and when she finally arrived, she found Pati in a coma. Her favourite small companion died soon afterwards of heat stroke. Joy later found that Pati had been left in the car, under a merciless sun, while George was inside in the DC's cool office.

It was on this coastal trip that George once again became poisoned by an overdose of mepacrine, which he had taken for malaria. On the two occasions he took the medication, he became, in Joy's words, 'temporarily mad', a well-known side-effect in people who were allergic to it. As a woman who liked to be needed, she recalled with unusual gentleness that both times George could only relax and gain his health knowing she was beside him. She felt truly grateful that, at such times, George knew his wife was the only person he could honestly turn to and rely on. Only with her could he trust his feelings. This deep need for Joy was also apparent after George had been mauled by a buffalo in Meru. She was immediately there to comfort him when he broke down and cried. There was a part of Joy which relished the fact that George never showed such intimacy to others. But why, oh why, she wondered, did her husband treat her so callously and cruelly as soon as he was well again?

*   *   *

Life went well with Elsa until two incidents happened which deeply affected Joy's rapport with her. One day, as she was sitting on a rock with her sketchbook on her lap and her box of paints by her side, Elsa padded slowly up behind her and took Joy's entire skull in her mouth. Joy froze, panic-stricken, as Elsa's jaws closed around her. She dared not make a move in case Elsa bit her. Just as suddenly, Elsa spat her out and walked away. Profoundly shocked, Joy let out a long scream and George came running.

The second incident was equally serious. Lois Low, by then a generous, protective friend of Joy's, and her husband, George, arranged to have a drink with the Adamsons. They found Joy nervously pacing up and down the drive, waiting for Elsa to return with the game scouts with whom she had been out all day. George arrived and climbed down from the Land Rover. Suddenly Elsa came bounding towards them, narrowly missing Lois Low. George fended her off and, according to Lois, 'gave Elsa a good thrashing with his *kiboko*'. Joy turned and said, 'Come on up and we'll have our drink,' before walking off ahead of Elsa towards the house. Lois, well aware of how unwise it was for anyone to walk ahead of a lion, said to her husband, 'Joy's a fool to walk in front of Elsa like that, she's asking for trouble.'

At that moment, Elsa pounced on Joy, knocking the breath out of her as she hit the ground. Before George managed to beat the animal off, Elsa had badly clawed Joy's head and deeply lacerated her back. Joy was hysterical, screaming, 'It was all George's fault,' and was led, crying, back to the house. There her friend, who had been convinced Joy would be killed, tended gently to her wounds before taking her to hospital.

Joy never mentioned these incidents, nor admitted to anyone other than Lois, and perhaps her husband, that she was afraid of Elsa. Although she forgave Elsa and was always brave and resilient, it was a pivotal point in their relationship and from then on George, who was better able to control the animal, had more to do with the lioness than his wife.

By the time Elsa was two years old George and Joy decided the time had come 'to find her a home in the wild, away from us, away from Isiolo and as far away as possible from human habitation'. Plenty of people had reared lions in Kenya before the Adamsons, and knew a great deal about their behaviour and psychology, but never had they been rehabilitated into the wild. The Adamsons were not unaware of the potential danger Elsa posed to humans, especially the peoples of the bush. Realizing the inherent difficulty, George admitted that, although he was experienced with lions, he felt slightly at a loss at how to proceed.

Most of the game wardens, horrified at the idea of having 'that bloody woman and her lioness' loose in their park, refused permission. After an abortive three-month attempt in the Mara, where Elsa was only briefly accepted by a pride and became ill, she was taken back to northern Kenya, to the lush banks of the Ura River in the Meru County Council Reserve, near where she had been born. The area was within a day's drive of Isiolo, but only four miles from the nearest African homestead and the decision was bound to cause problems. Having driven to the appointed place for her release, each day Joy took Elsa for a long walk to get her accustomed to the local topography of dense, dry, thorn bush and scattered baobab trees. Her favourite climbing place proved to be a long ridge of red rock filled with caves and sheer cliffs.

Joy consistently showed remarkable courage in the bush and endured several near misses with rhino and elephant. While out walking with Elsa, she was startled by a sudden resounding crash as a buffalo charged through the undergrowth. Joy was instantly knocked flat on her back. She glimpsed the animal's huge black shape above her, his helmet close to her head. To add insult to injury, he kicked her hard with his hooves before ambling off. Brushing the incident aside she said later to a friend : 'Luckily I wasn't seriously injured. I had swollen glands for two days and I hurt all over and couldn't breathe properly. Bruises all colours of the rainbow covered my body and I had a proper imprint of a buffalo hoof on my thigh by the time George arrived home a few days later. I feel really quite proud of having been autographed by a buffalo, luckily not on my head !'

Such was Joy's emotion over Elsa's release in Meru that no one except George and their closest African staff were allowed to witness the event. It took all the Adamsons' courage and determination to leave Elsa stranded and miserable, no more so than after being fiercely attacked by a rival lioness. Joy cried to a friend in Nairobi that even though they had deceived her so often, broken faith with her, done so much to destroy her trust in them, somehow Elsa remained loyal. However, over the weeks, Elsa improved, growing strong muscles and a fine glossy coat. She came into season every ten weeks and learned to kill, soon realizing that gripping the muzzle of her victim, then breaking its neck, was her quickest way to success.

Once the lioness was able to kill for herself and the seductive call of the wild became stronger, they left her on her own for longer periods. From then on, Elsa managed to retain her extraordinary link between the two worlds, leading an independent life while maintaining her deep loyalty to Joy and George. Throughout their relationship with Elsa, Joy was always adamant that she never regarded the lion as a pet. Instead, it was her wish that the lioness, who had retained all her natural instincts, should become totally free of all human ties. But it proved impossible for Joy to sever her emotional links with the creature she loved best in the world. 'Elsa has taken the place of a lover in my life,' she insisted to more than one friend. There are numerous descriptions in her books which suggest that she needed and sought Elsa's dependency, wishing to continue the interaction between human and beast long after Elsa had been 'freed'. In the dry season, water became their main hold on her, for this she could get only at home.

Throughout the different stages of her upbringing, Elsa had been sketched and painted by Joy and photographed by both Adamsons. Hundreds of these photos, many with Joy almost sexually entwined with the mature Elsa, while George either walked or sat with her, were pasted into a book bound in lion skin – an irony which escaped Joy.

By the beginning of 1959, pleased by her photographs and sketches of Elsa, Joy wanted to complete her involvement with her lioness by jotting down her unique experiences. She asked the opinion of others and approached Michaela Denis, an animated, orange-haired Continental, usually covered in jewels. She had just successfully published *A Leopard in my Lap* and, with her naturalist husband Armand, was among the first to have a television programme on animals. Michaela told Joy rather cattily : 'You cannot speak enough English to write a book. Besides, just leave it to the people who know how to.'

Deeply unsure of her writing capabilities, Joy asked a number of people, including her friend Elspeth Huxley, to write the book for her. Feeling that her English was poor, she also approached her husband, well aware from his monthly reports and letters that George had a natural writing ability. But he was totally uninterested in the project and, according to Joy, much preferred to spend his days fishing, accompanied by Elsa, on the Ura River. George admitted that Joy often reproached him for enjoying himself fishing. While he and Elsa spent a few hours together, Joy leafed through his writings and took notes. Although it was never acknowledged, much of the content of *Born Free* was taken from George's diaries and reports.

In the bush, all Joy's writing and painting was done in her private sanctuary on the sandbank by the river, affectionately known as her 'studio'. Under the large branches of a fig tree, which hung like a weeping canopy over the river, her African staff built her a primitive bench and table out of the driftwood cast aside by the meandering waters. In the heat of the afternoon, when Elsa visited Joy, she flopped down under the shadows of the sweeping leaves for a siesta. With her trusting lioness close beside her and engrossed in her various artistic and literary pursuits, these moments were among the happiest times of Joy's life: 'I felt as though I were on the doorstep of paradise.'

Writing proved an arduous task for Joy, whose English prose and speech was difficult to understand and whose typing was often unintelligible. The person she turned to for advice, and one who helped her invaluably in every stage of the final draft, was Lord William Percy, the renowned naturalist who, with his wife, had known the Adamsons since Elsa was a cub. Joy always deferentially referred to him as 'Elsa's godfather'.

Over the next nine months, continual correspondence and cables winged their way between Kenya and England about content and descriptive passages. Lord William was initially dubious about Joy's real motives: 'You always talk about preserving Elsa's privacy, but much the biggest threat to that has flowed from your own typewriter. Do let the poor girl go into purdah for a bit and keep a "private diary".' This thoughtful man was full of constructive criticism and concern that Joy should steer a middle path between portraying the lioness in the anthropomorphic light typical of writers in the last century, and the twentieth century's tendency to regard animal behaviour in terms of conditioned reflexes and release mechanisms. The latter refuted any suggestion of intelligence, character or reasoning. As the book progressed, the differences between author and helper became more pronounced and, as in many of Joy's friendships, the exchanges became heated.

One strong disagreement revolved around a young lion which George had released into the wild and which was eventually speared to death by the local Tharaka tribesmen after it had mauled three people and killed six goats. Joy originally thought bringing him into the story would be a fitting ending for *Born Free*, with Elsa and her lion padding off into the sunset. Lord William was adamant that the introduction of a released lion as a possible mate would only lend an artificial, discordant note to the story of Elsa's rehabilitation into the wild. In a letter to Joy he wrote:

The whole charm of her story depended, for me anyway, on preserving the atmosphere of your little idyll between George, Elsa and yourself. I was astonished therefore that you did not realize at once that you could not even mention the 'trapped lion' without poisoning the atmosphere altogether. If the whole atmosphere of Elsa's story is not to be ruined, I think that all references to the 'released lion' should be left out of your book. If I read your account of it in any book I should regard it as an act of senseless cruelty, as in fact it proved to be, and I think anyone with a feeling for wildlife will think the same. Your own words in the galley proofs are 'of course he was very young'. Anyone reading that would say to himself, 'How then could she think he had any chance of survival, on his own, and in a strange country?' The only kindness you could have shown that lion was to put a bullet in his ear in the crate. You write to my wife, 'I am so very, very upset. It is a nightmare to think of his end.' If so, how can you keep it in what you always call 'Elsa's book'? It is as if you put a 'stink bug' into a scent bottle! If you want to keep it in please leave out my introduction and all reference to me. I do not want to have anything to do with a book with that in it. I can't have you say in your acknowledgements that I have made 'suggestions' for the book, because I can hardly find an important one which should be in that is not out, nor out that isn't in!

Meanwhile Elsa had all the telltale signs of being courted. Whenever the Adamsons saw her, she appeared restless and agitated. Occasionally she strolled back into camp for brief visits, constantly purring and with the pungent smell of lionesses in season. Most telling of all were the two small bleeding perforations on her forehead, the final mating gesture of the lion, as if to tell the world of the success of his siring. By the end of August, George had witnessed the courting between Elsa and her mate.

By the time Elsa had found her lion, Joy had finished a rather muddled, ill-written draft. As Lois Low possessed a typewriter, she proved most useful. 'Joy and I sat at a table and she'd read out her undrafted bits of paper and notes to me. As I finished typing each sheet, she placed it in a large envelope and we'd start on the next page. Joy neither read nor edited the typed sheet, nor took copies, saying, "Oh, no, we haven't got time for that." The title, *Born Free*, had been found out of the Bible for her by Lord William. It came from The Acts of the Apostles: "Then the chief captain came, and said unto him, Tell me, art thou a Roman? He said, Yea. And the chief captain answered, With a great sum obtained I this freedom. And Paul said, But I was free born."'

It was time for Joy to go to London to find a publisher. Mindful of her failure with her tribal paintings book, she gave herself a month to do so – and was rejected by thirteen publishers in quick succession. Presenting them with a large pile of typed pages in fractured English and assorted photographs rather than a neat manuscript, they had all replied, 'No manuscript, no book.' Naturally, she became dispirited, but she did not give up. Whenever possible, she escaped what she termed London's 'termite hills' and stayed in the country with her cousin Mary Pike, who remembers well Joy's determination. 'As you can imagine we had Elsa, Elsa, Elsa non-stop from Thursday to Monday. Henry, my husband, by then fed up with the topic, made the boob of the century by saying "We're just not interested in lions." Joy stood up and said in a voice quivering with emotion : "The world shall hear about Elsa.'"

Eventually, in desperation, she walked up the flimsy flight of stairs into the Harvill Press, demanding to see Marjorie Villiers. Remembering Joy's persistence with her tribal book, the no-nonsense Mrs Villiers was highly reluctant to see the tenacious Mrs Adamson. 'Joy arrived with a huge "manuscript", a very determined woman, whom I was convinced would lug this tome around to every publisher in London before she would give up.'

Joy refused to leave until she had spoken to Mrs Villiers and shown her the moth-eaten, lion-skin album filled with photographs of Elsa's life. She marched into the office and said, 'I have written you a bestseller.' The dubious publisher, rather than read the haphazard bunch of notes, sat Joy down and asked her to tell Elsa's story, in her own words and through the photographs. When Joy had finished, Marjorie Villiers was riveted. She knew she was on to a winner, saying later, 'It is undoubtedly the most popular wildlife story of our time.'

As soon as Joy left, full of optimism for the first time, Mrs Villiers excitedly cabled her boss, Billy Collins, chairman of the publishing house of which Harvill was a subsidiary : 'Wonderful book, but unfortunately no script.'

'Grab it. Keep Joy Adamson interested and immediately acquire world rights,' Collins replied.

On his return, Joy arranged to meet Billy Collins for the first time, together with Mrs Villiers and her partner, Manya Harari. Joy felt under par, with a swollen jaw and two front incisor teeth temporarily fixed before undergoing dental surgery two days later. She did not, however, let her appearance affect her performance. Before long Joy was offered a contract and an advance of £1,000, and she returned, elated, to Kenya. She thanked Lord William profusely for writing the 'blurt', as she called it before the amused naturalist pointed out the word was 'blurb'. Her misnomer became a standing joke between the two.

Meanwhile, Marjorie Villiers valiantly struggled, with the help of Lord William and a stream of tactful letters to Joy, to rewrite the entire book. Many days were spent in translating Joy's idiosyncratic, appalling English into a semblance of prose without altering the essential content. Little did any of them suspect just how great a success the book would be.

15

Dangerous Liaisons

During Joy's absence in London, George kept up his visits to Elsa. He let off thunder flashes or Verey lights to warn her of his arrival and shot a warthog or gerenuk as a farewell gift to lessen the blow of his leaving. The scampering of the baboons heralded the arrival of the lioness, who was now involved with a virile young lion – he could barely tear himself away and spent each night padding round the bush outside the Adamsons' camp, roaring his passion long into the night.

It was a happy time for Elsa who, on Joy's return, energetically embraced her with her paws. As the months went by, the condition of her fur became soft and shining and her enlarged teats confirmed that she was pregnant. On 20 December 1959, Elsa, crying weakly, bleeding and obviously in pain, left the Adamsons for the sanctuary of the 'whuffing rock', her lie-up on her favourite rocky ridge. There, a few days later, she delivered her first litter. She was now a wild lioness in every respect except for her remarkable affection for Joy, George and a few others.

Possibly Joy's greatest triumph was the occasion when, after six weeks' absence, Elsa came back across the river to the camp with her own cubs. By keeping them away so long, Elsa had established their identity and thus there was no fear of them being 'imprinted' by Joy, who clearly adored them. Although she claimed the cubs dismissed any over-familiarity and were left to live completely wild, secluded from human visitors, there are many references in her notes and letters to her maternal relationship with Jespah – the most tactile of the three – Gopa and Little Elsa. Jespah would lie near Joy and let her pat him for ages; she sketched Gopa and Jespah in the tent while they were in the midst of an embrace. Joy would watch, entranced, as her family of cubs devoured goats that were slaughtered for them.

During the rainy season, when the roads were impassable, food for Elsa and her cubs became an overriding concern. To overcome the problem a number of goats were kept in Joy's truck – a potentially risky business, for they could be smelled by lions prowling the area. Apart from lions at night, the goats were in constant danger of being consumed by crocodiles that slithered out of the river during the day. Two months after the cubs' birth, George shot a monster reptile measuring well over twelve feet as it crept towards the kitchen *lugga*.

The ultimate reward for Joy's patience occurred on the night of 4 February 1960. As Elsa was opening her legs, exposing her teats to two hungry cubs, she stretched herself across Joy, placing one paw round her. Joy was totally overwhelmed, claiming it was the happiest moment of her life.

Having been cabled the news of Elsa's litter, Billy Collins decided to visit the Adamsons and Elsa. It was the beginning of his love affair with Africa and the many books he would publish on its tribes and animals. Joy was ecstatic. She wrote of his visit to many friends. All through her letters there was an underlying hint of the feelings he kindled in her. Besides being a charming man and an ardent naturalist, he was, she explained, '*such* a good friend' of hers and they felt '*very* close'.

By the time Joy met Billy Collins she was forty-nine years old. He was ten years older, and still remarkably good-looking. He made an indelible impression on his associates, one of whom, Michael Hyde, remembers him fondly: 'Billy had devilish charm, he was superb company, probably never read a book in his life, loved selling and was an incredible, though lovable, bully with his authors. The only people who survived were those who stood up to him.'

During his early involvement with Joy, Collins made two trips to Kenya, in May and October 1960. Joy collected him in Nairobi, or ferried him from Isiolo, and showed him the flamingoes on Lake Nakuru, often without George. After each visit she told friends that Billy and she had had a marvellous time together, and bemoaned the fact that it had been much too short.

A tall man, he had been a fine athlete and tennis player at Oxford, good enough to compete in the men's doubles at Wimbledon. Although not an intellectual, he was intelligent and articulate, and was permanently surrounded by women who found him irresistible. According to a friend: 'He knew what he wanted and he knew how to get it. He demanded excellence.' His wife Pierre, a strong character and the power behind the throne, whom he met at university, remained in love with him from the age of eighteen until his death in September 1976. She said about their courtship: 'It took him ages to get round to making a pass at me. We would sit in his rooms at Oxford hour after hour and I was dying for him to give me a kiss, but instead he kept saying, "Would you like more cocoa?"'

Joy had already been instantly attracted to Billy on their first meeting in London. When he came to stay, Joy quickly fell under his spell. They went on safari with George, but whenever he was away working, Joy found excuses to take her new publisher off on safari alone for a few days. Joy, always impressed with personal magnetism and authoritative men who wielded power, found herself falling in love with the dynamic publisher. A number of people recognized the familiar signs of a new amour. One was Ken Smith, who remembered the furore it caused: 'Joy fell head over heels in love with Billy, who was a wonderful man. She could not stop talking about him; everything was Billy this and Billy that, and was always saying "Oh, George, why can't you be more outgoing, like Billy?"'

Once again Joy thought she had found her 'ideal' man. He was upper-class and knew a great many people of importance, both of which were vital to Joy, who was an inveterate snob. He was clever, attractive, had great strength of character and a drive and determination to equal her own. London's publishing world and Kenya settlers were soon gossiping about the passionate affair between publisher and author. Being married, both, of necessity, were naturally discreet. But Robert Nimmo, among others, remained sceptical: 'It is very difficult to resist an attractive woman on a moonlit night on safari, but Joy thought this was absolutely it, this was going to be her future life and that Billy Collins was going to marry her. She was going to divorce George and be with Billy.'

Unfortunately for Joy, this was not to be. Collins was a happily married man, and it is unlikely he took his involvement with Joy all that seriously. A short time into their romance, and realizing that the tempestuous Austrian could prove troublesome, Billy began lamely excusing any honourable intentions he may have harboured, in favour of his wife and family, reminding her that he had been married for many years and loved his wife and children, begging her to understand.

Joy clung tenaciously to her relationship – a situation that was difficult for Billy. When he was away from her she was vividly aware of her love for him and the comfort and sympathy he had offered. Each time he came out on safari, she pursued him relentlessly, still believing she could change his mind. Nothing he could say or do could dissuade her. It was totally in character for her to have made all the running and because of his business dealings with her, he was unable to disentangle himself from their involvement. It would have been virtually impossible to refuse Joy in one of her highly emotional states. In trying not to hurt her, he handled the situation with considerable delicacy, for he managed to keep her nicely distanced for a long time without creating volcanic eruptions. The couple enjoyed a close and intimate correspondence, and according to those who had access to the letters, Joy's were full of love and emotion, his full of deep affection. It would appear that all the letters between the two have since been destroyed.

Joy found in Billy something that she desperately needed. It is clear that he recognized some neurosis in Joy and he was both patient and astute enough to try to look after one of his bestselling authors. But Joy appears to have over-responded to his interest. It was a novelty for her, for throughout her life she knew little genuine concern; most people kept Joy at arm's length, finding her demanding personality too exhausting to cope with. Oddly, Billy Collins tried introducing religion to Joy as a balm to her woes, thinking a belief in God would cure her neurosis. He gave her an Anglican prayerbook and tried, very gently but with no success, to interest her in the Almighty. Billy was a man whose respect she treasured; though there were others who tried to suggest similar solutions to her, if Collins could not succeed then it was unlikely that anyone could.

At the end of the trip in October, Collins left from Nairobi airport, weighed down with paraphernalia. A large Kikuyu water gourd was slung over his shoulder. Purchased from a woman as she was filling it from the river, it would make an unusual lamp. Bulbs and flowers, seeds and stones were stuffed into various knapsacks and bags. His straw hat was now a riot of colour, with dozens of bright feathers sticking out in all directions. Not only did he have to carry numerous roles of film, he was also weighed down by Joy's newest manuscripts and photographs. Sad to say goodbye, Joy nevertheless had to laugh as she imagined the British customs men peering through his unusual collection.

George was well used to Joy's infatuations and wild protestations of love. The couple had enjoyed no sexual intimacy for the past year and, by all acounts, he took his wife's newest passion for her publisher in his stride, partly, one assumes, because he enjoyed Collins's company.

The first time George took Collins out on safari, he gave him his grubby old tent and a high bunk bed for the night, safely pitched inside a thick thorn fence. After a hot, tiring day viewing game and a long talk into the night with George, an amusing raconteur, Billy flopped straight onto the bed. In the middle of the night, as he rolled over, he found himself unable to move. A great weight was on top of him, and rolls of strong animal breath were continually flung into his face. He lay there, entangled in his mosquito net and rigid with fear for the rest of the painful night, realizing that Elsa was sitting on him. It was not until dawn broke, when George came trotting in with a cup of morning tea, that the great man was able to breathe easily.

The following night Elsa succeeded once again in sliding through the thick barricade of thorn, plus gate, to visit the publisher. This time, after hearing a yell, George found Billy with his cheeks firmly clasped between Elsa's teeth and his shoulders beneath the net, pinned down by her huge paws. His face and neck were bleeding and he had a number of deep scratches on his back. George had arrived in the nick of time. The next time Collins flew out to Kenya and went on safari with Elsa, he slept in the Land Rover, but that did not stop Elsa creeping through the thorn and hopping on top of the roof.

Joy dismissed the assaults as either great affection or jealousy from Elsa. She was convinced the lioness had not hurt Billy on purpose, and viewed his wounds as minor scratches. A small gap was left open in the fence between Billy's *boma* and hers so that, in case of any emergency, she could rush over and rescue him from Elsa.

Born Free was published in 1960. Billy Collins had returned to England in May, determined to pull out all the stops to make a huge success of the book. He ensured that numerous photos of Elsa with Joy and George saturated the pages of the book, huge publication posters of Elsa were in every bookshop, the book was sold at a reasonable price and the *Sunday Times* serialized the pictures. *Born Free* was an instant and phenomenal success. It was ironic, considering that the author was a confirmed atheist, that it became prescribed reading in schools in Northern Ireland as part of religious studies and was read in American churches. The first edition quickly sold out and within months the book had been translated into twenty-five languages. It was to make Joy a rich woman, netting £500,000 in the first ten years.

Why was *Born Free* such a success? After all, it was written in simple English, and the story, although pleasant enough, was not exactly earth-shaking. The photographs were not well printed, and until then few people in Britain or anywhere else had been especially interested in either Kenya, conservation in general, or the preservation of lions in particular. But the timing was right. Joy had hit on a moment when the people of Britain were ripe for some escapist story to lift them out from the doldrum years of postwar austerity, and Billy Collins had had the canniness to spot a story with universal appeal. In general, people were looking towards a happier world and a wave of appreciation for nature was beginning to swell. Enough of field marshals' memoirs; people's minds were ready for something other than the Cold War, something free of political conflict, which was emotionally uplifting and smacked of security. Elsa's story fulfilled all these conditions and had the bonus of a photogenic couple to help counteract the general gloom.

A few years earlier and *Born Free* would have escaped publication: a few years later and it would have been derided as naive in the climate of the Swinging Sixties. Perhaps, more than anything else, the book appealed directly to the heart. It was an animal story on a par with the exotic tales of Kipling, but with a living animal as its obliging star. Readers of all ages became besotted by Elsa. The heady atmosphere of a love story in the bush with a lion and the inherent danger to human life proved an irresistible combination.

However, *Born Free*'s greatest achievement was that it was the initial seed that led to a harvest of abundant concern for conservation. Prior to publication, the problems of conservation had been the interest of a select few. Suddenly, through this book, masses of people were made to consider the plight of animals. Joy had hardly intended this to happen. It was a perfect gem, accidentally tossed up on the tidal wave of interest in the book. But instantly, she was quick enough to perceive her role in supporting such interest and no one can deny that she did it well. From setting up a charitable trust to help protect wild animals, to worldwide lecturing on conservation, Joy gave her total commitment and dedication.

Joy's first book was a turning point in her life which would end one phase of it for ever. Life was never the same again for her, or George. The fame of Joy and Elsa spread far and wide, with the consequence that she would have to endure constant invasion of her privacy, deal with copious correspondence, enormous sums of money, and tax problems. With each new book and film the interest in the big cats of Kenya snowballed and launched Joy on her own private, tormented treadmill.

George, in one sense the real author since he was the expert on whom Joy's facts depended, did not have an equal share in her royalties. With typical understatement, he said, as he had had little to do with the writing of the book, 'I got all the fame but none of the fortune.' Her accumulated wealth was all to go to the preservation of wildlife. Joy was quick to point out her side of the situation as far as sharing her royalties with George was concerned. She claimed that George's relatives advised her to keep control of the money, since both his parents, being spendthrifts, had managed to get through a considerable amount of money during their lifetime. She bemoaned the fact that George seemed to have inherited their failings and decided instead to give her husband his share in goods rather than cash.

It was often said, even in print, that Joy was exceptionally tough over finance with George and gave him nothing from the proceeds of her books and films. Naturally, this elicited a great wave of sympathy for him. In fact, Joy made her husband a small personal allowance, from the time the money began to pour in from the book until his death. Peter Johnson, Joy's accountant and a trustee, was deeply involved: 'George had a life interest in Joy's Trust.' When rumour circulated that she was neglecting him, George did not bother to make a public denial. Later, when George resigned from the game department, Joy's Trusts financed various projects of his – the four-by-four vehicles, airstrips and long-distance travel needed for rehabilitating lions could never have been afforded on his pension of £800 a year. Joy insisted that the Trusts only withdrew financial and moral support five years later after George broke away from his original intention to rehabilitate the lions used in the film of *Born Free* in Meru Park. From then on, much to Joy's dismay, she felt he started to exploit them for his own benefit. Most of his revenue, however, came from films on his lions and two books written by him.

The focus of world attention on Elsa naturally brought with it numerous requests from distinguished visitors, film companies and newspapers to view the lioness and immortalize her in print and on celluloid. Government officials were delighted with the prospect of endless publicity this would bring the NFD, but Joy saw it differently. In a rambling letter to Lord William, she explained her fury over what she viewed as George's willingness to exploit Elsa. While he was happy to let film-makers invade the animal's territory, she would strenuously defend her beloved animal's privacy as long as she had breath left in her body. She and George argued endlessly over the subject and she felt that no one would support her. As a final plea, she asked dramatically what authority she, as a mere woman, had in a world full of ruthless, determined men.

By September after six months vacillating, she had obviously changed her mind about film crews, when David Attenborough stayed for a week at Elsa's camp to film a television programme for the BBC. Always one to befriend the famous, she fell in love with the film-maker's charm and wit and wrote to friends of days of laughter, fun and teasing. Joy described this intelligent man as being as 'fast as a mongoose'; he was down-to-earth; he also had a deep appreciation of classical music. For Joy, the trip was all too short.

Apart from the relentless invasions of their privacy, two other pressing problems were of great concern to the Adamsons. George was due to retire from the game department within the year and a new home had to be found for Elsa and her cubs. Demand for land had increased and many more tribal natives and their cattle were infringing on 'Elsa's territory'. Meru Council, regarding Elsa and the cubs as a danger to their livestock, some of whom had been killed by the cubs, had demanded they leave the area. Joy had previously said to John Cumber, 'Elsa will never be safe here, between white hunters and their parties and the Tharaka tribesmen who are keen to kill her off.'

Joy wrote to a number of influential friends that she was deeply concerned about George's future. She explained in depth that it would be the greatest pity to see his years of experience go to waste. Besides, retirement would come as a terrible blow to one as active. The only other game warden Joy considered an equal to George was Lyn Temple-Boreham, considered by many to be the finest game warden in the country. A bluff, charismatic character, known as T.B., he shared with George a lifelong commitment to his job.

The question of a suitable home for the couple to retire to also had to be considered. Joy pondered over the options. George was keen for her to purchase Loyangalani, an area popular with the safari crowd. But secretly Joy knew the arrangement would never work unless their marriage became less fractious. The idea of being alone with George, in a camp miles away from friends and civilization, horrified her. However, she could justify purchasing the land as a safe haven for Elsa and her cubs. On the other hand, she could always buy it as a place for George to live on his own.

In the middle of January 1961 Elsa fell ill. She had already been treated for maggots by Joy, but George assured her that there was nothing to worry about. Reluctantly, Joy left for Nairobi in search of transport for the move from Meru. While she was away, Elsa's condition worsened. As she became progressively sicker, she seemed to need the presence of George and continually forced herself to be near the man who had raised her. George, in a state of great distress, later told the vet, John MacDonald, that he had gone to look for Elsa early the next morning. He found her close to the camp, lying under a shady bush beside the river. Although she lifted her head when he called, she did not have the strength to come out and greet him.

By now thoroughly alarmed, George sent off his driver in the lorry with a telegram to Joy, telling her Elsa was worse and begging her to bring some antibiotics immediately. He then brought a mixture of goat brains and marrow to tempt Elsa, but she refused to eat – she was getting weaker. That night he took over his bed and slept next to her to make sure she was not worried by other lions or hyenas. Elsa could not tolerate her cubs near her and they kept a solemn vigil a few feet away. George barely registered when a bull buffalo came close to his bed and snorted loudly at him.

The following day Elsa's breathing became increasingly laboured. Somehow, with what little strength she still possessed, she managed to stagger onto an island in the river, before collapsing. She was by then panting hard but George could not make her drink. Realizing he had to try to get her into camp, George and the rangers improvised a stretcher from his camp bed, but she managed to stagger across the river with his help. Slowly, with frequent long rests, she reached the camp, followed by the cubs.

As soon as George's driver returned he was sent off to get the senior government vet from Isiolo. Twice Elsa went into the river by the studio, stood in the water and tried to drink, but without success. Her body was as cold as ice. At about 1.45 a.m. she crossed over onto a mud bank and lay, half in the water, her breath coming in short, harsh pants. The boys and George carried her on the stretcher to his tent. George lay down beside her and was just dozing off when she got up, walked quickly to the front of the tent and collapsed. Her breathing was exceedingly painful and she was in acute distress. Wiping away his tears, George held her head in his lap. 'In a few minutes she gave a great and terrible cry.' Dawn was just breaking. Elsa was dead.

In Isiolo Ken Smith managed to contact John MacDonald at 1 a.m. before setting off in his three-ton truck to collect Joy, who was marooned in Nairobi. Driving through the night, the vet took four hours to make the sixty-mile journey. He arrived half an hour after Elsa had died. He recalls: 'I took with me a small amount of antibiotics for cattle as I was completely unprepared for treating lionesses or other wild animals. If I had been called earlier, it would have made no difference at all. I shall always be relieved on two counts. One, that Elsa died before I got there so that I couldn't be held responsible for her death as far as Joy was concerned. The second, more dominant factor, was that Joy was in Nairobi, otherwise she would have been absolutely hysterical at the time. I never found out what Elsa died from. She was in beautiful condition, no maggots at all, no signs of disease.'

George agreed to a post-mortem and various samples were taken from the carcass. Having kept them in the fridge, John sent them off the following morning, packed in ice, in plenty of time to get to the lab in Kabete that afternoon. Little did he suspect that the Somali driver would drop off at Nyeri to see a friend and arrive at the lab after it had shut. He shook his head: 'All the samples were left over-night outside and that ruined the whole diagnosis. I will always regret sending them.' Joy was convinced the Tharaka tribesmen had poisoned Elsa.

After the post-mortem, six of George's game scouts, sweating in the morning sun, dug a hole and Elsa was buried. Stone slabs were placed on top of the earth mound. The scouts quickly disappeared and a few minutes later returned, smartly dressed in their uniforms. Standing in a line, they fired shots over the grave. George stood beside them, his head bowed with grief as he said quietly in Swahili : 'Kweli yeye ni mke wa mfalme ya amani.' – 'Truly the Queen of peace.'

Joy was chatting to Robert Nimmo in the foyer of the King George VI hospital when Ken rushed in and told her of Elsa's desperate illness. It was a sad occasion. Robert remembered : 'Joy got very emotional and threw her arms around my neck and eventually rolled on the floor in a paroxysm of grief. A passing doctor said, "Just look after her and I'll be back in a second."' Thinking she was having convulsions, he arrived with a stretcher and four orderlies. Nimmo explained what had happened : 'She had got completely hysterical and, though I tried to comfort her, she still clung round my neck. I tried to shake her off and when she fell on the floor it must have looked as if I had tried to knock her out. She could never control her emotions, poor Joy.'

Ken Smith, who had driven through the night to reach Nairobi, flew back with Joy to Garba Tula. As she stared out of the window at the clouds tinged pink by the morning sun, Joy's mind reeled. 'She was on edge and very fidgety. I tried to tell her that she must not be too optimistic. We got down to camp in the afternoon. George was just sitting there, obviously looking very miserable, so I stayed by my vehicle.' Joy, realizing the worst, half walked, half ran towards him and George, looking straight up at her face, got to his feet. Ken also felt desolate : 'They ran into each other's arms. They were both crying and I was deeply moved by the two in their moment of grief, apart from the fact that Elsa had gone. It brought them closer at that time and I think probably left its mark.'

Ken spent the night with his friends. Nothing was said, just a dreadful silence full of sadness and mourning. George sat outside his open-flapped tent with his strong whisky, Ken joined him with a full glass and Joy sat feverishly writing letters and telegrams, the first one to Billy Collins. The next day at lunchtime, Ken left laden with sad messages from Joy while the couple reached out to each other for comfort. Joy was inconsolable at the death of 'the one creature in my life I loved more than any other'. On hearing from George about Elsa's last cry, she said, 'I can only interpret it as her cry for her cubs. When Elsa died, our loss and bond for her was so strong that a part of me died as well. I never had a moment to recover.

Usually, when you mourn, you are given time – I wasn't. I was always having to talk, give lectures, give interviews.'

Although Elsa's death brought the couple closer together for a short time, it was not long before they were back on their collision course. Joy never mentioned to George that she partly blamed him for Elsa's death, but she confided in a friend at Naivasha: 'During the time I was gone, George spent an entire day pottering around his camp. He must have known Elsa was seriously ill and too weak to move from the other side of the river. He did not bother to look for her until the next day, by which time she was near death. If only he had gone to her the day before, he could have easily sent for the vet to come and treat her.'

Joy's greatest sadness was not being with Elsa at the end. Once, in a moment of grief, she berated George: 'Why did Elsa have to die in your arms instead of mine?' Many years later Joy summed up her feelings of that time: 'I had no inkling of what lay ahead, of George, of anything, but now in retrospect I could see I needed the strong personality of George to help me in my abilities to expand and convey our findings to the world. George's deep love for nature, and mine, all culminated in Elsa.'

16

Pivotal Point

Life at Elsa's camp was coming to an end. George had resigned in April 1961, but was still acting as game warden in July, and the new chief game warden had ordered the cubs to be shot after they attacked the herdsmen's goats and sheep. In the ensuing battle Jespah received an arrowhead deep in his haunch.

Joy battled with every authority, including George, about where to take the cubs. Pulling strings through Prince Philip, Peter Scott and Billy Collins led nowhere. In desperation she wrote to Ian Grimwood in the game department asking for his intervention to find a suitable place. She disagreed adamantly with George's conviction that Lake Rudolf was an ideal home. George's view smacked of self-interest, since he had always wanted to live in the area. She told Grimwood she regretted writing behind George's back, but during their long marriage, she had come to the conclusion that he was either unwilling, or unable, to put anyone else's feelings first. As often happened when she wrote of her disagreements with George, a note of self-pity crept into her letter. In a rather forlorn attempt to gain sympathy, Joy explained she was homeless and her life was only worthwhile if she could assist Elsa's cubs.

After lengthy battles with the National Park Trustees the Adamsons were given permission by John Owen, the Director of National Parks in Tanzania, to take the cubs to the Serengeti Game Reserve, the immense, majestic park in Tanzania and ideal lion territory. It was here that the largest congregation and migration of animals in the world occurred. A million hooves trampled the earth as wildebeest, zebra and kongoni stampeded down ancient trails.

As soon as Joy met Owen, she grabbed him, kissed him roundly on the cheek and congratulated him warmly: 'Our saviour.' The couple were given a short time in which to rehabilitate the cubs before leaving the park. It was not an easy task, locating the newly released cubs each day in the heavy rain. Joy's worries escalated. Venturing out daily into the unhospitable terrain, she often had to crawl along the bottom of a seemingly interminable escarpment; she fell headlong into antbear holes and occasionally surprised elephant or hippo in the thick riverbush. Serengeti was crawling with lions and one night a lioness sauntered into her tent. Shining a torch into the animal's eyes, Joy told her to 'beat it'.

After a particularly harrowing experience during which a young man had been dragged by his head from the front of his open tent and had his skull torn apart, Joy and George were asked to move to Seronera, another area of the park. According to Joy, when asking Myles Turner, the local warden, 'What on earth should I do if a lion comes into my tent with the intention of eating me and there is nothing but a table between us,' he replied: 'Thank your lucky stars for the experience. Soon our wild animals will have vanished off the face of the earth, so value every encounter with them.' When the time came, against her will, to leave the park, Turner watched Joy behave like a child having a tantrum: 'She lay down on the aerodrome strip, banged her head on the ground and kicked her heels in the air.'

Before Elsa's death Joy had completed the first of her two books on the life of Elsa's cubs, from the time of their birth until their mother's death. *Living Free* was published in October 1961. This time her adviser was Sir Julian Huxley, the renowned biologist, Lord William Percy having been reluctant to 'engage in a similarly exhausting volume of penmanship once again'. He did, however, correspond with Marjorie Villiers and suggested alterations to the manuscript.

Throughout the writing of the two books the editor and the Percys had struck up an intimate and revealing correspondence, discussing, besides Joy's writing style, her mental and emotional state. Despite the fact that her writing gave personality to her animals and always cast them as sympathetic and believable characters, there remained a degree of blandness in Joy's books. Her passionate nature and the intensity with which she approached life were entirely missing.

Soon after the publication of her third book, *Forever Free*, Joy left George to go on a publicity tour. Nervous and lacking confidence, she first lectured in England on 'Man: The Inferior Species' to a packed audience of 3,000, showing a short film about Elsa and her cubs that she and George had made. Her thick Austrian accent and idiosyncratic vocabulary were difficult to understand – what made it worse was the speed at which she spoke. She hurriedly took elocution lessons, which helped so little that her tutor was obliged to sit in the front row and hold up a small red flag when Joy gabbled. Nevertheless, smitten by her new-found mission, Joy was eager to accept every invitation. Lectures, museum talks, lunch parties, television and radio programmes, talking to prisoners and women's clubs and glamorous gala dinners began to take their toll.

By October 1962, Marjorie Villiers was concerned about Joy's state of mind. She wrote to Lady William Percy that, while everyone was conscious of the strain Joy was under, a great deal of it was self-induced and she would not accept that she had to slow down. Indeed, after one interview, Joy had complained bitterly to Billy Collins that nothing had been arranged for the rest of the day. She was being given as many medical opinions as she had medical advisors; but she was now so febrile that, in Marjorie Villiers' opinion, she was heading for a nervous breakdown.

Added to the stress of lecturing, Joy had become so upset by constantly answering morbid questions about her beloved Elsa that she only narrowly missed collapsing. She had become convinced that Elsa was transmitting telepathic messages and that she had some mystic power through which Joy could continue her work. Insisting publicly that she kept the ideas to herself, Joy often held court in private with her theories of communication through space between animals and humans. 'I can't explain why I feel that Elsa is working through me. She dictates to me and I am just an interpreter. I have never been able to talk to anyone about it because I have to be very careful not to be considered a crank. I am not a crank, at least I don't think so. This is something which I can't compare to anything else but there is a force in me.' Her resolute belief in Elsa's guiding spirit became the mainstay of her work for the rest of her life.

Early in 1963 Collins persuaded Joy to go on a world tour to promote her two latest books. Occasionally on her lengthy trips, either discussing her book or talking on behalf of the Elsa Wild Animal Appeal, things went disastrously wrong. A Kenya farmer who wishes to remain anonymous remembers the time when Joy was booked to speak in South Africa. While in Durban he arranged to meet her at her nearby hotel and escort her across to the town hall. To his horror, Joy appeared in a long, slinky dress and a blazing display of what appeared to be glittering diamonds hanging from her neck and ears. It was just too much artificial glamour for the large, conservative audience in their short day-frocks. Joy spoke well and was just making her appeal with some emotion when a voice from the hall called out, 'If you need money for the animals, use those bloody diamonds.' Similar calls echoed round the hall. The talk ended badly. Joy, retreating from the increasing catcalls, fled from the room.

Joy's choice of clothing frequently got her into trouble – she saw nothing incongruous in wearing her leopard-skin coat and hat while lecturing on conservation or posing with a leopard cub. Monty Ruben, an honest and helpful friend interested in film-making, and later a trustee, told her more than once : 'For God's sake, Joy, you can't wear that bloody coat. They'll skin you alive.'

During her tour in Denmark, the local press had severely criticized her for wearing the coat. Back in Kenya, after a good deal of persuasion, Joy finally fathomed that, as a professed conservationist, it was foolish to wear animal pelts. But the skins of the coat were badly matched and she had great difficulty getting rid of it. After it was rejected on the spot by a Nairobi furrier shop called Madame Louise, Joy finally decided to store it discreetly.

Many years later, when receiving an honour in Canada, she confided to her old friend Alys Reece that she thought it rather funny to be a patroness of preventing the trade of spotted cat fur while having a magnificent leopard stored away for the last ten years which she had been advised never to wear. Such small ironies were highly amusing, but she was, of course, well aware of the prime importance of fighting for the survival of the cats.

More often than not, the author of *Born Free* was received enthusiastically by the public wherever she travelled. Audiences were hungry for information about the couple who had created something quite unique in the Kenyan bush. Joy, with her new craving for publicity, delivered the goods. However genuine her feelings, being the actress she was, she joked with friends that she only needed to say 'Elsa' three times with a certain catch in her throat before an avalanche of tears poured down her face. The cameras loved it.

A letter from Lady William Percy to her son reveals Joy's astonishing impact : 'Joy bounced into London like a true VIP, flashbulbs popping and surrounded by reporters, loving every minute. We were asked to go to a literary lunch, in her honour, at Foyle's with a cast of one thousand. We declined !'

However, some legs of the tour created the atmosphere of a pantomime. In Sydney, Joy's often tactless dedication managed to raise the hackles of her hosts. She was appalled by the state of the lion enclosures in the zoo and threatened to shoot the keepers, insisting they were mistreating the lions. She tried to have the zoo closed down and auctioned her body on television to raise funds for a proper lion enclosure. There were no takers.

In the middle of a hectic schedule in New Zealand, the root of one of her teeth became septic, infecting part of her upper jaw. The tooth needed immediate extraction but Joy went to the extraordinary lengths of having all her upper teeth pulled out at the same time. She wrote to Dorle that it was an unbearable shock especially as she had only one day in hospital to recover before immediately continuing with her lectures. All the time her swollen mouth kept bleeding. It was total agony, she said, especially with her new set of dentures, which she found unbearable.

The country which received Joy with the widest embrace, and continually gave her the thrill of seeing packed audiences, was the United States. There she was truly 'lionized' and made a number of friends. A couple she remained close to for the rest of her life were Bill and Annette Cottrell. A remarkable couple, he was research associate in ornithology at Harvard University and Annette was a keen conservationist. At the height of Joy's fame, Annette arranged for her to speak at the annual meeting of the New England Wild Flower Society in Massachusetts. 'When we met I could see that she was taut and worried beneath a startling veneer of make-up – totally inappropriate for a Boston audience. However, as we talked, her sincerity shone through and she walked onto the huge platform before an overflow assemblage. Her delivery was swift, passionate and vivid up to her appeal for the Elsa Fund, when at the climax her voice broke and there was a long – too long – silence before she could quaveringly finish.' At her next lecture, and acknowledging the need, Joy agreed to take stress-control pills to prevent breakdown at the climax of her story.

Following appearances in Florida, she lectured daily in New York before touring California, determined to bring in more than the £5,000 for the EWAA which she had raised the previous year.

The hectic ten-month tour took its toll. She saw the inside of more airports, lecture halls, bookshops and hairdressers than she could count. Her days were devoted to publicity and the only occasions that she really enjoyed were those when she came across someone who interested her – a rare event. As soon as she returned to her hotel she fell into bed, but was too tired to sleep.

By the time the trip was over, Joy's fragile hold on the one friendship she cherished above all others had received a severe bruising. She had never been able to rid herself of her passionate preoccupation with her distinguished publisher, and continued to make her usual stream of emotional demands on him. Feeling that Collins's affections were slipping from her grasp, she pursued him relentlessly when she arrived in London. It was all very well to discuss her latest book with Marjorie Villiers, but she badly needed the attentions of Billy. Billy, however, had no intention of pursuing the affair. He gave her the cold shoulder, refusing to see her unless there were others present. Joy was visibly distressed, unhappiness etched on her face. Marjorie, who had no interest in Joy's romantic attachment, could not cope with her hysteria and palmed the author off on a colleague : 'Take her to Fortnum's or to the park. Just get her out of the office.'

As they walked, Joy poured her heart out and wept copiously : 'How can Billy be so cruel and behave like this when he loves me so much?' There were no answers. Joy was bitter, complaining that, with *Forever Free* completed, she ceased to exist for him. Yet, however heartbroken she was, she felt she had little alternative but to accept the situation while she remained in London. She told anyone who would listen that Billy had treated her badly. However, she was bound by contract to produce another book, even though she felt mentally and physically incapable of writing anything. As she so often did when she felt rejected by one of her own kind, she turned to her animals and the bush which had claimed her soul. Her last words to Susi Jeans were of those people she had encountered who had once lived in Kenya. Their obvious homesickness only made her realize how deep her roots lay in her adopted country. She went home to Africa.

17

Cats and Consequences

In December 1963, there appeared on the London stage a Cambridge Footlights revue. Among the satirical and humorous sketches characteristic of most university thespians was a song entitled 'Pride and Joy'. The empty stage was dignified by a single, forlorn palm tree which had obviously known sunnier times in previous productions. As a hush fell over the audience, an ambrosial blonde sauntered from the wings, her ample curves doing full justice to the khaki bush shirt she wore. A pair of wide-legged, baggy shorts failed to eclipse the shapeliness of her legs. Her mass of hair was capped by a solar topee, *de rigueur* for the equatorial sun, and in her hand she clutched a large rifle. In a clear, slightly brassy voice and with faultless enunciation, the saucy young performer belted out the words 'Oh, I'm in love with a lion and a lion's in love with me', to instant laughter and recognition from the audience.

> I long to be where we're born free
> With the animal for whom I care.
> To hear once more his gentle roar
> Where I always get the lion's share
> I long for a lark in a national park
> With the tropical moon above
> Oh take me back where the folk are black
> And back to the beast I love.
> So I can once again run my fingers through his mane
> Oh I'm in love with a lion
> And a lion's in love with me.
>
> Down in the jungle I'm all right
> With a little bit o' lion on a Saturday night.
> I'm in love with a lion
> And I'm in ecstasy.

Oh, I'm not lyin', I'm relying on a lion
And a lion is lyin' on me !

I never felt a pang for an orangutan
Or a flutter for a chimpanzee, not me.
I'm not a girl who winks at a passing lynx
For the lion is the cat for me.
And I'm safe from men in my African den
With the beast I've got my eye on.
And it can't be a crime, cos in everything I'm
Content to toe the lion.
I'm as happy as I could be
With my African bush baby.
Oh, I'm in love with a lion
And a lion's in love with me.

We're the happiest couple you've ever seen
He's the king of the jungle and I'm his queen.
I'm in love with a lion
And I'm in ecstasy.
There's no denyin' that my heart is sighin'
And I'm really dyin'
With a cryin' and a tryin'
And I'm not lyin'
I'm relyin' on a lion
And a lion is lyin' on me !

This dig at the Austrian from Kenya who tended to take both herself and her fabled lion a mite too seriously to some extent reflected the attitudes of a number of Europeans in Kenya towards Joy's fame. Joy's story of her one lion appeared to be an indulgent abundance of hype to not a few of them, although they were to reverse this censorious appraisal when the full effect of Joy's efforts on behalf of the conservation of Kenya's wildlife appeared in later years. Joy, who at best possessed the most tenuous of humours and who had an inherent need throughout her life to be taken seriously in her passionate commitment to a particular cause, would not have been amused by this theatrical lampooning, especially its sexual insinuations. The satire, nevertheless, was yet another indication that, in the eyes of the general public, Joy had arrived.

By now Joy had accumulated considerable wealth, almost all of which was ploughed back into The Elsa Wild Animal Appeal, formed that year, 1963, one of the first trusts set up solely for conservation. It later became the Elsa Conservation Trust. Joy spent virtually nothing on herself. A board of trustees in London controlled all funds, with advice from an advisory committee in Kenya. This one act of setting up a trust to benefit wildlife was Joy's greatest act of generosity. Through her dedicated efforts, it made an enormous impact on conservation throughout the world, but especially in Kenya. However petty the Trust's infights and bureaucratic handling of individual requests, many feel strongly about the benefits the country has received. Like numerous others interviewed, Jock Dawson, an honorary game warden and an expert on wildlife, expressed his views strongly: 'Of all the people in the world who have contributed to wildlife, especially here, Joy Adamson must head the list.' The Kenya Game Department and Parks Department, now the Kenya Wildlife Service, would have had a much deeper financial problem in maintaining their work had it not received substantial help from the EWAA. After independence, the Republic of Kenya badly needed the help, faced as it was with enormous problems of development and hampered by an unprecedented population explosion.

Yet, however indifferent Joy was to her wealth, she was not naturally generous to those who had been, or were, close to her. In the year that the Trust was set up she received a letter from Rufus von Klarwill. He wrote out of pressing financial need, not for himself but for medical treatment for his daughter, and the sum he asked for was comparatively small. His was a simple request, referring neither to times gone by nor to his part in leading Joy to Africa and thus to her source of wealth. Would Joy help him this once, in a time of need? Joy's response was a simple negative, a short and almost callous reply. She expressed no interest in his problem, no memories of good times past, no concern about him. But, intriguingly, for a number of years, she kept his letter.

Joy came increasingly to rely on the businessmen who ran her affairs. She had managed to persuade Henry Pike, the husband of her cousin Mary, to take on the chairmanship of the EWAA in England. Without any knowledge of Africa, he nevertheless proved to be an excellent choice, with a flair for business and great understanding of the duties and rules of trusteeship. Her personal financial affairs were handled by Peter Johnson, an accountant who was always professionally correct, could not be swayed and was kind enough to carry out endless errands, such as arranging visits to the hairdresser, without ever losing her trust or respect, or his patience. This was something of a phenomenon in her life. Doubtless she prized his reliability and integrity, and 'No, Joy, don't do that – remember your breeding,' was a comment that would bring her to heel instantly. He commented: 'My role was to enable her to do her job. I dislike rows, so we never had one, but so few people tried to understand her. Joy was an idealist and was striving for the perfect conservation world. Such an ideal being unattainable naturally led to her unhappiness, and of course, Joy was also continually looking for love.' With no overtones of emotional involvement present, she felt entirely secure with both men.

In 1964 Joy was cabled by an excited Billy Collins that, with her agreement, Columbia Pictures proposed to make a film of *Born Free*, with George advising the film company on how to handle its lions. Joy accepted the offer, having already turned down an MGM offer as they refused to give her any control over the film script. She wrote that she was unprepared to take the risk of having Elsa turned, in true Hollywood style, into a bloodthirsty animal scripted to eat the tasty wife of a love-sick husband. She would not have any say in this script either, but Columbia paid better. The Fantasy-world location was a farm at Naro Moru, where lush green plains spread softly out beneath the craggy peak of Mount Kenya and where the rains usually grew timid when expected.

Three months after preparations for filming had started, the stars, Virginia McKenna and Bill Travers, George and the crew were joined by Joy who returned, exhausted, from her world tour. Joy's tent was immediately pitched near her husband's, away from the main camp and next to the lions, where George had gone, supposedly to escape the frantic midnight bed-hoppings of the film crew.

Without George's calm instructions on how to deal with each lion and how to cajole them into doing what was asked of them, the firm would not have succeeded. But, as happened with the book, George received no personal accolades from the film. Twenty-one circus and native lions were brought in to play the roles of Elsa, her sisters, rivals and mates. The hiccups between the producer, Carl Foreman, the two directors, Tom McGowan and James Hill, Joy and George, the forty Europeans and 120 Africans involved in the film, were legion. James Hill, an experienced director, was driven to despair by the unpredictability of filming dangerous animals weighing 300 lbs which, if they decided they didn't like the plot, refused to cooperate. He told Sandy Gall: 'You just want the lion to sit there between Bill and Virginia for a minute and you could be a week on that.' Added to that, the weather was appalling, often preventing the frustrated crew from reaching the fleshpots of the nearest town, Nanyuki, and the bar and swimming pool of the luxurious Mount Kenya Safari Club.

The Joy Adamson of *Born Free* and the subsequent films was not the Joy Adamson of real life. To portray a living person, especially someone as mercurial as Joy, was a particularly difficult task for any actor: how much to reveal, how much to invent, how much honesty, how much showmanship? The love story between human and beast needed warm, sympathetic characters to be believable and although George was naturally relaxed and friendly, the same could not always be said of his wife. She may have been a genuine romantic and a dreamer, but she was hardly the soft-hearted creature the script demanded. Virginia McKenna, a beautiful English blonde, played Joy with a delicate sweetness Joy never possessed. She showed great bravery in many potentially risky scenes, returning to the set in a cast after her ankle had been broken by Boy, one of the acting lions. Her real-life husband, Bill, was a large, tousle-haired George, but there the similarity with their real-life counterparts ended. The film portrayed, amid cliché-ridden dialogue and somewhat stilted acting, a wholly saccharine relationship between Joy and George, based on thwarted mother love. Such lines as 'Crikey, what a bit of luck'; 'Right off the bat'; 'All talk and no action, beautiful dialogue though'; smacked of the Biggles books of the 1920s.

But the Traverses succeeded admirably in conveying the unique relationship between the Adamsons and Elsa, and no one could deny the difficult feat, requiring stamina and courage, of manoeuvring lions into playing believable roles. The best actors in the film were undoubtedly the lions, especially Boy and Girl, given to the company by the Scots Guards; and Mara and Ugas, the latter a huge beast weighing more than 400 lbs. The public adored the film and the haunting music won an Oscar.

Virginia McKenna was grateful to Joy for her restraint during the filming: 'For someone like Joy, who was always so personal about relationships, whether with animals or people, she was amazing to me. She never tried to interfere or suggest I interpret her differently and she did not seem to begrudge that she was not playing the character herself. That must have been difficult for her.' At the age of fifty-four, it would be hard to imagine Joy not being secretly delighted that the cinema-going public would see her portrayed as a gentle optimist by a stunning actress twenty years her junior.

Inevitably, though, Joy's intractable nature led to frequent rows, causing Carl Foreman to explode with frustration: 'Two of the greatest mistakes of my life have been to get involved with this film and to allow you on location.' Joy's inability to handle animals naturally was obvious to many during the making of the film – her nervousness showed and she became the only person wounded by Mara, suffering a deep gash which needed many stitches. One particular scene, of a lion fight, caused a monumental argument. As soon as she realized Carl Foreman was going to provoke the two lions into a confrontation she moved in: 'Can't you just pretend?

Get someone to scream, then run in and say there's been this terrible fight.' As James Hill told Sandy Gall, he said to her, 'Joy, that's like making a film about the Battle of Hastings and somebody comes in and says, "The battle is over, Sir."' Undeterred, Joy rushed over to George, shouting at the top of her lungs, 'George, George, you've got to stop them. They mustn't do it because the lions will tear each other to pieces.'

The more determined producer and director became, the more hysterical was Joy. Columbia won. The sensitivity of the scene, together with the possibility of Joy's continued histrionics, made it imperative that she be banished from the filming. The rather pathetic sight of Joy peeping over a distant rock, trying to glimpse the scene being shot, was noticed by the entire crew.

It had been agreed during the filming that three lion cubs belonging to the Marchesa Sieukwe Bisletti and her husband Francesco were to be used in the climactic scene of Elsa and her cubs. The Bislettis were old hands at rearing carnivores at their ranch, Marula, in Naivasha, and naturally Sieukwe was on the set to look after the cubs.

To start with matters between the two women went smoothly, since Joy had recently had a row with the girls in charge of the circus lions and decided to befriend the newcomer. Sieukwe described the move as 'the end of a beautiful friendship'. For Joy was jealous of anyone who was popular and rapidly began to view her as a threat. Sieukwe was an arrestingly beautiful woman, a magnet for men, as well as being highly intelligent, warm and interested in people. The crunch came when a reporter from the Nairobi *Times* arrived on the set to interview Sieukwe and to snap a few photographs of her with the cubs. When the picture appeared in the Kenya news Joy was furious.

The two women had radically different approaches to rearing animals. Unlike Joy, who was inclined to be bossy, the Marchesa preferred to walk quietly with her lions, following them, not forcing them to do what she wanted. She remembers, 'Joy was basically very lonely and very neurotic but her fanaticism led to her achievements. If she hadn't been a fanatic she wouldn't have been such a bore. She had very little idea of handling animals or of animal behaviour; she was over-emotional and extremely nervous, but she did love them. Perhaps her achievements gave her some inner happiness, as far as her nature could be happy.'

Although Joy was a great trial to most of those connected with the film, her compassion occasionally surfaced. When one of the crew had a personal problem, Joy was overheard being kind and considerate to him, saying, 'If I can do anything, please do call on me.'

While the film was being made, Joy's attention was diverted by the arrival of another big cat. She was thrilled one day to be given a orphan female cheetah by an army officer who was returning to England and was searching for someone to rehabilitate the year-old cub. Once again, Joy could immerse herself in an animal. The cheetah's name was Pippa. Yet, however deeply Joy grew to feel about Pippa, she was nervous around her, occasionally impatient and frequently exasperated.

During the latter days of their involvement on the location of *Born Free* at Watamu on the coast, Muff Becker, who used to run the Seafarers hotel, spent a few weeks in the company of Joy and Pippa. While the beach scenes were being shot Joy stayed in a small cottage belonging to the Beckers which was cordoned off into a *boma* for the cheetah. 'Joy was not at all at ease with Pippa and at that time I don't think she even particularly liked her. She certainly didn't have any intrinsic rapport. As Joy didn't want to, I took Pippa for a walk every morning and evening along the beach, where she loped along and paddled in the water.'

On one of these walks Becker saw George and two of the film lions out in a canoe when they passed a couple of African fishermen, also in a boat. The lions, deciding they would rather play with the strangers, jumped out of the canoe and swam furiously towards the Africans. Mute with terror, the fishermen paddled frantically towards the shore, leapt out and ran off into the bushes. The lions remained struggling, a hundred yards out to sea.

Again, when the Cottrells were visiting Joy on the set, Joy was still struggling to learn how to handle the cheetah. 'We left in Joy's Land Rover, with Pippa collared and chained in the rear of the car, for a special training area. It was rough going but levelled off into a wide, open grassland surrounded by forest. Here, Pippa, with her collar, was released to dash away. As we watched her sweeping forays across the open land-scape, Joy explained how Pippa was learning to hunt and return. As time passed and the sun went down, we became anxious about Pippa's coy behaviour as Joy tried to catch her with long leash in hand as she swept past us. Finally, in desperation, Joy sprang at the cat's flying body to fasten the leash while they rolled over and over. When the dust cleared, Joy rose, to our relief, and dragged the recalcitrant Pippa back to us in the car.'

As the filming was drawing to a close, Joy, together with George and the Traverses, joined battle to save some of the film lions from going to zoos. Columbia seemed determined to sell them rather than allow them their freedom. Columbia's attitude towards the Traverses, the lions, as well as George and herself, never ceased to infuriate her.

Her nerves frayed with continual bickering, Joy beseeched Virginia: 'Ginny, I would love to show you Elsa's grave – let's go up to Meru.' The two friends went swimming in Elsa's river and 'spent hours sitting on Elsa's grave, looking and talking and then not talking, just being there', recalls Virginia. 'Joy got very emotional – it was easy for her to cry.'

When the Traverses left Naro Moru for good, Joy was so grateful for their part in the film that, Virginia recalls, 'Joy wrote to us saying, "After you left I felt such pain and emptiness inside."'

When filming was completed the Adamsons were the last white people remaining on location while they waited for their two camps in Meru to be readied by their assistants. A few days before the departure date, George's newly discovered cousin, Pam Carson, turned up one evening. Joy became upset as soon as she realized that George and she had arranged for her to spend her leave with him at Meru and she would be helping him transport the lions Boy and Girl to Meru. According to Joy, the young woman intended to make films and give lectures on the animals, a domain she regarded as belonging to herself and George. Joy begged Pam to postpone her holiday as, under the rainy weather conditions, the move was more than risky. There were no facilities for any guests at the Meru camp. Always jealous of George's female friendships, Joy asked her to show her concern by staying behind and not adding to the couple's difficulties. Her entreaties angered Pam, who arranged to go ahead. George backed her up, although he had previously promised Joy that he would go alone with the lions the next day to Meru. Joy agreed to follow a short while later.

On the day of his departure she helped George load the lions and made him promise to radio-call his safe arrival. She heard nothing for a week. In the meantime, she phoned all over Kenya to find an assistant for him, tried to buy him a new Land Rover and also to buy the location farm to be used for wild animal research and their future home. A week later a couple of journalists called in, arriving from Meru where apparently George and Pam had granted interviews. Joy found out from them that George had reneged on their agreement and driven with the lions and Pam to Meru where Pam had remained. With her new-found fame, Joy needed the backing and encouragement, help and understanding that a husband might provide. It was not often forthcoming. George helped when it suited him, but calmly and with clear vision went ahead with his own life.

18

Pippa in Meru

From early 1965 onwards Joy and George lived in separate camps. George declared that if it had not been so 'life would have been intolerable.' It was a deep sadness for Joy that she no longer shared a home with her husband, blaming the separation on the fact that she was rehabilitating a cheetah while George was busy returning the lions Boy, Girl and Ugas to the wild – the two types of carnivore were natural enemies. But an added and deeper reason was that she and George were simply incompatible when around each other for any length of time. Joy felt George no longer needed her and continually pressured him to drop his lion schemes and live with her. While he was still fond of, even loved her, he was happiest alone in the bush with his animals away from her incessant demands.

Although she tried to hide her feelings, she had been profoundly unhappy during the filming of *Born Free*. However mercurial her nature, it had occurred to her just how rootless her existence was; how much she missed being able to curl up in a nest of her own. She realized that life's temptations were of little value compared to sharing feelings and emotions with one person who was prepared to trust and understand her. She felt a tinge of bitterness that while she and George were at Naro Moru for a year, George gave everyone on the film set the impression they were on the point of being divorced. He never bothered to spend any time alone with her after the day's filming was over but remained in the bar drinking with his friends while she worked. Her tribal book, endless correspondence, the Elsa Appeal conservation work and promotion articles for the film took up her evenings. She resented the fact that he never helped her reply to a single fan letter, and he also made it quite obvious to everybody that he regarded her presence as an intrusion.

The couple were to live twelve miles apart in the Meru National Reserve, where Joy would start studying cheetah behaviour through Pippa. This naturally solitary animal, never as affectionate as Elsa, was an enigma to

Joy, who badly wanted to capture the total love she had experienced with the gregarious lioness : 'I felt a mother's deep love for Elsa, but my feelings are more sisterly towards Pippa.'

Meru was a favourite place for both the Adamsons. To the east of Mount Kenya the land dropped quickly, webbed by the many rivers. Rain swept across the rich, red soil, and the landscape was lush. The Meru and Embu tribes were well settled on this side of the mountain long before the arrival of the Europeans. In the Meru area the land fell steeply to a flattish plain in which stood the park and, high above, the forests smelled of Meru oak, camphor, podocarpus. In the colonial days the *boma* at Meru or Embu was a good posting – gardens had as many as twenty-two varieties of fruit, crystal-clear rivers flowing from the mountain were stocked with trout and a mass of game swirled below in the flat country.

As Joy turned off from Meru towards her new camp, she tried to put the sad thoughts of the inevitable separation from George behind her. Her senses quickened as the road dropped, passing the small *shambas* growing coffee and straggling pawpaw trees. Occasionally the shadow of a mango tree draped the dirt road like a shroud as the Land Rover rumbled and bounced over the ruts. She noticed Sykes monkeys swinging in the tall branches of a forest glade and before long she reached the dramatic range of the Nyambene hills. From there she could look down on the misty volcanic hills in the blue distance of the low country. At last – her beloved NFD. It was always a sight which caught her breath in a great surge of elation, as if nowhere else on earth had God been so generous or creative. On the side of the road, Africans squatted and gossiped, tying up their small, fat bundles of *miraa* (khat). It was here in Maua that the best *miraa* trees were to be found, from the twigs of which the bitter juice was sucked. For many years the twigs had been exported to Somalia, the people of that country delighting in the sense of alertness and euphoria it brought.

Soon the land harshened, becoming more open and empty of people. The park was combed with dancing streams and brooks, which finally emptied into the Tana river at the southern boundary of the park. Spidery lines of riverine forest dipped raffia palm fronds into the water and the curious angular branches of the doum palms towered above the bush. Between the rivers open plains galloped, dotted with baobabs and stands of the umbrella thorn, and the air was filled with the sounds of Superb starlings and weaver birds. It was this water that was the life blood of Meru Park. However dry the grass, the water always provided relief for its animals.

Soon Joy travelled over the last concrete causeway, crossing a small river before reaching her new home. On the damp soil fringing the river a cloud of sulphur-yellow butterflies extracted moisture, oblivious to the flash of brilliant blue as a kingfisher darted past. Dragonflies performed a tremulous dance over the small, rippling falls as the song of water in a hurry repeated itself. A chorus of cicadas, as if on an endless musical mission, filled the humid air.

The 700-square-mile park was an area difficult to control. *Shifta*, marauding armed gangs of poachers and raiders, had long been the enemy of the elephant and rhino here. These merciless men were Somali or Boran nomads who claimed the semi-desert NFD belonged to them and were permanently in conflict with the Bantu people of the south. Joy had often ventured into the abandoned hideouts of poachers in the western end of the park and knew well the baobab tree, known as 'Poacher's Lookout', which hugged a huge cavern in its bole.

Joy's final campsite in Meru was beside the Rojewero river, 90 miles from the nearest phone and 120 miles from the nearest tarred road. The first thing she did on arriving, to discourage inquisitive tourists, was to erect a noticeboard: 'Scientific Experiment – No Entry' at the entrance to the camp. Livid with indignation, she had been forced by Perez Olindo, Director of National Parks succeeding Mervyn Cowie, to leave her first site for releasing Pippa due to the presence of a small lodge where visitors stayed. She saw this as breaking the association that Pippa had created for herself with territory she now considered hers.

Most of the time, however, Joy felt comfortable with Olindo, whom she sensed was on her side, and although he continued to have his battles with her, Olindo confessed his admiration: 'I had to give Joy special permission to be in certain portions of the park on foot which caused me grave worry. But I don't condemn what Joy and George were trying to do. You cannot really survive in wildlife without a little sentiment. There are greater bonds between the individual human and animal than there is on a broad species basis. They may not have been scientists but they learnt one hell of a lot.'

Joy's camp was efficient and attractive and she soon settled in. Against a backdrop of bush-covered hills, rocky outcrops, doum palms and giant fig trees, *bandas* of palm thatch and split palm logs were built, for Joy's bedroom, guesthouse and studio, where she typed vast quantities of correspondence every evening. Its walls were filled with press cuttings and pictures of Elsa, Pippa and friends. Yellow weaver birds jostled noisily together in the large tamarind tree shading Joy's bedroom and swallows swooped in circles inside her studio while she worked. Her bathroom was a canvas tube hanging from a tree. Here, in the heat of the day, Joy stood, fully clothed, beneath the dripping water to cool herself off. A few feminine touches lightened up the camp – waste-paper baskets, a checked cloth on the dinner table, a mudscraper outside the dining-room door, books lining one wall of the dining room itself.

One of the first things to be done was to erect a wire fence round the compound to protect Pippa from other predators during the night. The greatest danger to the camp, and one which made Joy paranoid, were the number of snakes – puff adders, cobras and boomslangs – which plagued them. Her deepest concern was for Pippa's safety rather than her own. Any snake tracks seen near Pippa's watering places were followed and the snakes ruthlessly hunted down.

One of Joy's few neighbours was the first game warden of the official reserve, Ted Goss, a tall, fair-haired man with a casual, helpful manner. It was only through the generosity of Joy's Trust that the Meru County Council, who owned the land, could declare it a national reserve. Goss oversaw his domain from his headquarters at Leopard Rock, so called because hunters had once baited leopard there.

In the beginning, all went smoothly between Joy and Ted. Unlike the wardens of two other reserves, he had no objections to Pippa being in his park, as there were relatively few tourists and cheetah pose few problems to humans. Ted reminisces: 'Although Joy bravely insisted, "I have no time to be bored," she also repeatedly said to me, "I feel so lonely here because I need to share. There is no one, besides you, to have a sensible conversation with."' Her evenings were solitary and to ease her isolation Joy constantly asked Ted to come round for a drink. Feeling responsible, Ted dropped in two or three times a week for an evening beer. Sitting outside her studio in a couple of canvas chairs, they listened to the sounds of the animals and discussed the need for conservation. Following her usual pattern with those useful to her, Joy grew increasingly dependent, demanding Goss's help with everything from broken radiators to unworkable radios and fridges if George were not available. Visitors were not particularly welcomed and few people ever dropped in on Joy other than fans, especially Americans.

For a while Ted was helpful – and single. However, he drew the line at booking her hair appointments in Nairobi, saying, 'No, Joy that's not on. I'm running the park here.' It was when he married that Joy's attitude towards him changed, and she felt that Ted was not giving her enough attention. 'Obviously I did not go round to her camp as often. She really started to shout at me, she cried and swore and cursed.' Jealousy raged and small digs were readily tossed. 'You cannot seem to get up in the morning, Ted. I wonder why?'

Joy's relationship with Pippa and observations of her habits continued to dominate her life. She soon came to know intimately the territory of sixty square miles covered by the cheetah. Never one to waste time, she continually typed on her small Olivetti as she sat in the Land Rover on the way to see Pippa. She watched anxiously for signs of an accident, knowing that the bones of cheetah are fragile and broken legs one of the main causes of their high mortality rate. Afraid of disturbing the animal's natural instincts, Joy was adamant that no one should accompany her on her daily visits other than an assistant. If her semi-pets were to live as wild animals, she understood they must never lose their fear of human strangers. She knew what was correct, but Joy's emotional nature often kept her from doing the right thing.

Ted supplied Joy with the services of a humorous and gentle ranger from the Meru tribe called Toithanguru, nicknamed Kitungu – Swahili for onion – as she found it difficult to pronounce his name. Both Joy and George also called him Local. Each morning after a quick dip under the canvas shower and a hasty breakfast at seven, Joy, accompanied by the small, humorous tracker carrying his gun and a large sack of meat, went out to find Pippa. Toithanguru knew, 'in his heart' as Joy put it, where the animal would be.

The cheetah, unlike Elsa who had considered the camp her own, preferred to live a few miles away. Joy, in large sunglasses and with cameras slung over her shoulder, carried a large megaphone to call her cheetah. Often many hours of searching went by before they spotted her, during which time they said little to each other. Walking through the long grass on the open plain, all that could be heard above the strident crescendo of the cicadas and the rippling birdsong as the heat of the day rose, was Joy's high-pitched voice endlessly calling 'Pippa, Pippa.' As soon as she came across her, Joy was rewarded by an affectionate lick from Pippa as a greeting and she would constantly follow Joy around as they went on a walk together through this vast stretch of Africa.

It was at the times when she could not locate Pippa that Joy wondered about the rightness of what she was doing. She had begun to feel she might be little more than a profound nuisance to the animal, repeatedly shouting her name until her throat became hoarse. At times she was unable to trace Pippa for days on end and when the animal eventually appeared at the camp Joy, like a protective mother hen, complained that she did not seem at all relieved to have found her way home. In fact, having been fed and made a fuss of, Pippa was only too happy to disappear as quickly as possible.

In the bush together, things were different. In the heat of noon when nothing stirred, they would rest in a grove of trees, Pippa eating her meal while Joy, who had brought her drawing kit and a low camp bed, sketched the cheetah and made notes. Around them, in a moving panoply of shapes and earth colours, roamed the wild creatures of the park. On her walks, black rhino, wary buffalo and elephant toppling doum palms were encountered. Plains game and reticulated giraffe sauntered past ostriches as they stalked across the land, and pairs of secretary birds systematically hunted for insects in the grass.

The extraordinary variety of birdlife in Meru particularly fascinated Joy, who often came across a great spotted cuckoo and recognized the red rump of the buffalo weaver as it flew past her. She spotted vulterine fish eagles feeding on the skins of palm nuts and Kori bustards which gazed disdainfully into the distance. Whenever Joy saw anything of particular interest, or whenever Pippa came back to the camp – about once a week – she would call excitedly, 'Kitungu, Kitungu, come quickly and see this.'

Toithanguru proved an immensely loyal and understanding man. A man of simple mentality, he was considered by all in the park to be an exceptional bushman. In the polite, politic ways of old Africans, he tolerated Joy's *kali* (fierce) moods and rages and grew to love Pippa as much as she. 'Memsahib Haraka' – lady in a hurry – 'was not good, she was not bad, she was in the middle.'

As the wife of a respected *muzungu* (white man) it was his duty to look after her as well as he could and for many years he did. Whenever there was a new scare from the *shifta*, Joy would ask him to sleep outside her *banda* with his gun at the ready. A smiling, crinkly old man with wise eyes and, in the custom of his tribe, long, looped earlobes, he had twice walked for three days to Goss's *banda*, clutching two faded photos of Joy and Pippa, for his interview. When asked if sleeping outside Joy's hut scared him, he replied, 'I am an *ndume* [a bull, a strong man]. I have no fear protecting a woman.'

In the ways of an African old-timer, he kept derogatory memories of his employer to himself. Once, on being called by her, he jumped up and stepped on a stick which was on the fire where his *posho* was boiling. The red-hot pot of maize meal fell on his leg, causing third-degree burns. Furious that he had been so careless, Joy forced him to walk the eight miles to Leopard Rock for treatment.

Goss's tenure and help ended when he began experimenting with a new drug for darting elephants. After the initial dart the animal looked asleep, allowing Goss to approach. 'Unfortunately it was still awake, it charged and caught me. I remember the sharp bristles of its trunk were like needles as it curled around me and threw me to the ground. It then tried to spear me with its tusks but missed, instead smashing my thigh bone with its leg.' As the ranger with Goss continued shooting at the elephant, Goss yelled at him in Swahili: 'For God's sake stop, otherwise it will fall down dead on top of me.' Clutching on to tufts of grass, he slowly pulled himself through its back legs before the animal dropped dead inches in front of him. The ranger, who could not drive, managed to put Goss in the back of the Land Rover and follow his boss's instructions on how to change gear before he passed out. Goss was flown to Nairobi by the flying doctor and narrowly escaped dying of shock.

To help her with Pippa, Joy started to employ a series of assistants. Besides spending time in the field, each was something of a general dogsbody, getting her groceries, post, keeping the Land Rovers in good repair, pasting press cuttings and photographs into scrapbooks. One of the few assistants who helped Joy whom she not only respected but liked was James Willson, whom she had met on the set of *Born Free*. Kenya-born, his genial, open personality never became ruffled under Joy's demands. His deep interest in wildlife combined with a rare ability to smooth over difficulties with servants Joy had upset. She was totally unsympathetic to their various domestic needs and problems, often forgetting to pay their wages.

'Joy's attitude was demeaning to Africans. She did not understand them and this aggressive, domineering mentality provoked ill will from the staff. I used to listen to a fusillade of abuse and sarcasm thrown at them. Then I'd step in and try and calm things down.' Such was her cook's fear of Joy and terror of Pippa that he slept each night up a tree until he was carted off to Maua Mission Hospital.

For his sixtieth birthday, on 3 February 1966, Joy presented George with a new refrigerator for his lions' meat. A few months later she flew to London for the Royal Command Performance of the film *Born Free*, to be attended by Her Majesty the Queen. Naturally this special occasion demanded a new dress and Joy, moaning to a friend after so many years in the bush, 'To think I was one of the best-dressed women in Vienna,' went to town.

Joy's metamorphosis when dressing up for special occasions was extraordinary and this time she wanted to look her best. She was used to the work of the better dressmakers in Nairobi who could, and would, make an outfit in a very short time. Once in London she went straight to Norman Hartnell, considered the best couturier in the city at the time. Joy described at length the style of dress she wanted and the type of material, all of which was possible. But his staff were sniffy about the required time – three days – explaining it was totally impossible. Joy promptly blew a gasket, insisting it must be done. Eventually, in order to stop the tirade, one of the vendeuses told Joy that they happened to have a lovely dress that was exactly her size. It had been made to the order of another client, but had been rejected as it was not a perfect fit. They had made another and since this one was lying spare, they wondered whether 'Madame' would care to try it. The dress showed Joy's figure off to great advantage and she happily left the shop. But no one had mentioned that it was a reject from Her Majesty the Queen, who wore the identical dress to the première.

Joy looked stunning, with an unusual choice of modern gold jewellery, her hair beautifully coiffed and long white satin gloves complementing her elegant gown. Although the Queen gave no sign of recognition, a picture of Virginia McKenna, about to collapse with laughter next to Joy, appeared in the press. When asked for a comment, Buckingham Palace declared, 'Her Majesty does not notice what other people are wearing.' Joy remarked, 'Both being ladies, neither of us said anything.'

Although the London critics panned it, the film became a worldwide box-office success. Joy and George were perhaps right in laying that success at the feet of Virginia McKenna and Bill Travers. If the story had been shot as a documentary with the real Adamsons, it is likely it would have faded without trace many years ago.

In the midst of this whirl of success, Joy received a cable that Pippa had given birth. She flew back to Kenya for three days before her film promotion tour of Europe and the United States. Once home, she was delighted to find Pippa eager to show off her cubs, which she had hidden in dense thornbush. Joy quickly took a roll of photographs, convinced this could be the last chance she would be given to come this close.

Joy was immensely proud of having succeeded in her ambition of returning Pippa to the wild, particularly as she had been told it would be an impossible task. Although Pippa could now hunt and was totally independent, the maternal side of Joy remained touched that the released animal still occasionally came to camp to greet her old friends.

In so far as she was giving details of the behaviour of the carnivores she worked with, Joy could be very accurate – and more scientific than she was ever credited with. It was in her personal relationships that the truth was never clear. She wrote about and filmed at length the courtship and love-play of the animals and often alluded to an almost sexual intimacy with them. 'I don't really see the difference between having sex with a cheetah or a man,' she said more than once.

During her preoccupation with Pippa and her second set of cubs – the first having been eaten by a lion – she continued to study their behaviour carefully. They remained affectionate yet aloof, trusting yet distant. She watched their fast and rough play together as they sharpened their reflexes for the time when speed and agility would mean the difference between survival and starvation.

Joy's own behaviour was becoming increasingly erratic. Her jealousy and domestic quarrels escalated, despite her work on a new book, *The Spotted Sphinx*, about Pippa and her brood, Whitey, Tatu, Mbili and Dume. Her book on the tribes, *Peoples of Kenya*, was published in 1967, and now she was struggling to keep a balance between mawkishness and behavioural study. She vacillated in her opinion of her writing, cursing it as 'far too sentimental', or 'so cold and without feeling'. Her confused nature still desperately needed an outlet for affection and so she clung tenaciously to her cheetah family. She was well aware that film companies favoured George and his lions over herself and her cheetah – a case in point was a short, educational film being made on both by a small company with an excellent young director, Richard Tuber. The Trust had put up one-third of the film costs and half the crew stayed at Joy's camp, the other half happily with George. The production team with Joy were permanently on edge, waiting for the next volcanic eruption. Eventually Joy stopped speaking to them.

Jean Hayes, who was involved with the sound recording, warned Tuber of Joy's emotional nature. Unfortunately Tuber made a major error when he decided to shoot George's sequence first. When it came to filming Joy, she spoke non-stop and almost incoherently about her life with her animals. Richard explained that he might have to use a Viennese actress to dub Joy's voice as her English was not clear. This was accepted but later, on hearing that the uncorrected colour print of the film had been sent to Jean, Joy demanded to see it. As soon as she viewed the film she flew into a temper, calling Tuber a 'bloody liar' and claiming that she had not said the words put into her mouth via the dubbing. In an effort to placate her, Jean reached for the original tape plus Tuber's transcript to prove to Joy that the dubbed words were exactly what she had originally spoken. Undeterred, Joy stormed out of Jean's house and immediately put a veto on the showing of the film in Kenya, reneging on a promise that a copy would be given to the Game and Parks Department. She also put all her efforts into hiring an American lawyer to stop the film being shown in the United States. Without acknowledging the fact, Joy was aware that fresh scientific research on cheetah behaviour by a young man named Patrick Hamilton had resulted in new information which made the views she expressed in the film seem slightly irrelevant and out of date.

Matters with George broke down even further when Bill Travers started filming *The Lions are Free*, partly because it would loosen her financial hold on her husband – George had been assured of a handsome income. She resented Bill cashing in on George and distracting his attention from the real aim of his lion project – rehabilitation. She also wanted to take an equal role with the lions in the film, but Bill, unprepared to show her in a light which was not accurate, stuck to his guns and refused. According to Joy, he arrived in Meru and insisted on camping at George's, where he wanted thirty of the Africans to erect *bandas* and tents before filming. She complained that he was determined to turn all their animals into film stars and the endless rehearsals were geared solely to showing him in the best light. She naturally felt that would annul everything she and George had by then achieved. She refused to cooperate and stormed out, leaving George, as she saw it, to be cajoled and flattered. According to Joy, from that moment on, George invited every tourist to mingle freely with his lions. The animals became so used to human company that they seemed more tame than wild, even though they could easily fend for themselves. One Kenya settler, who wishes to remain anonymous, said of George's continuous contact with the lions : 'Of course I've never thought that was right – dangerous, lots of problems, bad conservation. Mind you, at the beginning I was all for it because I thought he was training the lions to eat Joy !'

An added factor that fuelled Joy's anger was that George was writing his autobiography *Bwana Game*, the proceeds of which would also help finance his way of life. To punish him for what she considered his various transgressions, Joy temporarily cut her husband off from the Trust. Yet, however jealous she was of George's increasing popularity, he never said a nasty word about Joy.

In 1968, when the Traverses were again filming, they drove up to Meru to see and film George, with whom they had remained close friends. Virginia was determined to patch up the quarrel between her husband and Joy and begged George to take them to Joy's camp. In the late afternoon, all three leapt into the Land Rover and drove off to find Joy. They soon spotted her, walking by the river. Virginia jumped down and shouted for Joy to stop. 'Joy knew it was me calling, but she went on walking. I ran after her yelling, "For goodness' sake, Joy, stop."' Eventually Joy slowed down. 'I gave her a big hug and said, "Oh come on, here we are, it's crazy for us to continue to be like this." She was very affectionate.' Bill and George, seeing the friendly exchange, climbed out and stood by the Land Rover.

'I will come and talk to Bill if he will apologize,' Joy told Virginia.

Walking up to Bill, she repeated her statement. He replied, 'Joy, I ex-plained about the film, I don't know what to apologize about.' Turning to Virginia, Joy said tightly, 'You can come to my camp, Ginny, but not Bill.' The actress, put in a difficult spot, replied, 'I'm sorry, Joy, but if Bill cannot come then of course I can't.' Joy turned away to walk back to her camp. George, fed up with this unnecessary drama, shouted, 'Don't be an idiot, Joy. Get in and we will take you back.' Joy reluctantly climbed in the Land Rover. Virginia recalls: 'Everyone was upset. It was so disappointing after all we had been through. We had received numerous letters and cards saying how much she had loved the filming of *Born Free* and how we had encapsulated everything they really felt in our film. There was nowhere to go from there.' This was a far cry from the time when they had left Naro Moru.

19

Jehovah of the Thunders

The same year, 1968, Peter Jenkins took over as the game warden of Meru with a brief to develop the park. He moved with his wife Sara and two small children into his headquarters, a primitive mud and wattle hut full of bats, snakes and rats. Jenkins immediately set to business, turning Meru into a model park with gleaming signposts covering a superb network of roads and excellent concrete drifts over the many rivers. An unusually neat headquarters with buildings and lorries set out in shipshape fashion set the tone. A no-nonsense man, tall and attractive, he kept his animal haven free of an excess of tourists and it was possible to experience the solitude that was so much the feel of the African bush.

Sharing the views of other first-rate wardens – David Sheldrick, Bill Woodley and Miles Turner – Jenkins disapproved of 'rehabilitating home-reared lions which breed like house cats'. He foresaw huge problems. Animals would not go wild easily as long as they were being fed. The lions would either be hounded out of the district by the indigenous lions, killed, or forced into surrounding tribal areas where they would become man-eaters or kill stock. To this day Jenkins states, 'I don't think it has ever been proven to be a success and certainly did not warrant the vast amount of money that was poured into it.' He agreed with the aims of the Trust: 'The preservation of wildlife and the education of the public to this aim.' He was less worried about Joy and Pippa: 'A cheetah was a fairly innocuous sort of animal.'

By now Joy was increasingly in favour of wildlife education and foresaw the need long before other people. Without her generosity the Meru National Park would never have been created. Samburu would not have been gazetted a Reserve and many a bush pilot, including Peter Jenkins, would not have learnt to fly. Joy soon realized that Jenkins was a hardliner on some issues, but nevertheless respected him, sending him monthly reports on Pippa, which he stated 'were totally unreadable – I sent them off to the Trust'.

Although full of admiration for a woman who was 'one of the few farmers that put her money back into the fields she reaped,' Jenkins and his wife Sara were soon exhausted by all the demands she made on them, dropping in on them only to request vegetables from Meru township, insisting they deliver her mail or repair her vehicle. Soon after he arrived, Joy charged in with one of Pippa's cubs which had been bitten through the head. Joy, completely hysterical, began screaming, 'God, George is such a bastard.' Although this was an everyday occurrence in the bush, she had decided that one of George's lions was responsible. A few days later, when Joy became unreasonable over a demand that Jenkins should burn an area of long grass before the rains fell to make it easier for Pippa to hunt, he ordered her out of his office. Turning to George, he said, 'I am sorry, I will not be spoken to like that.' George shrugged and continued sitting there, puffing away on his pipe. Joy, in her anger, stormed off and set fire to the grass herself, nearly burning down the Jenkinses' house.

Matters were patched up enough for the Adamsons to enjoy Christmas lunch with the game warden and his family. Joy was like a child each Christmas and relished preparing and celebrating among friends. For someone who was happy being alone in the bush, she took equal pleasure from the times when she could be gregarious. Christmas was a special time when she and George were together, disagreements were pushed into the background and, for a few hours, peace reigned. This year, 1968, she asked Toithanguru to cut down a small euphorbia (candelabra) tree to which she added a few white candles. She spent Christmas Eve cutting stars, crescent moons and strips of glitter from the foil wrappings of chocolate and hung them up. White candles in fruit-juice bottles filled with sand were scattered among the presents around the base of the tree. Packets of meat were ready in the fridge for her servants. Joy de-frizzed her hair, always a sign of a special occasion, and long after dark she was still wrapping up small presents and sorting out money and meat rations for the camp servants.

On arriving at the Jenkinses' hut, she gave them their Christmas present of a second-hand record of *Born Free* with a large scratch across the surface. At lunch, unaccustomed to brandy butter, Joy consumed two bowls of the traditional fare, remarking 'how delicious' it was. Sara remembers : 'Of course it left the rest of us with a rather dry Christmas pudding and Joy extremely over the top !'

By Boxing Day things had returned to normal. Joy arrived at the Jenkinses' in tears, explaining that by mistake she had put water into her petrol tank and that 'Peter just had to deal with it.' Sara was resigned, by now used to the fact that 'Joy could ruin one's whole day.'

January the following year saw the twenty-fifth anniversary of the Adamsons' marriage. On being reminded while in Naivasha that it was her silver wedding anniversary, Joy rang up friends to come and join them and immediately leapt into her Land Rover with her new secretary, an American, Netta Peiffer, and roared back to Meru. After discovering her cook had upped and left, she pulled into the Jenkinses' home, declaring, 'Sara, I've got fifteen people flying in and coming to dinner. You are the cook tonight, so you had better come along.'

1969 started badly for both the Adamsons. The year before, Jonny Baxendale had arrived to join George. A young godson of his, for whom he felt great affection, he was the son of his old friend and partner Nevil Baxendale. Happy to have a cheerful, younger man to flirt outrageously with, Joy was always glad to see him whenever he came over to her camp. But he was naturally assertive and there were many occasions when, in helping Joy, their personalities clashed. Soon after he arrived, Jonny had dropped in to Joy's camp to deliver her mail, to save her waiting an extra three days. It was the rainy season and the park was a quagmire. He left after having a beer and, on the way back to George's camp, his car fell through a bridge and stuck fast in the mud. There was no alternative but to walk the three miles back to Joy with his ranger and, as he left, Jonny snatched a bottle of whisky. Though neither carried a rifle, Baxendale held on to his powerful flashlight.

After a mile he sensed something was wrong. Turning round he saw in the dark the yellow eyes of five lionesses padding close behind them. As the two frightened men slipped and slithered their way back to Joy, their legs and feet torn by the thorns of the 'wait-a-bit' bushes, they continually threw mud pies at the animals to keep them at bay. Happy to have reached Joy alive, Jonny pointed behind him and jokingly said to her, 'Look at all my friends I have invited to the camp to have a whisky.' Joy flared up. 'Lions? How dare you bring lions to my camp? You know they petrify Pippa. Why couldn't you have gone somewhere else?' Amazed, Jonny spluttered, 'For Christ's sake, Joy. Do you know how bloody selfish you are? My feet were cut to ribbons and I've been floundering around in the mud with these damn animals on my heels.'

On one occasion, however, he saved her life. As he arrived at the camp, Joy was standing outside the kitchen, shouting, 'These servants are so stupid, they're all idiots, they don't do anything I say,' as three bewildered Africans stood silently, not understanding a word of her appalling Swahili.

Behind her the cook was standing with a huge carving knife raised in his hand, shaking with anger. Jonny went calmly up to him and said, 'I'll have that knife,' and quietly took it out of his hand. He took Joy outside and warned her: 'Joy, you are the idiot. You can't *tukana*, you can't insult, these people – they just won't take it, especially from a white woman. You realize, if I had not walked in, he would have killed you?'

Shaken, Joy said, 'God, Jonny, do you really think so?'

Exceptionally fearless in the bush, Joy was petrified by only two things – punctures and elephants. Whenever George climbed down from his Land Rover to get a better view of the elephant walking across the road some distance away, Joy yelled, 'Fool, fool, get back in the car right now!' An African always accompanied Joy in her Land Rover in case one of her tyres had to be changed. Her attitude towards her car was similarly dispassionate. She vaguely understood water was put in the front and petrol behind, but was incapable of doing it herself.

One definite way to stop Joy from appearing too frequently at George's camp was to mention either of her fears. More than once when Jonny was at her camp, Joy, wanting to see George, suddenly jumped up, saying, 'I'm coming round to see him.' Jonny quickly replied, 'Actually, I think that's a bad idea. The whole road between you and us is covered with elephant and they are pulling branches of thorn trees onto the road. They'll puncture your tyres. As soon as they move on, I'll let you know.' Jonny recalls: 'It was a perfect solution, since she always associated elephants with giving her punctures!'

Whenever she did go round to her husband's camp at Mugwongo Hill, Joy remained nervous of his lions and never achieved any rapport with them. George never failed to irritate his wife over his liking for White Horse whisky and his old habit which, like a mischievous boy, he knew annoyed her. Each time he opened a new bottle, he removed the small tag with a white horse on it and added it to the collection of other tags hanging on a wire which went round his studio hut. 'That's two years' worth of whisky,' he smiled. Pulling on his beard, his blue eyes twinkling with humour, he chuckled when she walked in, looked at the line of tags and delivered her usual sermon: 'Each of those is a bottle of whisky. You are an alcoholic, George, everybody knows it.' When asked later if he missed not seeing more of Joy, George answered, 'There are only two things I would ever miss. Lea & Perrins sauce and White Horse.'

The Adamsons' rows with Peter Jenkins continued, especially when they realized the warden was determined that, before an accident happened, George and his lions should leave the park. Joy, happy with her cheetahs but always on the lookout for a leopard to rehabilitate, was on friendlier terms with Peter than was her husband. At the end of January, when a member of the game department offered her two leopard cubs, she jumped at the idea and set off to tackle Peter about it: 'Wouldn't it be wonderful to have a third book on a third big cat rehabilitated in the same bit of country?' she asked. Jenkins, feeling slightly jaded about their carnivores, replied sarcastically, 'Just tell me, Joy, what do we, the Parks Board, get out of all these books you produce? We are not running a glorified zoo. I'm sorry, but the answer is no.'

Distraught that the fulfilment of her dream had been so offhandedly dismissed, Joy threw herself onto the dirt road in front of his office, kicking and screaming in uncontrollable anger. She then jumped into her car and, with a resounding crash of gears, roared off at high speed. She was not going to be thwarted. Heading off to George's camp, as soon as she arrived she shouted at Jonny to drive her immediately to Nairobi so that she could collect the leopard cubs. He refused, saying, 'No, I have a life of my own. I am driving my own car to Nairobi to see my friends, to get drunk and to get laid, not to collect any animals for you. I am young, only twenty-two. Can you remember ever being young, Joy? If you want to go to Nairobi, then drive yourself and I will follow you in case you get a puncture.'

Now apoplectic with rage, Joy drove off in a cloud of dust, this time followed by George's young assistant. The convoy had not travelled far when, rounding a bend and swerving to avoid two Africans, Joy's Land Rover careered down a ravine. Five minutes later, Jonny found her, completely hysterical and in great pain, picked her up and drove rapidly to Embu Hospital. Joy's right hand, trapped between a rock and the car, was a crushed mess of torn flesh, embedded with dirt.

Joy refused to stay in such a primitive hospital as Embu, pathetically begging Jonny not to desert her: 'Please, please don't leave me here, I'll die.' So, wrapped in blankets, suffering from shock and devouring painkillers, Joy was driven to Nairobi. The accident was the first of many Joy was to suffer and bear with great stoicism.

Gerald Nevill, Joy's surgeon, was waiting at the Nairobi Hospital to receive her at midnight. Knowing her well as her GP, he considered Joy 'almost a manic depressive'. Nevertheless, he was fond of her and admired her extraordinary courage. 'What a mess this is – we might have to amputate,' he said, realizing that with every bone in her hand broken, it was unlikely that Joy would ever be able to use it again.

'No, no, I forbid it,' cried Joy in horror.

'Well, we'll do our best, but I can't promise anything,' Gerald replied. She was operated on immediately, with skin grafted from her leg, and knew it would take many months before the severed tendons and bones would mend. George came to visit her in hospital and her room was filled with so many visitors and flowers that the staff began to feel she was the only patient in the hospital. One visitor, on bending over to kiss her, reeled backwards, knocked over by the combined fumes of cod liver oil and garlic – Joy had long been convinced that these were the elixir of life.

Joy proved to be an impatient though resilient patient and any operation that required her to rest was doomed to failure. Although she found it difficult to keep still she seldom complained about the pain she was suffering. Desperately anxious, she cried to her surgeon: 'This bloody hand has *got* to work. I *must* be able to paint again and play the piano.' Occasionally, as in the past, her nervous state got the better of her. Nevill remembers that over the years of their friendship, 'Joy didn't just cry, she would sit there and weep. Often one had no idea why she was weeping.' While in hospital, Joy learned to type with her left hand, but soon got bored and wanted to leave as quickly as she could.

After four frustrating weeks, Joy left with her stiff, deformed hand to go back to Meru. Soon after her return, another serious accident occurred in the park. Jonny Baxendale and George's lion Boy were together near his Land Rover when Peter Jenkins pulled up in his new Toyota with Sara and their two children. The car had half doors and open windows and the young boy, Mark, was kneeling in the middle seat, gazing out of the back. Boy, who had shown no interest in the Jenkinses or their car, was padding silently in the direction of the river when he suddenly turned and sprang effortlessly into the Toyota. Squashing Peter Jenkins's back against his seat with his powerful shoulders, he reached past and thrust his sharp claws onto the boy's head, sinking his teeth deep into his arm. Peter Jenkins had the presence of mind to put his foot hard down on the accelerator and jerk the car into motion. With blood pouring from Mark's head and arm, they drove quickly to the mission hospital.

Back in the park, George and Jonny were desperately upset by the attack. Luckily, Mark survived but the park authorities ordered George's beloved Boy to be shot. George, however, stood firm, arguing that nothing would have happened to Mark Jenkins if his father hadn't stopped so close to Boy. The lion was saved, but even George could see that the animal's days in the park were numbered.

Joy's hand was so impaired that Nevill suggested she go to London in June for a further major operation and physiotherapy. As she planned to be away five months, she left explicit instructions with her new assistant, Brian Heath, on how to run the camp. He was delighted to be left alone in the bush. For one thing, Joy's assistants were never allowed to have visitors or girlfriends. For another, he could now eat properly. Joy had always been indifferent to food and had extreme ideas about what her assistants could and could not eat. Her diet seldom varied. Lunch consisted of sausages and potatoes. For dinner a beer chased down one slice of Kenya cheddar cheese and an inch of meat was cut off from the dozen or so mouldy-looking salamis which hung in bunches from the rafters of the hut. So strong was the stench that the sausages could be smelt by visitors long before they reached camp.

Much of the time in England was spent with her old friends Robert and Pat Nimmo, who lent her a wing of their house in Surrey – Robert had been running the EWAA in England for some years. Before her operation she spent each day dipping her mutilated hand into a wax bath, never once moaning about her misfortunes. Every evening she had dinner with her friends before retiring to her room and bashing away with her left hand on her typewriter.

Once ensconced in St Mary's Hospital in Paddington, she wrote to them as she lay in bed before receiving her anaesthetic. Having spent a blissful few weeks with her thoughtful friends, she found the stark surroundings and depressing views a shocking contrast to their comfortable home. Half-jokingly she told the Nimmos that she had left their name and address on the desk, just in case the grimness of it all proved too much and she did away with herself.

Joy's letters to her friends were often outpourings of frustrated love. She adored people when they helped her and, more often than not, started with several lines of effusive affection and genuine concern, before spending the rest of the letter describing her rushed, exacting days. Again, in July, after recuperating with the couple, she told them that so great was her love for them that there were no words to express her gratitude. Joy was well aware that she was not an easy person to have around for long periods and the Nimmos, in particular, had been of immense help. All Joy could fervently hope was that the stressful memories of putting up with their patient for such a long time would fade.

Twice a week, Brian wrote to her giving details of Pippa and the cubs. On Joy's instructions he was busy sticking mountains of press cuttings into scrapbooks. During the four months Joy was away, she complained that George only wrote to her three times, and in all cases he was concerned with his own problems with the lions. He only bothered to enquire briefly about her hand in a scribble at the end of his letters. She felt bitter that he contributed nothing financially towards her operation or to any of her numerous living expenses. Over the years George had only paid for his wife's grocery bills, while she had to fork out for the rest. In her letters she often stated that he never shared his plans or interests with her, lived like a bachelor and often became violent whenever Joy disagreed with his wishes.

While she was in England the imminent publication of her book, *The Spotted Sphinx*, plus an exhibition of her tribal paintings got Joy on her feet again. She tried desperately to appear on the children's television programme *Blue Peter*. The producers turned her down on the grounds that, due to her now sharp, wrinkled features and fast, excited speech, she might frighten the younger children.

By September, she was impatient to return to see Pippa and her cubs. Her useless hand was extremely painful and her mood was one of great frustration. She could hold neither a pencil nor a paintbrush. Large amounts of painkillers contributed to her tetchiness. She complained that her husband and assistant had abandoned her in Nairobi, telling a friend that, between them, they had four cars at Meru to collect her from Nairobi. She alleged that, although both knew her flight number and Brian had already been in Nairobi for the past two days, neither of them turned up to meet her. She waited for three days at the Nairobi Club until Brian arrived with a letter from George explaining the reason he had not come was because he had had to look after his lions. Joy could not fathom why Brian had to repair one car to collect her when he could have borrowed one of the other three. In fact, Brian remembers collecting her on the agreed day.

Finding the cheetahs on her return fending for themselves, well fed and healthy went some way towards restoring her equilibrium. Indeed, so independent had they become that Joy began to feel the only way of keeping in contact was by feeding them. Two goats a week were slaughtered. Each time animals needed to be added to the small herd, Brian drove twenty-two miles to the nearest market. There he spent all day under the shade of a large spreading acacia, while an African assistant walked to market to bargain forty shillings for each animal. Joy was determined that the price would not escalate simply because she was a European.

Six weeks after Joy's return, Pippa disappeared for ten days. Brian and Toithanguru, hunting everywhere, found the cheetah with a broken leg, which had probably resulted from an encounter with a bushbuck. Joy, distraught, rushed to find Peter Jenkins. Seeing Pippa's emaciated condition and realizing the animal was unlikely to live, he said, 'Joy, I don't think there is a hope. Do you want me to put her down?' His remark led to another fit of histrionics. 'Absolutely not. While there's life, there's hope.'

Toithanguru, equally upset, begged Joy not to take Pippa to Nairobi : 'Memsahib, you should not move Pippa. If you do, she will die.' Joy, taking no heed, drove her beloved animal down to the city. One vet refused to deal with the leg, saying, 'It's beyond repair. If we put it in plaster it will either be too loose and never mend properly, or too tight and it will get gangrene.' Joy begged him to amputate. He refused, saying 'That's ridiculous. How is a three-legged cheetah going to survive in the bush ?' Joy could not see the practicalities ; all she wanted was for Pippa to survive. A second opinion was sought and the husband and wife team, Sue and Toni Harthoorn, immobilized the leg. Joy, together with her animal, stayed at the animal orphanage, where she slept alongside Pippa each night and soothed her. On 7 October, Pippa died. A friend, Charles Hayes, recalls the pitiful sight of Joy lying over the body of Pippa 'in paroxysms of grief'. Joy and Pippa's body were driven back to Meru. Toithanguru, always loyal, was there to meet her and for the rest of the day the two old comrades sat and cried, mourning for many hours the loss of their lovable but aloof friend. Together they buried her alongside one of her cubs and Brian fetched large stones, which were placed over the grave. To console her African ranger, Joy gave him a small gift of money.

At first, Joy blamed her assistant for Pippa's demise. Brian remembers : 'Once Pippa had died, Joy somehow got it into her head that while in England she had received a telepathic message that her cheetah was in trouble and that she had rushed all the way home to find out she had broken her leg. She completely forgot that when she first came back she had found Pippa perfectly healthy and spent the whole day with her.'

Joy's highly strung state also led to a falling out with Sue Harthoorn. A few hours after Pippa died Joy thanked her profusely for all that she and Toni had done, telling her that the whole episode had brought her closer to them both than ever. While Joy was crying, Sue apparently handed a letter for George behind Joy's back to the man who had offered to drive Pippa's body and herself back to Meru. Unknown to Joy, Sue was planning to see George about a children's book she wanted to write on his lion Ugas. Joy was amazed to see the Harthoorns the next weekend at Meru. By then, Joy was slightly paranoid about the couple, convinced that they were avoiding her – they spent Sunday picnicking with George, passing her camp twice without asking her to join them.

An air of finality hung over the park. George had been ordered to leave his camp and, much to her secret delight, had agreed to live with Joy for the next three months until she, too, was forced to leave. Stormy interviews between the warden and the Adamsons had resulted in Joy travelling to

Nairobi to talk to the authorities in order get Peter sacked. But his wife Sara recognized that 'George was just as bad. If they spread enough rumours about how badly Peter was managing things, then the bosses would say, I suppose Jenkins had better go.'

The day arrived when George said goodbye to his surroundings. To stop any attempt to renege on the agreement, Peter set fire to the *bandas* that had been George's home for the past four years. Wisps of smoke curling into the blue sky were seen by an emotional Joy and George as they stood silently side by side.

Domestic life back at Joy's camp proved to be no easier than it had ever been. Joy was infuriated by George, who scattered all his belongings round the camp, turning it into a chaotic mess. Whenever she asked him to clear it up he refused. She also demanded that he remove his car from where it had been parked, as it was interfering with camp life. She said crossly that he did nothing but sit down for drinks and finally dinner. During one meal, shared by Brian, they had a monumental row about the food. When she saw that George had asked the *pishi* (cook) for a bowl of soup to start, she lost her temper, picked up his plate and threw his food into the river. 'There is no way you can continue living with me unless you damn well eat what I eat and do not expect sumptuous meals.' George, protesting, stood up from the table and tried to soothe her.

But, having worked herself up into a state, she yelled to the staff to come and rescue her from George, who was on the point of murdering her. Two servants rushed out of the lean-to kitchen to find the Bwana and assistant looking rather nervous and the Memsahib still screaming at the top of her lungs. Joy later told a friend that she had thrown the plate of rice into his face, telling him to remove the car before he had another mouthful. She claimed George rose from the table and threw her on the ground, beat her up and left her lying moaning until her cook came to help. Her highly embarrassed assistant, who was there throughout the ordeal, maintains that Joy's account was a 'lot of bollocks'.

After the incident Joy left the two men in the mess hut and went outside. Holding a kerosene lamp she removed the keys from each car. George, who had remained with Brian, shook his head and said, 'I'm going off to live with my lions. They are a hell of a lot nicer than Joy.' He left the young man and went out into the night. Once he discovered the reason why his Land Rover would not start, he simply removed the distributor cap from Joy's car and hid her tools before jump-starting his Land Rover and driving away. He disappeared for six days but, unknown to Joy, sneaked back to camp for food while she was out in the bush.

*   *   *

Boy was the next to have an accident, breaking his leg in a run-in with a buffalo. George's devotion to his big cat was limitless. The first night, supported by a half-bottle of whisky and a steady rifle, he slept in the bush beside him. The Harthoorns flew up to perform a series of operations to pin the bone together. The Adamsons were not averse to the publicity that such an occasion would bring them and arranged for the Harthoorns to collect Bill Travers and a camera crew to film Boy's subsequent treatment. Joy, somewhat trapped by her popularity, flew in a cavernous military plane to Meru with the entourage of reporters, vets and film crew.

Peter Beard, the well-known American photographer and author of *The End of the Game*, who was staying in Meru at the time, recalls the event. 'It was a movie, not an operation. I remember nobody in the surgical team would do anything until the cameras were rolling.' To add to the difficulties of the operation on the anaesthetized lion, Joy, needing her own brand of attention, started playing up. Peter Beard and George had previously located two sick lion cubs that had been attacked and abandoned, one of which died. In the middle of the operation, the busy team looked round and saw Joy, in Beard's words, 'leaning over the back end of the station wagon in a prayer position as if it was the altar of sentimentality itself, french-kissing milk into this lion cub's mouth. She was simultaneously sobbing and ordering people around. It was the ultimate scene.'

Joy later claimed that the continual coverage in the international press provoked a great deal of controversy and criticism. This resulted in the degradation of their rehabilitation work, which many now saw as a failure. Naturally, she was incensed. However inaccurate some of the reports were, Joy felt great harm had been done to all her positive achievements with cheetah rehabilitation and research. She also claimed rather dramatically that, as a result of the growing criticism, both she and George had been asked to leave Meru, and even to leave Kenya for good.

20

Naivasha

During twenty-six years of nomadic life, either the game department had provided housing for the Adamsons, or they had lived the peripatetic camp life of those involved with the creatures of the wild. Joy realized they would need a home when they both became too old for the harsh ways of bush life. She had the money and she did the thinking. However, George had already decided that he needed no house – his home was the bush. It was in these ways that he was his most selfish, taking no notice of Joy's wants and needs. A few years previously, on the advice of her financial adviser, Peter Johnson, she had bought a small stone house for £1,750 amid fifty acres on the shores of Lake Naivasha, deep in the Rift Valley. The Maasai had named the area 'that which is heaving, that which flows to and fro'. Joy christened the place 'Elsamere'.

The sadness of leaving Meru in the way they were forced to affected them greatly, with Joy holding George and his troubles with Boy responsible for her own exile. She would no longer be able to follow the lives of Pippa's first surviving offspring, although they now had little need of her. Added to that, her injured hand would prohibit her from studying leopards in the bush for the foreseeable future. George, equally sad at leaving Girl, knew that if Boy was to survive, the lion would need many months of care in the 'semi-civilized' confines of Naivasha. 'Bloody surburban,' George muttered.

Joy had offered Elsamere as a refuge for George and Boy, full of anticipation that perhaps, in a new environment in peaceful surroundings, the torn threads of their marriage could be pulled together again. (Prior to Boy's operation Jonny and Brian had gone down to Elsamere to build a wooden cottage for George and a compound where Boy could recover. As soon as they arrived, they received a message from Joy that on no account were the two allowed to stay in the house. They erected a prefabricated hut to live in.)

When George left Meru with Boy, Joy stayed behind to pack up camp, complaining that when he was supposed to be helping her by packing his kit for their final move, George instead spent every day reading. She was left to sort out all his belongings, which took three days.

A month later she joined her husband in Elsamere and as before, things started badly. On her arrival, much to her indignation, she found George entertaining. Seated round the table were two women she disliked, Pam Carson and Sue Harthoorn, as well as a few other people George knew she would never have invited herself. One of these was her former assistant, Brian Heath, whom she had not seen since, she said, he had bolted from her camp. In fact, after building Boy's *boma* at Elsamere, Brian had left for Nairobi to have a painful damaged knee seen to and Joy, not accepting his reason for leaving, never spoke to him again.

Matters with Sue Harthoorn finally came to a head. When the two vets arrived in Naivasha before the last operation on Boy to discuss all the necessary details, Joy asked Sue to refrain from bringing the press once again to watch the procedure. Sue replied, 'Joy, you have no rights on Boy – he is not your lion.' Joy backed down, but the crunch came after a further post-operative visit from the Harthoorns. A number of guests, including Peter Beard, sat around the dining-room table for lunch one day. Joy, apparently innocently, thumbed through a popular international magazine which contained a large photographic article on Boy's operation. Joy, turning each page slowly, remarked to the vet: 'This is a nice picture, Toni, of you and George and Boy, and who is this?'

'Sue's niece.'

After a couple more pages Joy said, 'Here you are in the kitchen, what are you cooking?'

'Oh, we were making breakfast for George.'

Joy replied, 'Oh, here you are with Boy, what are you doing?'

'Just about to give him an examination,' was the reply.

After five minutes of meekly suckering the vet into various comments, Joy pounced, accusing him of manoeuvring himself into every aspect of their lives. Toni Harthoorn sat speechless. The other guests found it both embarrassing and exhilarating. After what seemed like an endless stream of abuse, Sue leapt to her husband's defence and joined the screaming match. She ended the row: 'We're all fed up to the teeth with your so-called greatness. I don't care what you say, everybody hates you and loves George!' As she flounced out of the room, Joy called after her: 'Don't you ever dare show your face here again.'

Elsamere stood on a promontory jutting out into the lake and was nestled in a small belt of primary forest. Many thousands of years previously a thriving community had lived by these shores, carving their axes and arrowheads from the obsidian lava flow of Mount Longonot. The area around the house was one of incomparable beauty. Each morning, when the air was still sharp and gentle sunlight embraced the yellow bark of fever trees, the cry of the fish eagle echoed along the carpet of mauve water lilies fringing the shore. Hippos, their small pink ears continually twitching, snorted as they blew out water and lumbered amongst the thick stands of papyrus. Paddling behind them at a distance, the white pelicans attended to their morning toilette. Small animals which sheltered in the thicket – marsh mongoose and bush pig, grey duikers and shy bushbuck – trampled soft trails through the undergrowth and colobus monkeys with outstretched arms and mantles like flying capes leapt between the highest branches of the acacias.

Darkness favoured the hunter. Jackals, serval cats and genets stalked the paths in the stillness of the evening and watched with night-eyes as zebras, lions, buffaloes, giraffes and an occasional leopard sauntered down from the waterless hinterland, past the euphorbias, aloes and sisal plants, to drink from the lake. But by far the biggest attraction of the area was its birdlife, especially the water birds. The many creatures possibly thought they had found paradise when they first winged their way down onto the land beside the water. Herons and cranes, black-winged stilt and grebes, spoonbills and lilly trotters jostled for their share of the still waters. The white-browed coucal (the water bottle bird) and the red-chested cuckoo (the rain bird) dived for cover from the harrier hawk, while lovebirds warbled their song.

There was much about Elsamere that Joy loved apart from the beauty of her land. It also had the amenities of civilization : mains electricity and good shopping only fifteen miles away at Naivasha. When the road was dry she could reach Nairobi in an hour and a half, which was as well since her hand was in need of continual treatment. And she could be soothed by the gentle beauty of nearby Lake Nakuru, with its rippling pink and white tapestry of flamingoes and pelicans.

When she bought the house Joy, used to wide open spaces, had instructed her architects to change the cramped interior into a few large rooms. The inclusion of a large verandah was essential, but after dis-covering the nuisance of lake flies, she had it closed with sliding doors. In this way she could still spend her evenings at sunset looking out at the lake with its birds and animals and the blue hills on the other side. The architects complied and the result was a well-designed, functional and airy home. She had a pantry with a china cupboard and a practical kitchen with a *dhobi* (laundry) room for washing clothes. George's bedroom, at the far end of the house from Joy's, had its own bathroom.

Joy used her bedroom as a workroom, and a table and small armchair covered in zebra skin were positioned by the window. The back wall was filled with cupboards for all her painting and writing equipment, her files and photograph albums, typescripts of her books and medicines. She was a magpie when it came to collecting oddments from her safaris: Borana square-cut aluminium beads; Turkana woven water gourds; early stone axes; short spears and cowrie-shell female aprons were meticulously kept in order.

The living room was decorated simply, with Joy's piano and uncomfortable wooden armchairs beside the fireplace covered in soft topi and Grant's gazelle skin. A large Grevy zebra skin was mounted on board and a huge skin of a lion, shot by George in the course of his duties, was spread over the floor. Colourful *kikois* were flung over the chairs. Two watercolour landscapes by Joan Vincent, a Kenyan whom Joy readily acknowledged as a fine artist, hung on the walls.

An original Ralph Thompson painting of two leopard cubs was also now hers. A few weeks after settling in, Joy had burst into Peter Johnson's Nairobi office. 'Peter, Peter, Peter, I have just seen a painting of leopard cubs that I love. Oh, Peter, do you think I can afford to buy it?' Peter, astonished, laughingly said, 'But of course, Joy. You can buy any painting you want.' Joy had simply no idea of her wealth and he had never known her to spend any money on luxuries.

Game trophies, normal decoration for European houses at the time, decorated the verandah and included a good buffalo head shot by Joy. The bookshelves were packed with conservation-linked books, Rachel Carson's *The Silent Spring*, biographies and others by Herbert Tichy, Hammond Innes and Gerald Durrell. Next to the main house a garage block was built, complete with a workshop for George, an extra guest room and a couple of storerooms. This workshop was another place to which George often repaired when he happened to be at Elsamere. As usual, some of the shelves held bottles marked 'Paint Remover', 'Paraffin', 'Oil No.2' and tucked in-between were his disguised bottles of whisky.

Operations and films, the continuing development of projects with the Elsa Wild Animal Appeal, writing a sequel on the cheetahs – *Pippa's Challenge* – piles of correspondence to reply to and the entertaining of hordes of fans and visitors as well as film companies from the United States took over much of Joy's time at Elsamere. But on her land, she found time to make friends with a family of colobus monkeys and the Verreaux eagle owls, Africa's largest owl. She often fed the latter by hanging molerats up by their tails on the washing line for the birds to swoop down on. She also found time to paint, with her left hand, a large watercolour of Bundu, her favourite Verreaux eagle owl, for George's birthday. It was the last large painting she undertook and, from the time of her accident, her animal paintings and sketches understandably show a marked deterioration.

In February 1970 a third operation was necessary on Joy's hand to stop it from freezing into a claw. When George collected her from hospital, she told him she would be making numerous future visits to the physio-therapist and two doctors who had operated on her. George casually mentioned that his old friend Toni Ofenheim was soon arriving and he wanted to meet her on 28 February. Joy took it for granted that he would drop her off at the hospital in Nairobi, but George, reluctant, managed to put Joy off by telling her if she came with him she would only be rude to Toni. According to Joy, her husband thought that since Toni came so seldom to Kenya, she took priority over his wife. He then told her he would take her to Nairobi later. Since she assumed he would only be with Toni for the one day, Joy agreed. In the meantime Joy waited for the telephone call to see the doctor the following week.

The day after a pleasant dinner on Friday with their neighbours, the Streeters, George drove down to Nairobi to meet his close friend. Early on Sunday morning Joy was told that George intended to take Toni to the Aberdare Mountains. On 1 March, the call came through asking Joy to travel down to Nairobi to see her doctor. She assumed that George would drive her there but, early on the Monday, George wanted to take Toni to see the mass of flamingoes on Lake Nakuru. Joy suddenly snapped and told him to get out of her sight, before accepting a lift from the Streeters. George did not return until late that night.

At breakfast the next morning Joy announced that, from now on, George would not be welcome in her house and that she wanted him to live and eat in his bungalow. She would also give him precisely one month to make alternative arrangements for himself and Boy. She demanded that, at the end of the month, they should leave. George did not reply and for the rest of the morning behaved as if nothing particularly unusual had happened. After lunch a neighbour arrived to say he had shot an eland and that George could collect the carcass for Boy. George left, returning at 9 p.m. Joy had retired and was typing letters after locking the house up. George, unable to get in, came up to the window in Joy's bedroom. Suppressing his anger, he begged her to let him in. He was ravenous. Annoyed, Joy shouted that, as she had explained that morning, George had to provide his own food from now on. After all, he had a cook and everything he needed in his self-contained bungalow. George, now enraged, threatened to break down the doors.

A short while later Joy heard him pottering around in the kitchen. Somehow he had managed to get a key from the cook. Joy already knew that he had previously made himself a spare key to the drinks cabinet to use whenever he felt a pressing need for a whisky. Joy, by now having worked herself up into a fury, marched into the kitchen and told him he had no right whatsoever to help himself to a drink or to enter the house without her permission. As her voice rose, she screamed at him that he had had plenty of time to buy food since that morning and, furthermore, that under no circumstances was he to forget the time limit she had given him to leave Elsamere. George's eyes narrowed as he spat out what a bitch he considered his wife.

Joy then snatched up a photo of George's grandparents, which he dearly loved, and smashed it on the kitchen table. Furious that she could wantonly destroy a family memento, George rushed at her, shouting that he had just as much right as she did to the place and adamantly refusing to move away. By now he was white with rage. According to Joy, as she tried to shove her angry husband out of the door, he threw down the soda syphon bottle he had taken out of the drinks cupboard and belted her as hard as he could on the left side of her head. Joy, seeing stars and about to collapse, kept silent. In tears, she looked at him while he swore at her before finally leaving.

Joy, nursing a paralysing headache, took a few minutes to collect herself together and then ran to her writing table. Crying, she rang her lawyer, Mr Deverel, and asked him to come the following day as, with her injured hand, she could not drive herself to Nairobi. Joy wanted an immediate divorce on grounds of cruelty. As soon as she could, she also went to her local doctor, Dr Bunny. After examining her, he wrote in his notes that Joy had complained of severe pain in her left ear, as well as a degree of vertigo. Her right tonsil was definitely enlarged and inflamed, although he could not detect any impairment of her hearing. Neither was any laceration of her tympanic membrane noticeable.

As soon as the lawyer arrived, Joy explained her reasons. Although George had upset her on numerous occasions, they had also shared many wonderful experiences together. Joy realized that, without George, her life with Elsa would have been impossible, her trip to South Island would not have happened and she would never have crossed the Sahara. But, looking back, she felt George looked upon her as a mother-figure – she had done all the things he would have loved to have done but, because of his weaker character, he did not have the tenacity to carry intentions

One of Joy's flower paintings: eight Kenyan flowering herbs including *Commelina latifolia*, *Striga somalensis* and *Cassia grantii*

y at an
hibition of her
bal paintings

A watercolour of Lord and Lady Percy with Joy and George Adamson done by Lady Percy
Elsa and her cubs are in the foreground

Joy with her least favourite animal, an elephant, at Naro Moru

Joy and George with Virginia McKenna and Bill Travers on the set of *Born Free*

Virginia McKenna and Bill Travers with Girl at Malindi

George at Kora

George and one of
his lions with his
assistant Tony
Fitzjohn at Kora,
1978

...y with her leopard cub Penny at Elsamere, 1977

Penny up her favourite tree at Shaba

Shaba camp

...oy with Bill and Ros Hillyar and their son, Charles

...oy, Pieter Mawson and friends at the swimming hole at Shaba

Joy and George. The fondness remained to the end

through to the end. The tears rolled down her cheeks as she admitted to Deverel that perhaps George deeply resented her superior intelligence, while needing her because she was his only reliable friend, in much the same way as a child depends on its mother. She told her lawyer that George only confided in her when he was in trouble, otherwise she hardly existed. Over the many hours of discussion, Joy explained that their temperaments were so extreme that, even when they walked together, there was trouble. She either had to slow down for him or he had to accelerate to keep up with her, which resulted in great stress and irritability for both of them. Although she was extremely attached to the pleasant side of George and loathed hurting him with a divorce, she hated the parts of him which she saw as foolhardy, over-fond of spirits, violent and slightly sadistic. She was terrified that he would continue to beat her.

She added sarcastically that sometimes his intelligence was too limited to understand fully what he was doing and she could not bear his love of those who continually flattered his ego. She declared that he had forced her to marry him, telling her over and over again that if she did not marry him, nobody else would. He had behaved so badly towards her during their first few months in Naivasha that she now felt increasingly desperate, however fearful she was of ending their marriage.

Turning to her lawyer, who up until then had been silently listening, she pleaded that, if a divorce might help George realize what she meant to him, and lead to some workable relationship, then he should proceed. But if, on the other hand, a divorce would destroy both their lives, she was prepared to put the idea aside for the time being and give George one final chance.

As soon as rumours of the impending divorce started to circulate, the international press had a field day. Headlines proclaiming: 'Straight from the Lion's mouth – Adamsons split'; 'Lion lovers to divorce', were splashed all over the London papers. George, who was still fond of Joy and was greatly distressed after such a long, tempestuous marriage in which they had shared a deep love of living in the wilderness alongside its creatures, maintained an outward reserve. Eventually he agreed to Joy's request. Joy was sixty years old, George four years older.

By July, thanks mainly to the intervention of Ken Smith, a good friend to the Adamsons, Joy had dropped the divorce case. A quiet, restrained, lifelong bachelor, it would have been totally against his nature to interfere between husband and wife. Despite anything he might have thought privately about their marriage, he was no gossip and had never commented about the divorce to anyone. But now he had to speak out, convinced that at this stage of their lives a divorce was totally unnecessary and potentially disastrous. Joy was greatly surprised to receive a letter urging her to reconsider her decision. The letter was simple, sincere and direct and she realized that he must have felt very strongly to take such action.

The implications of the letter gave Joy considerable anguish. To her, it was a letter which could well be a barometer of the feeling of respected Kenya Europeans in the world of conservation. It implied that adverse publicity caused by a divorce could well alienate her from the very set of which she needed to be part. It had long worried her that scientific conservationists in Kenya were not amongst her admirers, although George was greatly respected for his natural understanding of animals. Joy was clever enough to have known for many years that her own acceptance relied a great deal upon her husband's long and honourable work with the game department. She may have been fêted overseas but it was a different story in Kenya, where many people were involved in the world of conservation and knew infinitely more than she did. Although she never acknowledged it, she knew she could never compete with those most knowledgeable about the country's wildlife – hunters and game people, scientific researchers and those steeped in wildlife and bush lore.

Could Joy stand alone? She would be totally dependent on the good will of the game and parks departments for her continued work. Although by the early 1970s she should have been secure enough in her position to have no doubts, this was not the case. She did have grave doubts, she was still deeply insecure in many respects and she knew in her heart that she needed the protection George's name, person and reputation gave her. This one short letter from Ken Smith was undoubtedly much more of a deciding factor than any of the advice given by those with obvious interests in keeping Joy's name unsullied.

As the months went by Joy and George drifted back into a state of unarmed neutrality. Perhaps it showed the depth of George's well-known tolerance, but it also demonstrated Joy's dependency on George, some emotional bond that had always tied her to him. By now George, who had been desperate to escape further matrimonial bruising, had found a permanent home for Boy and was convinced that 'Working with my lions is more important than my marriage to Joy.' From now on he would seek solace in his small pleasures of whisky and tobacco and solitude with his lions in the bush. He left the soft breezes of his lakeside home to live in the remote ochre-coloured reaches of Kora in the NFD.

Kora suited George's temperament admirably. His Kampi ya Simba – Camp of Lions – was built at the base of Kora Rock, a 400-foot, sandy-coloured rock two miles from the Tana river. The remote, northeast corner of the country, and one of the last great wildernesses of the world, would become George's small paradise for the rest of his life.

Terence Adamson, now an expert at erecting camps and constructing roads, had been cajoled into cutting a road through the bush to Kora and building a home for George and his numerous carnivores. Inevitably, disasters occurred. In 1971, Boy pounced on Stanley, the young African who had looked after him devotedly for so long. Dragging him between his jaws as he made for the bush, he dropped him when George ran towards him, waving his arms and shouting loudly. But it was too late; Stanley's wounds were fatal. George raised his gun and shot his favourite lion through the heart. He was greatly affected for a long time afterwards: 'I can't get used to not seeing Boy sitting on Camp Rock and not hearing his roars echoing in the hills.'

Apart from Christian and Boy, most of George's lions were given to him by game managers as a means of stock control. More than once throughout his time living in this sparse African landscape, George was attacked by ardent conservationists and wildlife enthusiasts, including the famous writer Wilfred Thesiger, for killing a good deal of wild game to feed his lions and for bringing an element of show-business into his work of rehabilitation. As he got older even George chuckled to a journalist: 'I'm doing no harm – you wouldn't begrudge an old man his few pleasures in life, would you?'

The different attitudes towards their animals continued to deepen the rift between Joy and George. Her theory was that once a carnivore, or any other mammal, was truly rehabilitated into the wild, it should left totally alone with no human contact at all. This view was held by most zoologists and conservationists. George, of course, just liked lions. He showed few signs of ever 'letting go' his lions at Kora and always tried to find them if possible. Whenever they appeared in camp each evening he threw them large chunks of camel meat, to the delight of the visitors. He took absolutely no notice of what Joy thought and did exactly what he wanted.

In fact, as has been seen, Joy was not good at putting into practice what she preached. She must also have found it difficult to 'preach' conservation when it was possible to criticize her own husband for his methods. Most Kenyans liked 'old George' enough to be indulgent about his lions, but not a few wondered how he had got away with what he was doing for so long. However, he had the sanction of the game department and it was thought politic to leave the old man alone. After all, Kora was pretty remote and he had become quite a star. But it is possible that Joy, who was trying to live up to the image of the conservationist, was anxious about criticism from overseas.

Certainly Joy and the trustees' main gripe against George was that funds were diverted to his animals which could have gone to other more needy conservation schemes – raising one lion for two years could cost up to £500. Kora also had to be protected from poachers, which was an expensive business. In 1973, when Kora was gazetted a National Game Reserve, Joy refused to allow the trustees to allocate any further money to it. But her jealous nature also resented the way that people, from princes to film stars and especially pretty girls, flocked to Kora, as if to find out the secret of George's total harmony with the bush and its creatures. Joy undoubtedly had a gift with each particular animal with which she formed a relationship, but George had an intuitive and almost instinctive understanding not only of lions, but of all other animals. He was happy to share his life with them on equal terms, except for two. 'All creatures are welcome here apart from scorpions and venomous snakes – those two I won't tolerate,' he said. George's remarkable *laissez-faire* attitude towards the numerous hangers-on and unexpected visitors who made Kora almost a shrine to a guru was typical of his character.

The days by the shrub-fringed Tana, the country's largest river, had a relaxed and peaceful rhythm to them. Doum palms, tamarinds and henna bushes, which flourished on the banks of the ruddy waters, gave way to thick nyika thorn bush and acacias. It was a land teeming with animals. Being so near the equator, the sun was directly overhead all year and at sunrise the camp was filled with the sounds of marabou storks, violet-backed sunbirds and white-headed buffalo weavers.

The daily ritual began with George feeding millet to the flock of guinea fowl which had became accustomed to having breakfast with George and Terence. George mused : 'Curiously, they always go around in an anti-clockwise circle, I become quite dizzy watching them. When I was a game warden we almost lived on guinea fowl on safari, but I can't very well feed and eat them now. At times, though, they so infuriate me with their noise that I feel like putting them in a pot.'

The younger brother disliked the birds' interference with his meal almost as much as George loathed listening to Terence chomping his way through his bacon, toast and eggs. Terence's own camp was by the river but, never having been particularly close before, the two men, now reaching their seventies, finally began to open up to each other. Whenever he needed a haircut, George stuck a bowl over his head and Terence clipped his way round. The days were spent looking for the lions, calling them through a megaphone – sometimes it took weeks to find a particular animal. If cubs were in camp, they needed to be fed and watered and either left out for the day, covered, or brought back into the fold. It was

George's habit to have a gin at eleven o'clock and another at midday. In the evening, being a man who liked to live with his own memories and thoughts he looked forward to his three Scotches.

In their midst appeared one day a tall, handsome, rough diamond – a twenty-six-year-old Englishman, sent by Joy as a possible assistant for George. His name was Tony Fitzjohn and he was a jack of all trades, having tried his hand at being a photographer, nightclub bouncer and Outward Bound course instructor. Possessing a mercurial nature, he was not always easy, but he knew no fear. A strong man with a fine physique, whom women went wild about, Tony became an instant hit with the lions and invaluable to George. Within a year he had acquired the survival skills for bush life. He expertly managed the lions, maintained vehicles, learned from his boss the secrets of bush lore, collected provisions and mail from Mwingi, the nearest town ninety miles away, and mastered rudimentary Swahili – all for no pay. He learned to dodge the rifle shots from poachers which habitually whizzed over the camp. By now George, who had always enjoyed sleeping under the stars, was spending his nights lying in a trench, his gun by his side.

George wrote about his assistant: 'Tony and I had begun to enjoy the kind of reciprocal benefits that zoologists call symbiosis.' Looking back on their time together, George doubted that it would have been possible without Tony's help. In exchange for the simplest food, a few shillings when absolutely necessary, numerous crates of beer and an outdoor life, Tony soon became George's right-hand man.

Slowly, Joy began to take an intense dislike to Tony. Nothing could erase her jealous conviction that he led her husband astray with booze and broads. She also deeply resented the fact that George regarded Tony as the son she had never given him. In Tony's words: 'She continually tried to get rid of me by badmouthing me to George.' Terence was also less than partial towards the young man, calling him Caligula behind his back.

To keep the peace, whenever Joy came to Kora, Tony was sent off down to Terence's camp. However, he well remembered the effect she had on George. 'We always went through the three stages, interesting conversation, tears and emotion. Finally she would throw a chair down, sweep everything off the table, then storm out of the camp, striding down the road, leaving George shaking and upset.' However, his assistant's talent for mimicry tickled George's sense of humour, especially when he imitated Joy's German names and accent. Whenever a call on the radio came up from Joy and Tony answered, 'Yes, iss dat a messich from von Friederike Adamsson, yah?' Joy would be spitting with rage. One night George was beside himself with mirth. He had been trying to reach Joy by radio without any success for three nights. 'I can't get through because the Italians are always yakking. I wish those bloody Dagos would shut up,' he said to his assistant. Tony casually reached out for the soda syphon which had a habit of making a loud farting noise and aimed it into the receiver. The dialogue immediately stopped and George fell off his chair, laughing.

In June the following year, Tony became slightly suspicious of George who had returned from a short visit to Naivasha and had been humming round the camp for three days 'with a smirk on his face'. Tony said: 'I knew something was up because we knew each other so well.' George then took great relish in telling his assistant: 'I went and seduced the old bird who lives next door to the Djinn Palace. I told Joy, and she got terribly upset.' Tony replied: 'Well, good on you, mate, but why on earth did you tell her?' George just laughed. Tony recalls: 'He was almost like a naughty little boy who did it just to get his own back on Joy. It was the first time, to my knowledge, that he ever went off with another woman.'

Of Joy, Tony remarked in his usual, blunt way: 'She was a bit off the bloody wall and thank God she was. However much of a pain in the arse she was, in her way she was a magnificent person because of the money that she ploughed back into conservation. I don't want to appear flippant about those who suggested her difficult nature was due to a screwed-up childhood, a lithium problem, too many male hormones or a carrot up her bum – many people have been affected by their childhood without carrying on like that. But she ploughed a bumpy road and was, in my mind, a great conservationist. The trouble was she was always desperate for George to be a sort of prince consort behind her.'

As far as Tony was concerned, life at Kora achieved three things: 'The first was the new chance we gave all those lions. Second was the stopping of the Somali poachers' movement south for a number of years although inevitably that fight was lost. Thirdly, since George's arrival, there was an increase in game, rather than a reduction, in the reserve.'

For the next sixteen years, Tony, volatile and forever fighting with local officials who, according to George, continually harrassed them both, worked with the old man of the bush. After being told to leave by the authorities, Tony and Kim, his American girlfriend, headed for Mkomazi in Tanzania, to launch a study of wild dogs and cheetah.

There were fourteen lions, lionesses and cubs at Kora by mid-1978. A camel now cost £40 and lasted the pride for less than a week. George managed to eke out his royalties, donations and his small amount from the Elsa Trust just enough to live the life he loved. He bothered himself little with what other conservationists thought, secure in his love for his animals and the fact that, however slowly, they were being rehabilitated. He was also particularly ferocious in his patrolling of illegal grazing that so ravaged the land, and the heavily armed poachers: 'Animals have as much right to a place on earth as we do and I think the life of one elephant is worth the lives of at least one hundred humans. It should be a capital offence for anyone to shoot an elephant.'

Since the mid-1960s a serious division had appeared as to how to safeguard the future of the rapidly decreasing wildlife. In Peter Beard's words: 'It was a question of population dynamics versus the sentimental camp.' The murky world of conservation was fraught with opposing sides, petty jealousies and back-stabbing, however honourable the intentions. Increasingly, scientific approaches to animal behaviour were on the rise and arguments raged. Endless worthy groups jumped on the bandwagon, each eager to claim the largest slice of the salt lick. Scientists and pet-scientists climbed over anthropologists, behaviourists battled zoologists and environmentalists scrambled past geneticists in a desperate effort to claim success. In Tony Fitzjohn's words: 'If St Francis of Assisi were alive now, they would hang, draw and quarter him.'

Meanwhile, behind the scenes, the unsung heroes, the parks and game wardens, the rangers and committed Kenyans, continued with their work, well aware that in a country bursting with wall-to-wall *wananchi* (people) wildlife tended to disappear.

21

Aspects of Mercury

Although her life at Elsamere frustrated Joy, denied by her affliction from living in the bush, the place was her 'small paradise'. So cocooned was she becoming that she began to think that, unless she forced herself to take off into the wilds with a new project on leopard research, she would happily vegetate at Elsamere, writing books.

Close to Elsamere lay a spectacular nine-mile gorge, known as Hell's Gate, which became a place of great solace to Joy. Each week, alone or accompanied by a friend, she found her energy renewed by walks towards the dramatic cliffs. Many years ago the Maasai had grazed their cattle here, around a tall pillar of rock, the home of families of rock hyrax. Maasai legend tells of a chief's daughter who left the tribal *manyatta* to get married. Sad to leave home, she turned round to take a last forbidden glance at all she had known, and was instantly transformed into rock.

With her usual enthusiasm and enquiring mind Joy set out to learn everything she could about Hell's Gate and the geothermal steam jets which rose like wreaths of mist from its bowels. A few months after her first walk there, she rang up Jolyon Halse, a geologist, inviting him and his family for a picnic the following weekend and explaining that she wanted him to explain the history of the area. The picnic was memorable. 'We set off and Joy knew everything about the rocks and minerals and especially all the plants – she actually gave me a lesson. Whatever her subject, she read up everything.' Scattered amongst the grasses stood the silvery-grey leleshwa bushes, common throughout the Rift Valley. When crushed, the soft leaves smelled of camphor and the Maasai placed small bunches under their armpits as a deodorant. It was from the roots of the bush that they fashioned their *rungus*. Over this untroubled haven roamed the small, shy klipspringer, the reedbuck and the eland. Joy became enthralled by all she saw.

Joy was choosy about those she selected to be her friends in Naivasha.

Many of her friends dated from the post-*Born Free* era and trust played a large part in her attitude towards them. She felt there were few people whom she could trust who would not take advantage of her. She was convinced her fame and success had brought her general hostility as well as unnecessary opposition. The only solution was to keep her head down, her views to herself, and let the results of her work speak for themselves.

This distrust, together with her abrasive personality, distanced her from many of the people around her. She explained her feeling of detachment to her sister Dorle. Her pride would not let her beg for sympathy, however serious her problems. Letting her defences down – something she seldom did with her sister – she mused that this attitude might leave her increasingly isolated, but anything was better than being hurt continually by others.

One lakeside family whom she got to know early on and who were genuine friends were Dr and Mrs Bunny. Their daughter, Diana, an artist, remembers Joy with great fondness, witnessing her humility in those moments when she let her defensive guard down. 'Her trust in someone had to be reliable in her own area as the only security she had in herself came from being a gifted, talented woman. When she did trust, she would give entirely of herself, but there were few people with whom she felt safe. You cannot blame her for the reservations she had as she was taken advantage of in many areas, big and small. Little things meant so much to her. All she got was criticism, and she knew it, but in spite of all this, she stood her ground courageously, throwing her weight around, all because there was a small key missing. She had some very low moments, lonely, yearning for understanding and love. Her accomplishments are admirable and leave their mark. She saw and achieved. She threw herself into incredible challenges and won in so many areas. The little stones which make up the mosaic of Joy's life play a very big part in the world today.'

There were those who lived nearby and were not fond of Joy. Jill Simpson recalls one day when she went into the Kenya Farmers' Association shop, a natural meeting place for buying cattle food, animal drugs, milk churns and farm hardware. Before Jill could ask for her supplies, she found each assistant sidling one by one through the back door. Thinking that they could not all be going off for a tea break at the same time, she strode off and found them all huddled together in the corridor. 'What's going on?'

'We are all hiding from Memsahib Haraka.'

Joy had been seen driving up and no one wanted to serve her. The locals around Naivasha, in trying to be friendly, were more often than not pestered into doing things for Joy. When Mitch Morson, a close neighbour and one who stood up to her while still being as helpful as possible, had had enough he barked, 'Joy, I don't get paid to work for you and I wouldn't work for you and therefore you can't order me to do this or that.' His wife Millicent, who tended one of the area's most beautiful gardens, kept Joy supplied with carrots for the colobus monkeys and vegetables for the various animals, and knowing Joy's weakness in the culinary department, made sure there was adequate food in the house. 'Each night Joy would cut off a few slices of salami sausage which were hanging up and slap on a few bits of cheese. I said to her, "How can you eat the same thing every night?" Joy smiled: "It makes no difference to me what I eat."'

She came to rely increasingly on the Morsons, stopping in for a chat and a meal or laughing over an ice cream with Millicent in the dusty township. She had great respect for Mitch, without whom, his wife said, 'Joy would have ground me into the dust.' The two women became fast friends, frequently going off together on safari or rushing off to Nairobi when Joy's plate of false teeth broke. On the eve of the Morsons' daughter Anne's marriage, Joy sent over a present with the note: 'Dear Anne, Here is an Ethiopian slave bracelet. May you never be a slave to anybody in your life.'

The next week, the Morsons invited old friends of theirs, the Duke and Duchess of Manchester, to dinner. Joy was asked to join them. She arrived at the house promptly at 7.30 p.m., dressed in a long, glamorous evening gown, her wrist and neck ablaze with jewels. The Duchess was wearing a simple African *kanzu*. Millicent remembers: 'Joy nearly fainted. Here she was, dressed like royalty herself, just because she was about to meet a Duchess!'

In March Billy Collins again came to stay for a few days. He still came out to Kenya once a year and, perhaps to make up for the previous time, when he had deeply hurt Joy by not bothering to see her, he was full of charm and gaiety, bantering with her and praising her for all her energy and writing successes. Joy was flattered and delighted – her feelings for him had never changed. Before he left he wrote in her visitors' book: 'Elsamere is like the garden of Eden. An enchanting place and so so peaceful and beautiful in every way. My stay was far too short.' He would continue to stay there for up to four days from now on, whenever he came out.

In September 1973, Joy was off round the world again promoting the Elsa Appeal and helping publicize the Elsa Clubs set up by schools in Britain, America, Canada and Japan, which stimulated active work in conservation. While she was in London her sister Traute suddenly died of a cancer operation in Vienna. As with her animals, Joy still retained a degree of sentimentality about her family, however distanced she had become from them. Acknowledging that their differences had made any deep friendship impossible, she told friends in London that she was nevertheless devastated by Traute's death. But, as a rather lame excuse, she blamed her absence at the funeral on her doctor's insistence that any stress would delay her hand's recovery.

Before this, Joy had never expressed any profound love for her sister but, as if to keep the remaining threads of family ties woven, her writings to her sister Dorle multiplied. Letters enclosed the occasional £100 cheque as a present as, full of concern, she wondered what her sister lived on and what her husband did for a living. When she remembered, she occasionally gave Dorle small birthday presents. Once, she explained, she was giving Dorle a watch, which she herself had rarely worn. She often worried about Dorle, saying that she wished, above all, that she could bestow upon her a fraction of her own extraordinary energy. Definitely the elder sister, Joy tried to encourage Dorle to find a way out of her lethargy by following her own example.

An important aspect of Joy's make-up was that she adamantly refused to feel sorry for herself. Instead, she explained that each day she went to great lengths to appreciate her good fortune and solve any of her numerous problems through sheer strength of character. Often in her letters to Dorle, Joy's forceful nature came into play, sweeping aside major hurdles as mere inconveniences. In a somewhat prissy tone, she declared that Dorle should stop complaining about lost opportunities and do her utmost to be productive. That way she could hold her head up high.

Joy could not possibly accept each and every invitation abroad. She had been invited to Washington to accept a medal from the USA Humane Society but she was trying to dodge the trip because of the huge expense it entailed. However, she did want to go to Russia. Once there, Joy was flown to Sochi, on the Black Sea. In 1934 a citrus tree of goodwill had been planted, known as the Friendship Tree, and during the following years various famous and distinguished people had been asked to graft different species onto the original tree. Oranges, kumquats, Italian lemons, grapefruit and pomelos were grafted in memory of such celebrated people as Charles Darwin and Louis Pasteur, and soil from the graves of Tolstoy, Tchaikovsky, Pushkin and Mahatma Gandhi had been sprinkled at the foot of the tree. Now it was Elsa's memory which was to be honoured.

There was a part of Joy that realized the basic roots and mystique of her living in the bush had actually become passé. She was now so steeped in a world of publicity and trips abroad that it was incomprehensible to her why George would not want to come out of the wild and into the limelight. His answer was: 'I don't want to come down to Elsamere and be constantly on view.' On the other hand, if she had gone to Kora she would no longer be pursuing her international image. She still needed her husband's sage advice but his increasing popularity irritated her. She was doing so many more worthwhile things and yet people kept flocking to see him. Besides, she tended to regard Kora as hostile territory. Joy felt that, between them, Tony Fitzjohn and Bill Travers had made it virtually impossible for her to fly up there, so convinced was she that they had done everything in their power to turn George against her.

If she was irritated by George's popularity, Joy was enraged by that of Sieukwe Bisletti and her antagonism surfaced on more than one occasion. In 1971, Jack Couffer, the Marchesa's lover, came out to Kenya to direct *Living Free*, the second feature film to be made from Joy's books. Susan Hampshire and Nigel Davenport were cast as the Adamsons and Sieukwe was asked to help with the husbandry of the cubs. Jack met Joy for the first time at dinner at her house in Naivasha. His curt invitation stated: 'You will attend a dinner party tonight at Elsamere.' Couffer rightly excused the demanding phraseology as a lack of fluency in English.

Billy Collins was also one of the guests. As so often happened when he was around, Joy was charged with nervous energy, passing plates rapidly during dinner, smiling and gesturing broadly as she talked to her guests and instructed her servants. George was staying at Elsamere, too, and sat at the other end of the table, silently nodding in agreement when called upon to verify some statement, his small pointed goatee beard, pipe, and humour-wrinkled eyes giving him the aspect of a benevolent wizard.

At the end of the evening Joy pointedly said to Jack, 'I hope that you won't have that whore on the production.' Billy Collins's large eyebrows shot up as he sighed with exasperation. He seemed to know and dread what was coming. 'Joy, please ...' – he protested. George cleared his throat and quickly disappeared behind a large puff of smoke. 'That whore,' Joy repeated, 'Sieukwe Bisletti.'

Three years later, during the filming of a television series, Jack Couffer was again on location and Sieukwe Bisletti was employed by the art director as his Kiswahili interpreter and local liaison. While they awaited the arrival of the lions, crew, actors and production equipment, rumours of a persistent problem in Los Angeles winged its way back to Couffer. Joy was being slow to sign her contract. She insisted on 'small personal guarantees', and was particularly adamant about one. Sieukwe Bisletti was on no account to be hired. But this was not enough for Joy. Sieukwe was to leave her own property on Bushy Island on Lake Naivasha, where she and Jack were living in a tent before building a permanent *banda*. This idyllic spot was within a half mile of the lions to be used in the film. Joy was under the impression that Sieukwe's situation on the island was part of a conspiracy in which the company was involved in order to thwart her and hire the Marchesa. Couffer had two options; to get Sieukwe out, or wrap up the filming. Joy was even considering buying Sieukwe's own incomparably beautiful land from under her.

When Jack dropped the bombshell, his lover finally lost her temper. 'I had never seen Sieukwe so distraught; first crying, then throwing things, then like a kettle simmering on the fire ready to explode. She was inconsolable. I felt like a traitor.' Eventually she calmed down and a few days later tactfully left for her house in Lamu for the duration of the filming.

In May 1975, Joy managed to have George to herself for five weeks. She was thrilled to have him at Elsamere while he recovered from a broken pelvis, the cause of which was a game of hide-and-seek with his nine lions at Kora. One of the animals had pushed him down a steep rock and he had fallen onto a large, sharp stone, which temporarily stunned him. The lion, thinking this was all part of the fun, had then sat on him.

As she watched George, now sixty-nine years old, limp round the garden, it occurred to her that, with his flowing white locks and beard, he still looked exceedingly handsome. Although she had long considered him a basically weak man, easily influenced by others such as Fitzjohn, whom she always refered to as 'that ghastly young assistant' and Travers, her *bête noire*, she could not disregard his essentially good character. However, because of the way her husband appeared to have no qualms about the way that, as she saw it, Travers and Fitzjohn made their living from him; and because she felt they were doing everything possible to hurt her, both emotionally and professionally, Joy found it increasingly difficult to remain loyal to her husband. She bitterly resented the fact that George had spent the previous Christmas at Kora with the Travers family and Fitzjohn, while she stayed at Elsamere, lonely and desperately waiting for him to arrive. She bemoaned the publicity it had created in the London papers. As soon as she had read the articles, she had written, begging George to be with her this Christmastime, reminding him that they had celebrated it together since they first met in 1943.

Joy then beseeched a friend to telephone Travers, advising him strongly against monopolizing George unless he wanted to see the Adamsons' marriage collapse. Soon after, George telephoned Joy. Joy started to explain that if he insisted on Travers being with him at Christmas, she would end their marriage once and for all. George put the phone down.

Soon after George's return to Kora, Tony Fitzjohn returned to camp one night in a jovial mood, slightly inebriated after visiting the 'fleshpots' of Garissa. He needed more human company than George and regularly took himself off on a bender with the boys or to enjoy a few days in Nairobi or Malindi with one of his girlfriends. Discussing the women who flocked to the camp, Tony laughed: 'I won't say I wasn't desperate for female company – I'd jump on anything that arrived who was willing!'

Within an hour of returning from his day's outing, as he was playing with some cubs, a huge lion took him in his jaws. When Haragumsa, the cook, ran screaming into the mess tent with the news, George immediately ran out towards the lion, brandishing his stick and yelling at the top of his voice: 'Drop him, drop him, you brute.' The animal released Tony and slunk off into the bushes. George wrote of the accident: 'Tony was in one hell of a mess. There were deep gashes in his neck, head and arms and he was bleeding copiously.' It was too late in the day for the flying doctor to set off for Kora and George nursed his young assistant, who had lost pints of blood, through the night, dosing him with a shot of antibiotics and Valium to ease his terrible pain. The next morning, Tony was flown to Nairobi.

Of his near-fatal mauling, Dr Gerald Nevill, the same doctor who had operated on Joy's smashed hand, said, 'Tony was amazingly lucky. He could easily have died. The lion grabbed him through the throat; its canine teeth met through the middle of the neck – all it had to do was give one tug and Tony's throat would have been torn out. He is the only person in an accident that I've ever been able to put a finger in each side of the neck and had them meet in the middle.' George sent Tony a note in hospital saying, 'Getting chewed up is an occupational hazard!' He added, 'Please take a few weeks off at the coast and don't come back here until you really feel up to it. Everything is okay here. Here is five bob to help.' George shot the suspected culprit, the lion Shyman, through the brain.

Soon after this incident, a sixth operation on Joy's hand proved a failure, and she again wrote to Alys that her stiff, deformed hand was a disaster. She was still unable to move her fingers easily because of the unsuccessful skin graft. Unhappily reconciled to a life without piano-playing and painting, listening to classical music was now her greatest form of relaxation. She then reminisced about the evenings in Marsabit, when they had sat outside in the moonlight while piano music drifted out from the drawing room. Joy's favourite piece was the Rachmaninov Piano Concerto No. 2, which she enjoyed listening to all her life.

As soon as she arrived home from hospital, Joy continued to throw her energies into saving Hell's Gate as a National Park. Many battles were fought with the authorities who, Joy was convinced, wanted for political reasons to turn the area into *shambas* for the Kikuyu. She was disgusted at the way the government appeared to care so little about wildlife conservation. She had heard that Kenyatta intended to slaughter the elephants in Marsabit and also had plans to cut down the forest to make room for crops. She felt sick and helpless about such wanton destruction. (Hell's Gate was finally gazetted as a National Park in 1984.)

Joy's romantic life by now was virtually nonexistent, a fact which caused her much dismay. At the age of sixty-six, lonely nights at Elsamere were taking their toll and Joy sorely missed male company. One evening over dinner she quite seriously approached a man who often came to stay and who genuinely adored her – as a friend. John Eames was Editor of a conservation magazine, the *Africana*. Gazing at him with her blue eyes, she smiled: 'John, would you marry me? I've got plenty of money, you know.' Although he greatly admired her, especially for her drive, he declined the offer. 'Joy frequently talked about sex and finding someone to go to bed with. She had an infinite capacity for love, but she was quite a lot older than me, so it was a non-starter.' Eames belonged to the rare group of people who found his way below the surface of Joy's defence armour: 'Joy was an impossible woman, forever in a knock-down drag-out fight with someone or other. But she was also a great woman, accomplished and sensitive, who used eccentricity and an abrasive personality in self-defence.'

Joy complained bitterly to friends about George and his life at Kora, telling them that she rarely heard from him but knew he now had two more baby lions which brought the total to ten. She still berated George for being so dependent on Tony Fitzjohn who, she claimed, caused such friction between them. Besides which, he was doing a fine job of making the camp into a bush brothel. However, she kept to herself the time she arrived at Kora and banished Fitzjohn from the compound, telling him to sleep outside with the lions. That night she went to him, stripped her blouse open and, in an attempt to seduce him, told him to look at her breasts. They could be his for the night if he wanted. Gazing at her, he said, 'Forget it, Joy.'

The woman whom Joy came to look on as a daughter and genuinely to love was Ros Hillyar, the wife of a farmer, who first got to know her during the making of the film *Living Free* in 1971. She had been Mrs Fix-It, arranging everything from finding meat to feed the lions, to providing lumps of pumice to use as rocks for the Maasai herders to throw at the lions. When Ros gave birth to her son, Joy poignantly said, 'You know, Ros, with all the things I have achieved I have never produced a beautiful child like Charles.'

The two women discovered a shared love of walking. They left one Sunday morning in June to climb the Mau – Joy was keen to find the elusive bongo antelope which was reputed still to live in the depths of the forests. With them they took fruit and honey biscuits made by Joy's cook, together with two bottles of water. They climbed past the small patches of crops belonging to many African families under a settlement scheme. Passing through high lemon grass and bush Joy suddenly froze. Ahead of them stood a magnificent Chanler's reedbuck, nose quivering, the sunlight on his back, while the grass waved in the wind like yellow sea anemones. Far above, the thick bamboo slopes of the mountain beckoned.

After a picnic, Bill Hillyar, who was recovering from an operation, stayed in the car with his young son. Joy and Ros continued, walking up steep slopes, following game trails and hoping for a glimpse of a bongo. They soon became lost in the thick forest and tried to retrace their steps. On the way down, still high on the humid, misty slopes of the mountain, Joy slipped and fell flat on her back. Cluching her foot, she cried out in pain : 'Ros, I've broken my ankle.' Though still recovering from the trials of a broken elbow and an artificial hip operation, which she had undergone the previous November, she always made light of her various ailments. Neither woman had anything to bind Joy's foot with, clad as they were in shirts and shorts. The pain wafted over her as she continued down the slope on her backside, dragging herself along with one leg in the air.

The women were plagued by safari ants and carried no *panga* (machete) with which to blaze a trail, but dusk was drawing closer and they were already beginning to feel cold at the high altitude of over 10,000 feet. Both secretly worried about their chances of surviving the night on a freezing mountain full of buffalo, especially as Joy was by now in shock and would not have been able to shin up a tree for safety. By a stroke of luck they reached a metal tube shining in the undergrowth. It was the pipe which fed the spring above the dam where they had left Bill. Ros called out to her husband, but the echoes fell on a silent forest. Joy, sweating with pain, said, 'Ros, go on, leave me here and try and find someone to help.' Reluctantly, Ros agreed and an hour later found Bill, who said, 'God, Ros, I've been worried sick. I've been blowing the car horn every five minutes to help you find your way down the mountain.'

Blankets, a thermos of hot tea, food and pullovers were quickly taken back up into the forest. They reached Joy just before darkness fell. Bill picked her up, and carried the uncomplaining woman down the slippery hill and across the swamp to the car. Bill had saved Joy's life and she would never forget that.

Once again the Nairobi hospital was her home for a short while. When Ros visited her two days later she was sitting, crying, in a wheelchair in the hospital garden. Clutching a telegram in her hand, she appeared a sad and lonely figure. Joy had received a terrible blow and was grieving, not merely for her newest predicament but for lost hopes and vanished love. She had just learnt that her publisher, lover and friend of seventeen years, Sir William Collins, had died of a heart attack the day she had been lost in the forest. She had been so looking forward to his coming out to help her with her autobiography, which she was having some trouble putting together. Looking up at Ros with tears in her eyes, she said, 'We were intimate friends and I loved him so much.' She dwelled on the strange coincidence that on the very day he died, she could also have perished in the dark, remote forest.

A few months later, in October 1976, Joy was again caught up in a drama, this time with her friend Juliette Huxley, wife of the former director general of UNESCO. Lady Huxley was a keen naturalist who, after her last trip to Kenya, had taken an elephant and a rhino skull back to England and given them to Henry Moore as an inspiration for his sculpture. This time Joy wished to show her visitor the pink flamingoes at Lake Nakuru and they set off with Bobby Tyeis, a neighbour. By eleven that night the party still had not arrived back at Elsamere. Hospitals were rung. No Joy. Eventually they returned and explained their long absence. They had driven too close to the lake ; although the soda top was crisp, underneath lay thick mud. The car became firmly stuck, its wheels sinking up to the hubs. While Joy and Lady Huxley sat in the car for the next three hours, watching the pink feathers of the flamingoes deepen in the sunset, two others walked the five miles to the park warden's house for help. In an unusual display of trust, Joy poured out the sadnesses and frustrations of her life to her friend, telling her that George had no interest in seeing his wife more than twice a year. He was courteous, but she felt she no longer had a special place in his heart. With tears streaming down her face she explained how impossible it was to confide in him as he seemed unwilling to put himself out for her in any way.

She explained she had been suffering from depression, feeling that her life was dwindling away, and was unable to break new ground with the leopard research. Divorce was impossible because the symbol of George, herself and Elsa was revered by people all over the world. Lady Huxley, with wisdom and encouragement, sagely suggested ways Joy could place her life in perspective. It was one of the few times Joy heeded the advice of another. Later, in a letter to her, Joy thanked her for her kindness and patience, saying she understood what a terrible strain it was for anyone to be continually around a friend steeped in her own misery.

Unknown to either of them, a new chapter in Joy's life was about to begin. The rescue party included the warden, who quietly said to Joy, 'I have been looking after a one-month-old female leopard cub. Would you like to take her on?' After six years of waiting, and of being a thorough nuisance to Perez Olindo, whom she had consistently pestered to find her a cub, Joy now had a new carnivore to love and to study. The leopard's name was Penny.

The nervous young leopard's new home was a large wire *boma* built outside Joy's bedroom at the front and side of the house. Within a day of her arrival at Elsamere she had devoured a freshly killed and skinned rabbit, the blood and viscera of which were still warm, nipped Joy's leg, and scratched her with her razor-sharp claws. It was not going to be easy persuading this most unpredictable of predators to make friends. Indomitable as ever over danger posed by the big cats, including leopard, Joy declared to concerned friends: 'Oh, don't worry, it's a legend I hope to kill.' To protect her from severe scratches Ros and Bill Hillyar gave her a pair of canvas, elbow-length gauntlets, after which she travelled into Nairobi to purchase a canvas apron to protect her front and back.

When Penny was not sleeping under a shady acacia on the lawn or lying on one of the wooden platforms Joy had rigged up in her *boma* as a substitute for trees, she was walking on a lead with Joy and her assistant, Charles, around Hell's Gate. Padding through the star grasses she sniffed dik-dik droppings and molerat mounds, and gazed with silent interest at the giraffe and reedbuck in the distance. An occasional mongoose scurried past her as it tracked down crickets or snatched beetles from the air.

Elsamere and its restricted walks were fine as an interim playground, but Penny required a permanent home where Joy could observe her in the wild. Her great hope was to study several litters and to learn how leopards control breeding as well as determine how they 'communicate over many miles by telepathy'.

In November 1976, the merger of Kenya's national parks and the game department at last took place. Joy was now insistent that a suitable place be found for the rehabilitation of Penny. The authorities were reluctant; the human population had soared and all land use was being carefully examined. No one helped her more than Peter Johnson, her trusted adviser and chairman of the Elsa Advisory Committee of Kenya. He pulled every string possible but worried about the risk involved. It took ten long months before Joy's wish was granted. Jack Barrah, once George's assistant and now a senior wildlife adviser, personally intervened for Joy with the Isiolo County Council to help find a place. After hearing that the Council needed funds to provide a vehicle for the game warden of Shaba, Joy hastily donated two Land Rovers for use in the park, built an airstrip and financed an anti-poaching camel unit. She was then given permission to camp in the area, part of the Samburu and Isiolo game reserves.

On hearing the good news Joy immediately rushed round to her friend Millicent Morson: 'Come on, we're going to do a reckkie round Shaba.' In Nanyuki they spent the night with Rodney Elliot, the warden responsible for creating the Samburu Game Reserve, and Joy, in her usual forthright manner, said, 'Rodney, I've got a great idea. I want you to be my camp manager and build me a camp. Come and find a campsite with me.'

Rodney replied, 'Joy, don't be ridiculous, we can't do it in a day.'

'Don't argue, Rodney. We are going.'

The next day they left at dawn and travelled round the reserve four times before selecting a suitable site. Joy was not naturally generous when it came to money and when they stayed the night at Samburu Lodge, Millicent Morson found Elliot's bill on her account. She said to Joy, 'Sorry, chum, I'm not paying this, he is not my guest.'

Elliot was willing to help but had no intention of becoming Joy's camp manager. Worried that Joy was about to embark on the most precarious and difficult task of her life, George made one last attempt to persuade Joy to bring Penny to Kora, but his wife was adamant that Penny needed her own patch, far away from George's lions.

On her return to Naivasha there was much to do. Joy needed an efficient team to help her, someone with camping and administrative experience, who knew how to fix vehicles and who was proficient with a gun. Wary of her difficult temperament, young Kenyan men were loath to help her and so she applied overseas, complaining that she had had nothing but drunkards applying for the job. But eventually she chose a Kenyan, Jock Rutherfurd, a forty-eight-year-old ex-farmer and intrepid bush hand. With the addition of Makedde, George's old Turkana game scout and an experienced ranger and tracker who had been with George and Ken Smith the day they discovered Elsa, to protect her, Joy felt safe. She then organized her life for the proposed two years' absence from Elsamere, renting the house to prevent burglaries, completing two books and selecting illustrations out of thousands of photographs. She also viewed the rushes of a biographical film and sent some of her ethnographic photos to the British Museum for their records.

The next step was for Patrick Hamilton, who had just completed two years' research for the game department on the translocation of leopards, and Joy's vet and close friend, Dr Paul Sayer, to sedate Penny and slip a radio collar round her neck. Paul recalls, 'Joy rather hated the thought of Penny's clumsy collar, which she would have to wear for the rest of her life in order for Joy to locate her. Of course, this would also save her from poachers. But she said to me, "Do I have the right to impair her beauty?"' Dead tired after the complicated operation, Joy went that evening to a nearby hotel to give a lecture on conservation to a visiting group of Americans who had paid $1,000 to the Elsa fund. When she returned home, she found that Penny had torn off the precious radio collar, which had taken so long to fit. Joy set about refitting it in the dark.

A few days before her departure for Shaba, Joy awoke in the night. Trembling slightly, she turned on her light and reached for the notebook beside her bed. She found it odd that she had instinctively reverted to writing in German, the language she detested. She hurriedly wrote down her epitaph which, in the event of her death, she wanted put on a small bronze plaque at an inconspicuous spot on Elsa's grave. She also wished her ashes to be scattered across Elsa's grave. The next day she sent the inscription in a letter to her cousin, Felix Weisshuhn:

> Der Wind, der Wind das himmlische Kind
> er Fachelt den dinsamen Stein
> er schmeichelt und kost in der einsamen Nacht
> in der er ein tiefes Geheimnis bewacht.
> Der Wind, der Wind das himmlische Kind,
> verschwiegen seine Wege sind.

> (The wind, the wind, the divine child
> Fans the lonesome stone,
> Flatters in the moonlit night
> Where he guards a deep secret.
> The wind, the wind, the divine wind,
> How silent are his ways.)

Did Joy have some premonition that she did not have long to live?

When the new camp was ready at the end of August, a small motorcade drove past the red aloe flowers up Elsamere's hilly driveway. With Paul Sayer driving a heavily sedated leopard in the back of Joy's new Toyota

Landcruiser, Joy in her Peugeot with Kifosha her cook and two dozen live rabbits to feed Penny, and Sayer's family and Makedde leading, they left for the land of the north, the country where Joy's love affair with Kenya first took root. It was twenty years since she and George had left Isiolo.

22

Shaba and Penny

The rainy season in Kenya always produced huge problems, with roads in the northern areas being closed for up to three months. The cars slithered and skidded at the pace of tortoises, thorns on the road caused a puncture, and the cold crept into Joy's and her party's bones on reaching the higher altitude near Nanyuki. Descending into the plains, a different world greeted them. The heat was stifling and powder-fine dust filtered into car engines, radio equipment, cameras and clothes. Once past Isiolo on the road to Marsabit, they found few travellers along the road – the only splash of colour to relieve the biscuit-coloured landscape flowed from Samburu tribesmen and women walking back to their *manyattas*.

Turning off onto the bumpy, black, lava-strewn track to Shaba, the entourage passed a small circle of huts, surrounded by euphorbia bushes, where a marriage between two Samburus was about to take place. The new moon was rising and already the preparation of gifts from the bridegroom was completed. A sheep and two goatskins were placed next to one of the huts and two copper earrings and a container of milk had been given to the bride. Cows had been handed over to the relatives and two bulls were ready to be slaughtered for the feast. The bride, who had been circumcised early that morning, had provided the necessary items expected of her – a special apron, earrings and a piece of lion's skin, which was to be tied to her leg. The ceremonies were about to begin.

Much as she wanted to linger, Joy needed to get to camp before dark. As the shadows turned the rock-strewn sands to a warm ochre, they saw the lights of the Tilley lamps welcome them to their new home in the lonely outpost. Joy's words, 'the many wonders that nature will reveal to us, if we are responsive, and the limitless space which offers a certain spiritual freedom', applied admirably to Shaba. This was a land of near desert, dense thorn bush, lava flows and mountains which have been twisted and stirred like toffee, where life in the bush seemed tireless and man insignificant. Dark purple balls of Caralluma flower heads were scattered on the rocky outcrops and the round, white trumpets of the Ipomoea unfolded to catch the rains. To the north ran the Uaso Nyiro, its banks shaded by slender doum palms and the generous leaves of the fig trees. Crocodiles slipped through its waters and the hooves of buffalo sank into its muddy banks. The Samburu believed the many springs of Shaba to be haunted by the spirits of their ancestors.

Framed by rocky hills, lava boulders and the short, sharp grasses of the arid plain, Joy's camp was hewn out of the spare, abstract landscape near a swamp where the myriad call of swallows echoed in the water, grass and marsh rushes. Disdainful secretary birds and sacred ibis stalked the reeds, the scimitar horns of the oryx sliced through the tips of the grass and lion, buffalo and smaller animals drew near to the swamp as twilight fell.

Shaba was to be Joy's most impressive camp during her forty years in Kenya. A grove of tall acacia trees, drooping with the nests of weaver birds, spread its shadow over the huts and canvas tents, each of which had a small verandah and bathroom. The studio tent was well equipped, with pockets in the canvas to hold Joy's papers and a cupboard in which her valuables could be locked. The large dining tent held two refrigerators and many shelves, with space for storing food and camping kit. Her African staff were crowded into one large tent and they shared a shower and toilet. The Europeans had their own.

Cooking was conducted by placing pots and pans over burning logs placed under an ash heap. Somehow, under these primitive conditions, complete with visits from scorpions and brick-red spitting cobras with the telltale black band behind their heads, Kifosha managed to bake bread and a variety of dishes. Around the camp was built a wire fence three metres high, separating it from their most vital asset of all – crystal-clear spring water.

Paul Sayer's help with Penny was invaluable and Joy was sad to see him and his family leave. Four days after their departure Joy wrote an effusive letter, telling him of her immense gratitude for getting Penny safely to Shaba. She excitedly told him that Penny had been for her first long walk and seemed fascinated by her new environment. The leopard kept sniffing everything around her but, nervous of the open plains, always stayed close to Joy and her African ranger. Exuberantly, Joy declared she felt like turning the swamp at Shaba into champagne to toast Paul again for all his help.

Joy spent many hours looking for Penny, photographing her and following her movements and habits. She continually noted things, feeling strongly that when observing, instead of relying on memory, it was important to write down everything of importance. Dressed in a green apron over the front and back of her shorts and halter top, long canvas gloves and boots, and carrying a long stick, she struck an incongruous figure as she strode across the landscape. Stuffed with painkillers, she was oblivious to the many injuries which afflicted her and curtailed her speed. Apart from the constant difficulties thrown up by a steel hip and an impaired right hand, she had recovered fully from her broken elbow, knee and ankle.

Joy had a simple philosophy: she was convinced that the best way to stay healthy and young, or to solve problems was to keep working 'one's guts out' to prevent thinking about any unhappiness. And it simply was not on to bore people with long discussions about illness. She was also busy putting the finishing touches to her autobiography, *The Searching Spirit*. In March an editor from Collins flew out to do battle with Joy. Joy delighted in telling everyone that the editor left, defeated.

One of Joy's first acts was to donate a vital water tank to the rangers and their families on the outskirts of the park. But she suffered wide fluctuations of mood. When well disposed she gave away medicines, food and water to the surrounding villagers; if irritable, she shouted, 'I gave you some a few days ago. Now go away and leave me alone.' The Africans were philosophical.

The late Jock Rutherfurd was a man of rare calibre who knew how to handle Joy and countered her demands with his own brand of toughness. He was physically strong and almost without fear. Despite their rows, she grudgingly respected him, without admitting that he was far more knowledgeable than she about the bush, animals, birds and trees. Typical of Kenya-born men, he could keep a vehicle running on wire and string and use Sunlight soap to stop up holes in petrol tanks. Not a woman who appreciated being answered back, Joy called him 'Mr RatherRude'. Nevertheless she relied upon him, admiring his strengths and virtues: he was an intrepid horseman, used to lassoing giraffe from horseback. A man more than partial to alcohol, he managed to survive on beer at Shaba. 'The leopard was much easier to handle than Joy,' he commented sagely.

Each Wednesday Rutherfurd went into Isiolo to pick up the mail and provisions. It was essential that a camp in such a remote setting had a radio for communication with the outside world should any emergency arise, and every Sunday and Thursday at precisely 8 p.m. the couple listened in to the radio call, to receive and send messages. Sometimes Joy's lonely spirit missed Naivasha and the bright lights of Nairobi. In all her letters to her close friend Ros Hillyar she stressed : 'Let me know all Naivasha gossip !'

As usual with her assistants, the relationship between Joy and Ruther-furd soon deteriorated. In March he badly burnt his arm with boiling radiator water. He immediately drove off to Nanyuki to get it seen to. Joy told Ros somewhat unsympathetically : 'RatherRude is leaving at the end of the month and I have seen nothing of him during the past month. His arm only bothered him for one week, so I don't know what other excuse he has.'

In November the rains poured and the river's water spread over its banks. Rain dripped through the tents and the wings of the flying ants crashed lightly against the canvas. Overnight the plains became golden with small flowers and each exquisite white convolvulus turned its face to the world for one day only, springing up out of the earth over a soft mantle of green. The Hillyars paid a visit, with Joy begging them to bring their own camp beds – she could provide enough blankets. She also needed them to arrive with their own cook as Kifosha tended to become highly obstreperous when overworked. After her friends left, Joy wrote again, teasingly referring to their naughtiness, having discovered a large salami they had thoughtfully left for her. Placed between the pages of her letter was some money to repay them.

That month, Collins published Joy's autobiography, *The Searching Spirit*. In a letter to her sister Dorle, she gently told her of the immense difficulties she had had in trying to write about the sorrows of their parents' divorce and the emotional upheavals it had caused. She hoped that Dorle would understand and not be upset by what she had written, especially by the fact that she barely featured on the pages. Feeling that the core of what happens in one's life was an intensely private matter, Joy had tried her best to tread carefully over events which had made a major impact on her life. She compared the task to taking off all her clothes in front of a group of strangers. However, she urged Dorle to look deeper into what had been written and form her own opinion. Joy then switched abruptly to her younger sister's appearance and pleaded with her to improve her looks by getting a new set of dentures. In fact, Dorle had nothing to fear. Joy's bland autobiography reveals little of her character, her feelings or her thoughts.

Ros Hillyar became Joy's main link with the outside world, providing her with her beloved classical music tapes to fill the lonely hours of the evening when she was writing. Ros recalls, 'Joy sent me streams of letters asking me to get tape recordings for her. She was always saying, "I cannot exist without my music. Can you send me some Chopin, a bit of Schubert or Mozart or Brahms, or whatever you can find on the Romantics. I would also dearly love a bit of lighter music like Tchaikovsky or Rachmaninov, as well as some Strauss waltzes and any ballet music you may have." Joy always left the final choice to me. It kept me quite busy, but it made her happy.'

The tracks from camp to Penny's usual haunts often crumbled to thick fine dust or else were so wet that Joy's Toyota got stuck in the mud. Each week she drove a few miles to park under a spreading acacia at the end of a rocky *kopje* (hill) where the road turned north to the Funan spring. Here, two lines of metamorphic rock ran across the river which cut through them to form a magnificent sand-coloured gorge with beaches. A large cave nearby contained abstract painted designs, broken pottery and bones left by a people long ago. Bats and swifts and bristle-crowned starlings darted in and out of smaller caves. Having located Penny as she slipped like a shadow through the rocks or along the shady ledges on an overhanging cliff, woman and predator crossed over the river by way of tumbled rocks clung to by gnarled parasitic fig trees. Nearby, in the muddy water, the large silent shapes of crocodile and hippo skulked. Whenever she came across unwanted tourists whom she was convinced would invade Penny's territory, she shouted : 'You will *not* leave your car. I will report you.'

To walk among the rocks outside the gorge, or on Shaba mountain itself, needed a woman of great toughness and character. Joy searched for animal paths – even the elephants climbed part of the way – but she always carried a pair of secateurs to cut away the wait-a-bit thorn which caught her and Makedde in its curved cat's-claw thorns, making escape impossible without torn clothes and skin. Not far from Joy's camp, the swamp emptied in two different streams, the colour of weak tea and tasting like Vichy water, into the Uaso Nyiro. The southern stream formed an idyllic waterfall before reaching the crocodile-infested river and here shoals of fish curved their way through the water, producing the best fishing. As a treat on Sundays, when friends came to visit, Joy, who never thought of the dangers of tropical diseases, particularly bilharzia, took them to this favourite spot of hers. Wearing a topee to ward off the hot sun, and a leopard-print bathing suit, she bathed in the streams and stood, laughing, under the waterfall, which came to be known as Penny's Falls. It was at times like this when she felt her happiest.

Joy continued to explore the land around her camp. A few hours to the east stood a line of small ash cones and volcanoes, one of which was called Magado, the African word for salt. In the centre of the crater lay a salt lake and on the side deep caves, inhabited by Meru tribesmen from the slopes of Mount Kenya. They spent their lives as their ancestors had done, trapping and managing the salt, which they placed in baobab leaves to be hauled up the cliffs by basket-laden donkeys. The salt was then taken into Meru country to be exchanged for *miraa*, the leaf chewed to ward off fatigue and hunger.

The path down the steep slopes into the crater had been worn deep into the rock by the Boran cattle and goats coming to drink at the fresh water wells at the edge of the crater floor. Once down on the floor, the cattle had patiently to wait their turn, although they may not have had any liquid for two days. Occasionally, at weekends, Joy took guests to see the busy life of the crater, with its almost Biblical atmosphere.

One close friend who often came to stay with Joy was the American, Esmond Bradley-Martin. He was deeply committed to the fight against poaching and had amassed a huge quantity of statistics on the international trade in ivory and rhino horn. Esmond commented of his wife Chryssee and himself: 'We were two of a handful of friends towards the end of her life. Joy longed for companionship at Shaba but so few people wanted to be her buddy. She would complain: "Esmond, why don't people like me, why don't I have any friends?" And I'd tell her it was because she was pretty impossible!'

As Esmond and Joy walked to their favourite spot by the waterfall they discussed a shared love of wildlife and conservation and he kept her up to date with what was happening in Nairobi: 'Joy always wanted the news and the gossip about well-known people she knew. She craved conversation and radiated such enthusiasm that you just got caught up in it.' Although fond of Chryssee, Esmond's wife, Joy was still prone to the vagaries of jealousy. She deeply resented the amount of time the young wildlife enthusiast had spent at Kora, as George's part-time secretary. When meeting her in the middle of Perez Olindo's busy office in Nairobi, first Joy cut her dead then she flew at Chryssee, screeching loudly that she knew she was having an affair with George. She demanded that Chryssee leave him alone and stop going to Kora. Chryssee, highly embarrassed and near to tears, fled from the office. Later, Esmond sat Joy down, explaining firmly that at her age, she should know better than to be jealous of his wife.

The thought of Christmas filled Joy, as ever, with the anticipation of excited child, especially if George was going to be with her. His visits always depended upon the availability of friends' planes to transport him to Shaba and he had promised her that this year he would do his best to spend the day with her. In her Christmas letter to Ros and her family, Joy wished them all a very happy time and thanked them once again for the wonderful Christmas they had given her two years ago. Ros recalls, 'Joy was extremely lonely and sad then because George had stayed in Kora with Bill Travers, so she came to us. But Joy was really expecting George to join her at Shaba, this particular year – it all depended on the Tana river, which had flooded.'

This year she dressed a small seedling Balanites tree and as presents for each person, she had drawn, in red chalk, the heads of various animals found in Shaba. The Christmas cake and champagne were ready and carols blared out from her tape recorder. Hour after hour, Joy waited patiently for George, but he failed to show up. Her spirits sank. Kifosha produced an excellent dinner that night for the small group – Joy, a new young American assistant, Paul Strickland, and her overseas guests; but Joy's mind was elsewhere, hurt and uncertain to why her husband had let her down again.

In Kora on Boxing Day disaster struck George's brother. A lion attacked. Terence had never approved of George's 'bloody lions' and much preferred the ponderous beauty of elephants. Having re-thatched one of the *bandas* with makuti, Terence stepped outside the compound to set fire to the old palm leaves. Without looking to see if any lions were in the area, he was pinned to the ground within seconds, his face in the jaws of Shade, one of George's large carnivores. Blood was everywhere. The loyal labour gang hurled stones at the lion which immediately let go and slunk off into the bush. Terence's teeth could be seen through the gaping hole in his cheek and the lion's fangs, which had just missed his eye, had sunk in between his carotid and jugular.

As luck would have it, Joan and Alan Root, the renowned wildlife filmmakers, were staying with George to film the hornbills, famous residents at Kora. George and the Roots quickly bundled Terence into blankets, placed him in their plane and took off for Nairobi. In the plane, while being comforted by Joan, Terence told her, 'You know, I never believed Livingstone when he said that he felt no pain after being mauled by a lion. I feel nothing so it must be true, but I feel bloody cold and can't stop shivering.'

Although both Joy and George in their autobiographies state that they were together on Christmas Day, the visit in fact took place on 28 December. The Roots flew George and his American secretary, Pam, over to Shaba and had breakfast with Joy, blaming the delay on Terence's attack, which they told Joy had happened on the 25th. George's excuse was that he had not wanted to leave the camp until the lion had settled down again.

After breakfast the group went out to search for Penny. When they eventually found her, Joy and her assistant Paul immediately fondled the animal. Joan wrote in her diary : 'Paul was very good with Penny but Joy was excitable, seeming to have no feel for the animal.' She admired Paul's handling and the sensitivity he felt about Joy and the leopard, using his body to protect her from Penny when he felt it was necessary. The Roots came away feeling strongly that Joy should 'cut the mother strings' with her leopard.

Although George appeared singularly withdrawn and preoccupied by Terence's accident while at Shaba, in retrospect this visit has a certain poignancy. It would be the last occasion when George would visit his wife near Christmastime. By now Joy was increasingly worried about George's safety and the fact that there was a real possibility he could be mauled again, or even killed, by one of his semi-tame lions. Not only did she consider that there were far too many lions, but food was a problem due to lack of money and a paucity of game. But, however many times she nagged her husband, he took little notice of her fears. Matters once again came to a head. She decided to communicate her displeasure in the way that most hurt him – financially. She announced that from now on, she would no longer be prepared to finance his way of life. Every time he went up to visit Joy and Penny in Shaba, Paul Sayer remembers, 'Joy was convinced that the longer George went on feeding his animals, the more enormous the problems would become.' It was only after Elsa and her cubs became world famous that Joy evolved her philosophy of leaving wild animals alone.

Whenever Makedde was unavailable and Joy was alone in the camp, she hopped in the Toyota and went off to look for Penny. The leopard had become another obsession. Joy wrote to her sister, describing her days in Penny's company. She made a point of telling Dorle just how intelligent Penny was and that she was now completely able to fend for herself in the wild. As if to reinforce her own theories, she insisted that the preconceived ideas people had of how dangerous leopards were could be dismissed once the animal's unpredictability was understood and accepted. Penny was not constantly ready to attack her, nor was she particularly troublesome, because she was aware of how much Joy loved her. Yet whatever Joy wrote, there were many times when the cat turned. Once, when Joy took off her glove to stroke her, Penny suddenly turned and bit her arm. Joy nearly passed out with the pain of the most serious bite the leopard had ever inflicted. Five stitches were needed to close the deep wound. Joy knew it was unwise to go off on her own without one of her men and suffered an angry sense of guilt when discovered stuck in the car alone at night. But, undeterred, she continued to gain enormous spiritual strength from the harsh challenge of life alone in the bush.

23

Premonitions

1979 started off badly. On 16 January, Roy Wallace, the amiable young
manager of a tented safari camp ten miles away and Joy's nearest neighbour
and friend, came across Joy sitting crying in her car, which had stuck fast
in a narrow, sandy *lugga* (dry riverbed). She had fallen and broken her
knee while walking and sat waiting, in great pain, for someone to find
her. Roy took her to the mission hospital at Archer's Post, where
she was encased in a plaster cast from crotch to heel. Joy told Dorle
that she thanked her lucky stars she was not bundled off to Nairobi Hospital, where she would have been forced to stay in bed. Being used to the
space at Shaba, the restriction of small rooms tended to bring on a panic
attack.

Roy recalls that evening: 'She was in agony but on the way to the
mission she started telling me how beautiful all the sounds were she had
heard while she was sitting in the Land Rover and how much peace there
was, despite her pain.'

A strong bond of friendship grew between the two, despite a number
of altercations. Roy said, 'I was for ever telling her not to go and see that
animal on her own. I told her to be careful, this bloody leopard made
such a mess of her arms – she was not always wearing gauntlets. And she
was frightened of Penny – everyone was. It was not a friendly beast and
you could see it wanted to turn on you. Joy would get mad at me and say
that I didn't know enough about wild animals to tell her anything. In the
end I didn't say anything. I thought if Penny kills you or mauls you badly,
then that's obviously the way you want it.'

But Joy's spirit was with her animals. It was only through them that
she found peace. They set an example, for no matter how much they
suffered, they never failed to maintain their dignity. All the same, she was
aware of the impression her scars gave. When the journalist Brian Jackman
of the *Sunday Times* came to spend a pleasant, friendly few hours, Joy

pleaded, 'Please don't write about all my scratches and claw marks from Penny.'

Penny was again in oestrus and more than old enough to mate but she failed to conceive. Joy jokingly told Paul Sayer that Penny must be using a contraceptive. Eventually Penny was courted and indulged in a prolonged honeymoon. Cast or no cast, Joy was determined to continue looking for her, hobbling to her each day. She found her at last, hungry and exhausted. Joy carefully fondled her before offering her water and part of a goat she had brought. As she fed and flirted with the animal, Joy investigated her nipples, finding them to be still enlarged, with dry skin covering them. Joy discovered Penny's vulva was moist and slightly larger than usual. Shortly afterwards, Penny suffered a miscarriage. Joy wrote to Elspeth Huxley, saying how distressed she was, even though George had tried to comfort her by telling her of a miscarriage suffered by one of his lionesses who was later able to have lots of healthy cubs. In a moment of self-pity, she lamented that she herself had not been so fortunate.

In February, Joy discussed her worries over George with Ros. A tented safari lodge some six miles upriver from his camp had recently been ambushed, with a German and an African killed and other staff narrowly escaping. The camp was ordered to close for security reasons. The owner was the nearest European to George and was able to help with his large boat in case George ever got into trouble. Now another Somali gang was operating on George's side of the river and the government arranged for seven armed guards from Garissa to protect him. A permanent anti-poaching unit of fourteen rangers to control the 500-square-mile Kora reserve was also established. As the gangs were after anybody who interfered with the poaching, George was a likely target, especially as they were aware he had a whole armoury of rifles at the camp. Since he was often away buying camels to feed his lions, he stood in great danger of being ambushed. However, Joy told Paul Sayer that George was absolutely determined to live far away in Kora, where it was possible to be one's own boss and where he was so isolated from mainstream life that he did not have to adapt to the post-colonial Africa.

Joy was a voracious reader and was currently immersed in the auto-biography of Hedy Lamarr, the beautiful Viennese actress. She had become engrossed in comparing her life with two Austrian women who had left to seek happiness elsewhere – Hedy Lamarr and Susi Jeans, the gifted pianist. Pencilled in the flyleaf of the book were various comments. She saw her friend as leaving her country to find greater expansion in the world of music ; Hedy as looking for equal success overseas in Hollywood. Joy viewed herself leaving Austria with far more intensity and dedication in her search for greater things that either of the other two – intellectual stimulus, achievement, learning about the scientific side of life, love and fulfilment. Admitting her own pain, Joy scribbled that all three of them had ended unhappily. Underlined twice in heavy pencil she wrote the words : 'Where will it end ?'

In April, Paul Strickland, feeling he had spent enough time at Shaba, wanted to return to the United States. For the past few months he had been deliberately frustrated by Joy in his attempts to make a close study of birdlife, especially raptors. While at Shaba he had been asked by the eminent ornithologist Leslie Brown to watch certain nests of raptors and to keep notes on developments. Paul was thrilled with the idea, but Joy made it virtually impossible for him by not allowing him the use of any of her vehicles to take him to the nests. Paul was forced to walk, most of it in potentially dangerous areas. Joy had decided, much as she admired Paul, not to encourage him or offer any help.

The search for another new assistant began. Is it possible Joy ever saw the funny side of some of these applicants ? She related her woes to Ros, telling her that, having received a resumé which would have done credit to a saint, she had hired a middle-aged, unmarried, South African tee-totaller who was reasonably well-off. He had written that he was a university graduate and that his background included engineering and mining. She had been slightly dubious when he told her he was of mixed race. When this 'paragon' arrived, he fell into a drunken heap as soon as he got out of the car and took an instant dislike to Penny, refusing to have anything to do with her. He left.

Eventually Joy cabled for the twenty-two-year-old son of an ex-game warden of Zambia. His name was Pieter Mawson. Joy found him more immature than Paul, but more amenable, helpful and enthusiastic. At last she had found a good, practical young man to help her, even if she could barely understand his thick Afrikaans accent. The fact that he was one of the 'upper Boers', as she called him, with a mother who was a Kruger, appealed to her snobbish instincts.

The well-mannered Pieter established an immediate rapport with Penny, who licked his hands the first time they met. Well-built, with thick brown wavy hair and a ready smile, the young man had studied agriculture and mechanics at college and genuinely cared about wildlife and the bush. He and Joy hit it off immediately. Together they started caring for an orphaned leopard cub, Bala. Penny was now pregnant and amazed Joy by covering fifteen miles in one night. She excitedly told Paul Sayer that the leopard roamed over an area of 120 square miles and seemed happy to combine the freedom of a wild leopard with the love and attention Joy provided. All she could hope for was that she produced healthy cubs preferably when they could easily be found.

In May, Pieter, in the middle of an appendicitis attack, was driven by Joy at high speed to the hospital at Wamba. While she was talking to the doctor, Joy told him that recently she had become so dizzy she had to lie in bed for a whole day. He diagnosed low blood pressure and gave her tablets to improve the condition. In a letter to Ros, Joy preceded her usual requests with a list of medicines, as the Italian doctor was miles from camp. She also begged her friend to find time to send more music tapes. Her main request was for another recording of *Der Rosenkavalier* because she had played her existing tape over and over again during the lonely evenings at Shaba and it had become increasingly worn. Never one to feel shy of asking a favour, Joy, as a final request, asked Ros to go to the stores in Naivasha and purchase sewing thread and wine.

On 26 May, Penny gave birth to two cubs. The day before, Pieter had been deeply moved when Penny had led him a hidden rock where she lay down while she purred and licked his face and hands. Joy had not been able to climb the rocks because of her hip and by now she was taking so many painkillers for arthritis, osteoporosis and painful joints, that her body was unable to keep pace. She had been warned that leopard were particularly dangerous around their young, but Penny seemed to need Joy's mother love, and seemed anxious on the third day for Joy to meet her offspring. In common with lion and cheetah, though, Penny resisted any attempt by Africans to approach the cubs when small. Joy was ecstatic and felt a renewed surge of affection as she watched Penny nursing the tiny cubs, which she named Pasha and Pity. Her heart was full as the leopard affectionately licked her hands. The birth of the cubs heralded the end of the book Joy was writing on Penny – *The Queen of Shaba*.

In most of her copious letters to friends, which she typed in capitals to save shifting keys with the middle finger of her left hand, she made a point of stressing her 'good relationship with George'. She also made a habit of copying all letters onto pink flimsy paper. To a letter to Alys Reece, she seemed to feel that her efforts in conservation were often disregarded and despaired that fame so often came posthumously. She then told Alys of an old Austrian saying : 'While the stallion was alive, they gave him nothing to eat. When he was dead, they placed a bundle of hay near him so that people could not say that he died of starvation.'

Increasingly, Joy brushed aside remarks about the future. After her work with Penny was finished, she could see nothing, only an existence shrouded in obscurity. This unusual blankness worried her. She was tormented by dark forces and possessed a neurotic fear of growing old – did she envisage a lonely, possibly incapacitated old age? Did the inevitable passing of her sexual attractiveness, which had stayed with her longer than most, and had been the one certain power of her younger days, frighten her? By now she had few friends, she was alienated from her husband and less respected than she should have been for her conservation work. She felt eclipsed and resentful of George, who was so well liked and offered such a good image. He looked so good in the bush – the cultivated flowing locks and weather-beaten face brought out emotions in people overseas – pure box-office success. Why was it not recognized that in their serious conservation conflict, she was the one trying to do the right thing, following correct rehabilitation procedures, not George? Added to this, Joy was unable to work happily with either Europeans or Africans. Despite fame, wealth and a stimulating life, Joy felt that happiness had eluded her. Once every couple of months she went down to Nairobi, to have her hair done, lecture, visit her doctor, collect an award or see her business associates.

A close neighbour at Naivasha felt it was noticeable that Joy had some premonition that her days were numbered. After leaving Elsamere, Joy went to stay with Kathleen Willson, a friend and mother of her first assistant James, at her home in Nyeri. One evening in front of the fire Joy quietly raised her head and said: 'Kathleen, I have an ominous feeling that something disastrous is going to happen to me. I don't know what, but I am certain of it.' Kathleen sympathetically held out her hand to her friend and both women wept.

In August Kifosha, the old cook who had been with Joy for so many years, left. Perhaps he could take no more of Joy's constant abuse. Her good old Kifosha suddenly vanished without a word of warning. She could not understand it, as they were on the best of terms. That weekend she expected four visitors, which, without a cook or ranger – Makedde was ill in hospital – was a disaster.

Whenever she felt things getting on top of her Joy sent off demanding, hysterical notes to George: 'Dear George, one of the staff has done a bunk, none of the cars work, my typewriter is broken. I cannot cope. The furniture has not arrived. Come at once. Joy.'

His replies remained the same: 'Last night after supper it was a full moon and one of my lions was sitting on the rock – a most beautiful sight. Sorry to hear you have had some troubles. Love George.'

Her letters to her husband show a clear lack or loss of direction. His were descriptive and full of feeling for the beauty of nature around him, written in an almost lyrical fashion. Like Joy, though, he wrote with little show of affection. By now the couple had amassed a vast correspondence. But the fact remained that by not doing exactly what she wanted him to, George hurt her greatly. Joy's vulnerability and huge capacity for love were only assuaged by the animals which she felt never rejected her.

On the afternoon of 16 September, one of the fridges in the camp exploded. The blast lasted five minutes and the fire raged through the trees and into the sky, spreading across the swamp and out into the bush. Joy was alone in the camp and rushed desperately to put out the flames before the intense heat drove her away. Before she left, she tried to grab her precious tape recorder but nearly suffocated. Smoke was seen ten miles away at the tented camp. As far as Isiolo, the grey pall circled up into the air.

Within half an hour nearly everything was destroyed. Both fridges were lost, the vital radio link, all Penny's telemetric equipment as well as the news radio. The dining hut and mess tent were burnt to a cinder and the two dozen rabbits, huddled together in their wire *boma*, were instantly incinerated. Their death would haunt Joy for a long time to come. Gone were all the furniture and books, cutlery and crockery, but by far the worst loss was three years' worth of photographic records of Penny. Joy's ciné camera was destroyed and her tape recorder unusable. 'We are naked, except for the sleeping tents,' cried Joy. Luckily, the previous week, having finished the last part of her book on Penny, she had sent off her manuscript and a folder of photographs to Collins. Amid all her troubles, it had given her a quiet sense of satisfaction.

Roy Wallace was sitting having a beer in his tented safari camp with Pieter Mawson when he suddenly saw smoke drifting into the sky. Leaping to his feet he shouted, 'Pieter, that's Joy's camp.' Mawson just sat there, apparently unconcerned, forcing Wallace to send his lorry down with some staff to see if he could help. The ten miles which separated them meant it was a forty-minute drive away. The place was a mess. As soon as his men arrived back, explaining the disaster, Roy roared down to Joy with food, bedding and supplies to make her at least slightly comfortable for the night. He found her in a terrible state, crying and upset that all was lost. 'Joy, come back and stay the night with me,' he said.

Through her tears, Joy immediately answered, 'No, I'm not leaving a sinking ship. Your mother would have told you the same.'

Pieter did not go back that night. Roy remembers, 'I was furious with him, but covered for him that time.' Four weeks previously three of Joy's staff, plus Pieter, had narrowly escaped being killed by a fridge explosion.

A *fundi* (artisan) had come out from Isiolo to repair it. Ten minutes after he left, it exploded, causing a fire. A day later Joy was told that that particular make of fridge was known for dangerous explosions due to faulty design. She felt she had been deliberately fooled into taking the fridge. An Electrolux had originally been requested, but instead a useless, second-rate model had arrived. Although Joy was beginning to view the explosion as a bad omen, the most fortunate aspect of the whole episode was that no one had been killed or injured.

Did Joy feel that someone in her camp was out to do her harm? After the devastation, Joy gave Wallace a painting signed at the bottom, 'To my dear friend Roy for all your help through this tough time.' As she handed it to him, she was crying, as so many other times when she had broken down in front of him – she cried about George, about her love of animals, her love of life and how no one knew or understood her.

To add to the disaster, two days later Joy was again injured. The road to the park gate was impassable and the Land Rover became stuck in knee-deep dust. After walking four miles back to camp in the dark, Joy fell on sharp lava and broke her knee. Pieter, who was with her, gently picked her up and carried her the remaining two miles home. The exhausting journey took him two hours of sheer determination. She collapsed, crying, and in great pain. Pieter drove her to Wamba hospital the next day and after an X-ray was taken, once again Joy was encased in plaster from crotch to heel for five weeks. Paul Sayer remembered Pieter as 'so patient and tolerant. Joy was extremely brusque and rude to him and commanded him to do something in front of others. He would reply, "Yes ma'am." He used to come down here and see us just to get away.'

Camp life became extremely difficult. Without refrigeration, no meat could last in the heat for more than two days. Not only was there the staff to feed, there was also Penny, the two cubs and Bala, the orphan. The dusty road to Isiolo made driving there every two days almost impossible and the camp members had to make do with tinned food until a new camp was built and further fridges and provision supplied. Joy radioed frantically to the sanguine Peter Johnson to send up a mess tent before the rains started. But even in the middle of chaos, Joy was nothing if not pragmatic. Instead of bemoaning her run of bad luck, she asked Millicent Morson if she would do her a tremendous favour by finding her extra tape recorder at Elsamere. She needed it desperately to record Penny calling her cubs. She also pleaded that Ros should be reminded to send the much-needed tapes.

Millicent sent many other useful items from Elsamere to replace those burnt, as well as a fridge. Joy wrote to Millicent, expressing her deepest thanks for all her friend's fetching and carrying. She was only too aware of how time-consuming such tasks were and ended that she was practically in tears at the thought of her kind efforts.

By the middle of October the *fundis* had finished their work, leaving Joy with a workable camp. The rains had not yet broken and Shaba was infernally hot. Joy still could not drive and was without a radio receiver to locate Penny, having to rely on spooring and calling the animal, who was inhabiting an area ten miles from camp.

On 20 October Pieter Mawson cut off Joy's cast, much to her relief. Three days previously Joy had befriended a one-week-old ostrich chick. She fed it glucose and bonemeal for two days and spent most of the day sketching it knowing how essential it is that baby animals have company. On the third day the ostrich died. Again, Joy was pained, reflecting that even the death of a small animal which had barely begun to know life caused intense suffering to that curiously romantic creature, man.

It is possible that Joy was trying to fool herself into trusting her assistant. Tensions were running high and increasingly Joy gave vent to her temper at the person nearest to her – Pieter. Discussions turned into furious rows, heard by silent Africans in the background. To escape, Mawson spent more and more time up at the tented camp drinking beer and often partying until late at night. Roy, protective about Joy, told him, 'You can't leave Joy like this. It is 9 p.m. at night and she will think you have broken down.'

The two nearly got in a fight one night when Pieter had gone off to Isiolo for supplies and on the way back had dropped in for his usual five or six beers. Roy knew Joy was waiting desperately for urgent mail : 'Pieter, you shouldn't treat Joy like this.'

'I don't give a damn,' replied her assistant.

Many times he left Joy alone in her camp, going off to Nanyuki on the spur of the moment. Since she expected absolute devotion from those who worked for her, she became upset but tried to understand when Roy told her : 'Joy, you must let him go, you can't keep a young man in the bush. I'll look after you.' Joy, paranoid as always about drinking, continued to turn on Pieter, calling him a liar : 'Don't bother to deny it. I know you are going up to Roy's camp every evening.' She also felt that Mawson was inciting her staff against her, although with her mercurial temperament, most Turkanas needed no encouragement. She could only rely on her two redoubtable old faithfuls ('old' in the African sense, meaning wise and worthy of honour), Makedde and Kifosha, who had returned just as suddenly as he had left.

Roy grew to like Pieter less and less, feeling he was neglecting Joy and using his camp as a stage to show off to Wallace's clients by glorying in being Joy's assistant. Roy recalled: 'He would tell wild stories about Joy that just were not true. I told my staff that I considered him dangerous and bad news.'

Over the previous few months two incidents had led to a falling-out between Pieter and his employer. Although Joy always kept a small tin trunk under her bed containing all her valuables – money, papers, letters from Billy Collins and small items of jewellery – she entrusted Shs 1,000/- to Pieter's care to buy provisions in Isiolo. He placed them in an unlocked cabinet in his tent. After discovering his cupboard broken into and the money stolen a few days later, Joy insisted that he pay her back, blaming him for not locking it safely away. Mawson was furious: 'I don't have a box I can lock. You should have provided me with one – you know I can't afford to buy it out of my wages.' Joy remained adamant: 'Sorry, buy one yourself, out of your own money when you're in town.' Suspicion for the theft naturally fell on her African staff.

The second, growing disagreement between the two occurred over her writings on Penny. The entire time Pieter was living at Shaba, he had been keeping notes, hoping to write a book on their work together on the leopards. He was dismissive of Joy's ability to write, suggesting that he collaborate with her. Joy, jealous of what she considered to be her territory and valuable knowledge, was apprehensive and continually dismissed his efforts to help. The more he argued with her, the less she liked or trusted him. As so on as she had put each chunk of Penny's life on paper, she immediately sent it off to London, without rewriting or honing the material. Had she been nervous that Pieter would steal the material? It seems unlikely, but according to Roy, each time Pieter came up to his camp, 'He let everyone know that his one intention was to get hold of that book, write it properly and finish it off. He wanted to take over the whole project.' Now it was too late; the rest of the manuscript had been sent to London.

In the first week of December, Joy sacked Paul Ekai, a seventeen-year-old Turkana, who had worked for her for the past six months. She thought little of it – just another addition to her history of dismissals. Shouting at him, she told him he was lazy and his work had slacked off. She handed him his small wage packet and dismissed him with a wave of her hand: 'Go on. Get out right now and go back to Isiolo.' Ekai, deeply insulted that he had lost face in front of the other servants, turned on his heel and strode off down the track. Ever since the burglary she had suspected the young Turkana of taking the money out of Mawson's cupboard.

Three nights later, when Joy and Pieter were both away from the camp,

Joy's precious tin trunk under her bed was broken into with a crowbar. Her papers were rifled through, and her Leica camera, Shs 2,500/- and a couple of torches taken. A few of Pieter's clothes were also stolen. The police duly arrived, but on finding no incriminating evidence, Joy called in a witch doctor – a Turkana sandal oracle – to help find the culprit. The witch doctor proved unsuccessful.

Joy had been afflicted by so much over the past year, both physically and emotionally, that when an offer arrived to appear on a prominent weekly programme on French television, she leapt at it. By now she almost fanatically embraced her role of the charismatic public figure and was thrilled by the thought of starring in a prominent weekly programme devoted to famous personalities. *Born Free* was to be shown, together with a film about her life and work with animals, financed by the Elsa Appeal and originally shown by the BBC. This would be followed by a panel discussion. Even though she would be gone for less than a week, she needed to get away.

The tension in camp was almost unbearable, Pieter was more than keen to leave. She seldom saw Penny's cubs now, hidden up in the rocks, and she knew both mother and offspring were fine. After making a radio call to George to tell him of her plans, she spent the next half hour packing before driving all night to Nairobi to sort out various legal affairs with Peter Johnson. She stayed with the Bradley-Martins, one of the few couples nowadays who would give Joy a bed for the night. Worried that she had not got the right winter clothes Joy rushed the next day with Esmond and his driver to Naivasha to collect various bits of warm clothing. After a sleepless night flight she arrived in a rain-soaked Paris wearing her simulated mink coat.

It was not until she arrived at her hotel that Joy realized that her coat had a hole in it the size of a saucer. She saw the funny side of the situation. Rats had devoured the armpit of the coat and commandeered the lining as a nursery for their offspring. To prevent the hole's disclosure, Joy kept her arm firmly pressed to her side. Secretly amused, she thought how amazed people in Paris would be if they discovered her latest attempt to conserve wild animals and their habitat.

There were two sides with opposing views on the television programme. Agreeing with Joy were the actress turned ardent supporter of seals, Brigitte Bardot, a journalist, a trapper turned conservationist and a writer. Opposing them was the director of French national parks, a prominent zoo owner in Rouen, a circus director and a man defending the Eskimos' livelihood. After *Born Free* was shown, the group, by now warmed up, had lunch. According to Joy, the film was followed by an ever more heated discussion. As voices rose, tempers started to fly, Bardot collapsed in floods of tears, Joy started to shout and a furore ensued over the different solutions to the problems facing zoos and other animal sanctuaries. Understandably, the television programme was not shown live.

The next morning Joy flew off early to London, met Marjorie Villiers and her lawyer at the airport hotel and spent the day discussing the edited script and illustrations for her book on Penny, as well as two small giftbooks about the owls and colobus monkeys at Elsamere. That night she flew back to Nairobi and once again stayed in Villa Langata with the Bradley-Martins. She seemed ecstatic and full of renewed energy. As Chryssee remembers it : 'Joy was on a high as her trip had gone so well – it was the most excited I had seen her in a long time.'

So flushed with success was Joy that all her personal resentments and troubles of the past for months had melted away. Not only had she bought Chryssee a brooch of a horse as a present, she had also brought back Christmas presents for George and Terence, Pieter and Tony Fitzjohn. When she drove off to Shaba two days later, she left all her good clothes with the Bradley-Martins so that she had something suitable to wear whenever she came to stay in Nairobi.

24

The Suspicious Simi

George had promised his wife that he would come and spend Christmas with her. With a brave front but inner trepidation Joy, as usual, hung up tinsel decorations in her mess tent and readied the camp for his arrival. All the next morning, as her eyes swept the skies, she knew George was not going to make it. Unbeknownst to her, the pilot who was to fly George over to Shaba was called off on an emergency and George's radio had broken down, preventing him from warning Joy. It was a sad, lonely Christmas for Joy. She drank a bottle of beer and ate the tinned Christmas pudding sitting alone outside her tent. In response to the Cottrells' generous donation towards a fire extinguisher in camp, on the 27th Joy began a letter on her old Olivetti, thanking God that she had got through Christmas. Not only had she been let down by George, but Pieter Mawson had deserted her for the bright lights of Isiolo. She had spent a quiet day listening to her music.

On 30 December, Joy wrote a similar letter to Dorle, hoping the £100 birthday present had arrived. The money was only to be used on herself. Again, she lamented George's absence over Christmas, giving as excuses the expense of hiring a plane and the fact that Tony Fitzjohn was not around to keep an eye on the Kora lions for him. In fact, George always thumbed a plane ride whenever he could. Joy then changed the subject. She was keen to know if Dorle was keeping fit and trim by exercising, saying that she herself never failed to take care of her body. And she ended on an optimistic note, crossing her fingers that the following year would prove to be prosperous and happy.

Joy wrote another letter that day. Her editor at Collins, Marjorie Villiers, received a hurried letter from Joy exclaiming that she had just found out that female cats were called queens. 'Wouldn't *Queen of Shaba* be a marvellous title for the book on Penny?' said Joy.

From 29 December to 2 January, Roy Wallace received four notes in

Joy's handwriting – angry messages demanding that he do this errand or that task for her. Joy obviously did not trust someone in the camp. By now both she and Roy were convinced that Pieter Mawson could do her harm. Concerned about her agitated state of mind Roy repeated: 'Joy, you must be very careful of this guy.'

Joy had invited Bobby Lowis, a safari guide, and his two clients from the States who were camping in Samburu, to share New Year's Eve with her. The Americans had already kindly sent over a new telemetric collar for Penny. In front of her guests, Joy, in her leopard-print bathing suit and topee, appeared in great form, excitedly showing them her swimming hole and the waterfall. According to Bobby: 'Joy was very well built and her body did not look her age at all.' He brought along two bottles of sparkling German wine for a picnic and a couple of Mozart piano concerto tapes as a present. Pieter Mawson had taken himself off to the bright lights to bring in the New Year and Makedde was in Isiolo getting married for the third time. The only sour note was Joy's continual harping on her assistant's many faults: how much he lied, how much she hated him and wanted to be rid of him. Joy enjoyed their company so much that she invited them to dinner on 2 January, another long rough ride from Samburu.

It was Joy's habit to go for a walk in the late afternoon, usually accompanied by her assistant. She hoped to find Penny, but whether she did or not, she liked to return to camp before the sun set to listen to the 7 p.m. news. After hearing the news she always wrote up her notes on Penny on her typewriter before having dinner.

Bobby and his party duly arrived and sat round the safari table in canvas-backed chairs beneath a spreading acacia. Bobby recalled: 'We had a pretty revolting chicken which must have died out of old age and we drank out of cracked cups – Joy thought it entirely unnecessary to spend money on such things.' More than once Joy mentioned to Bobby that she still hoped George would arrive to see her. After the meal Joy went back into her studio and brought out two beautiful new watercolour paintings of the patterned skin on Penny's back. She was justly proud of them. As her guests left, Bobby glanced casually at the visitor's book as he was signing his name. No one had been to see Joy for many months. Bobby remembered the evening well: 'We had talked and talked and left her, all rather fond of each other, and with many plans for the future.'

As the sky began to lighten on the morning of 3 January, Joy awoke feeling thoughtful, introspective and slightly insecure. Kifosha, dressed in his usual attire of green apron over his shirt and trousers, made his way across the dusty compound to give Joy her morning tea. Joy and Pieter set out in the early light to find Penny. As she climbed out of the Toyota and moved silently through the sharp grass, Joy reflected on the beauty and peace of her small slice of Kenya. Although the leopards' camouflage was almost perfect among the rocks, Joy caught sight of their moving tails as the animals walked along the ledge high above, gazing down at the cows walking tranquilly below.

Pieter found her behaviour bizarre. 'That day she encouraged Penny, whom she had spent many months training for freedom, to come to her and as soon as the leopard did, Joy started playing with her.' She was breaking down all the training. As the day progressed, Joy's energy deserted her and for many hours she sat facing the swamp and staring out into space. In the afternoon she suddenly turned to Pieter, staring intently at him with her wide blue eyes surrounded by a crinkle of crows' feet: 'Pieter, if anything happens to me, will you promise to look after Penny?' The young man, surprised by such an unusual request, agreed. A few hours later she gave him her Bible. That day she made no notes. At 6.30 she told Pieter she wanted to walk alone that evening, something she seldom did. He warned her that he thought there were lions about – a herd of buffalo had been disturbed from the swamp nearby in a manner that suggested their proximity. Surely, if she knew there were lions in the vicinity, Joy would not have gone out on her own? Before she set off, she made sure both gates to the animal enclosures at the back were bolted.

While Pieter sat reading in a chair outside the mess tent, Kifosha went round lighting the paraffin lamps. An hour later, when night had fallen, Kifosha said to Mawson: 'It is late for Memsahib Haraka not to be back.' Joy's assistant joked about it and said, 'Perhaps she has been eaten by lions!' After five minutes, realizing that it was now 7.15 p.m., Pieter decided he had better go and look for her. He jumped into the Toyota pick-up and headed down the track Joy always took from the camp. After driving only two hundred yards from the camp the lights of the truck picked up a crumpled body in the road. She was lying on her face, in a small pool of blood. Peering out of the windscreen onto the patch of light snatched from the limitless black surroundings, Pieter caught his breath. 'Oh my God,' he whispered. 'Joy, it's Joy.'

Panic-stricken, Mawson immediately reversed the truck, causing the tyres to sink in the mud at the side of the road. Shouting loudly for Kifosha, he ran back to the camp and together they drove back to Joy in her station wagon. The old cook, stunned, kept repeating, 'Memsahib na kufa, Memsahib na kufa' – Memsahib is dead. Seeing a bloody wound on her left arm, Pieter automatically concluded she had been killed by a lion. He left Kifosha to guard the body and quickly drove back to camp to fetch a blanket and sheet to wrap Joy in. He thought it slightly odd that all the paraffin lamps in camp had gone out but, in his shocked state, dismissed it. He needed to get back to Kifosha and Joy. On the way out he grabbed his rifle and ammunition. When Pieter nervously turned her body over, he was struck by the expression of peace on Joy's face.

The two men carefully wrapped the body and laid it on the back seat of the station wagon. Before leaving for Isiolo, Pieter gave his rifle to Kifosha, telling him to guard the camp. The old man, greatly afraid, did as he was told. He immediately noticed that both of the gates had been left open. Shutting the inner one, he was too nervous in the dark to venture to the outer gate which opened on to the bush. Holding Mawson's rifle in both hands he stepped carefully over to Joy's sleeping tent, the flap of which was open. Her tin trunk had been forced open, valuables stolen and papers and other items were scattered all over the floor. Kifosha also found that a car battery was missing from one of the vehicles and the terminals cut. Joy's camp radio telephone was out of order with a microphone problem, preventing Pieter from communicating directly with anyone.

While Kifosha made these ominous discoveries, Pieter had driven hurriedly up to Roy Wallace's camp with the body. He ran in shocked and screaming, 'I think Joy's dead. She's been attacked by a lion.' Roy replied, 'How do you know it's a lion? Let me see her.' The inside car light was on and he shone a torch at the body. As Roy began to roll back the sheet and blanket from the body, Pieter lost all control. Shouting at the top of his lungs, he started to attack Roy, pulling him away from the car. 'Don't you go near her. How dare you touch her, I won't allow it. Leave her alone.' Roy's *askari* stepped in to separate the two fighting men, pushed Pieter out of the way and, with his boss, looked briefly at the body. Roy thought that if she had indeed been attacked by a lion, it was odd there was no trace of blood on her face. He said quickly, 'Pieter, we are not doctors, she may still be alive. Take her to the fathers at Archer's Post Mission and I'll radio Nairobi and tell them what has happened. Then I'll join you.' The mission was only four miles away. Mawson agreed.

For some reason known only to himself, Mawson drove Joy straight to Dr Wedel in Isiolo, a distance of forty-five miles, on a rutted and bumpy dirt road. He arrived at about 9 p.m. Not finding Pieter at the mission, Roy immediately set off for Isiolo and as soon as he arrived at the police station, he found out that Mawson and Wedel had already been there. Roy was incensed: 'I could not believe the guy. He had gone all the way to Isiolo with this body bouncing around in the back of the car. If there was any chance she was alive, the trip alone would have killed her. He must have known for sure that Joy was dead and had been murdered.'

The police doctor examined her and found two large wounds on her arm and one on the left side of her body. He confirmed Pieter's opinion – Joy was dead, attacked by a lion. Her young assistant had also contacted a reporter for the East African *Standard* in Isiolo, who relayed the sensational news to Nairobi. It was the main item on the BBC World News and a shocked world took it for granted that Joy had been killed by a lion. It was only on the fifth day that a journalist, Henry Reuter, bothered to fly up to Shaba to seek confirmation.

Meanwhile, Superintendent Mburu remained somewhat suspicious of the cause of death. Later that night Joy's body was removed to the hospital mortuary in Meru on the orders of the senior police officer, Chief Inspector Gichunga. Dr Wedel took the shocked Mawson home to spend the night with him. The next morning Mr Gichunga travelled back to Shaba with Pieter and the assistant was warned 'not to leave camp'. Throughout the night he also had not been entirely convinced that a lion was the cause of Joy's death. There they were joined by a number of policemen, including Senior Superintendent Ngansira. They examined the patch of blood where Joy had died. Next to it lay her walking stick. They found a crowbar from the camp tool shed in Joy's tent and the small metal box, now destroyed. Prints of shoes led into the bush from the gates of the animal enclosure.

Peter Jenkins was asked to assist in the investigation. He arrived in Joy's camp to find the whole area of the camp sealed off. For an hour he and his tracker hunted in vain for any tell-tale lion tracks. The ground was dusty and not disturbed. It would have been easy to see footprints. He then proceeded in the police Land Rover to the mortuary to identify the body. On being shown the injuries he stated that they could not possibly have been caused by a lion. On the following day three doctors carried out a post-mortem on Joy's body in Meru District Hospital. It was obvious to the doctors that Joy had been killed by an assassin holding a sharp, pointed instrument, such as a *simi*, a small dagger carried by the Turkana. Besides the two deep flesh wounds on her arm, the thrust eight inches into her rib cage had severed the abdominal aorta. Joy had been murdered.

Peter Johnson and Jack Barrah arrived in Shaba and, defying police orders, picked up Pieter Mawson and flew him down to Nairobi. Jack confessed: 'Pieter was in a hell of a state.' Before he left, the young man, who could speak only rudimentary Swahili, was generous with the remaining staff, giving them money and clothes. He told them he was leaving Kenya immediately. Still in a state of shock, Mawson went to stay with the game warden, Phil Synder, who remembers: 'He was a nice guy – obviously very upset. He stayed several days with me during the heat of this thing. He had some visa problem and was absolutely terrified he wasn't going to get out of the country. I felt sorry for him. He was young, caught up in this horrible event and petrified that he was going to be picked up again.'

On 6 January, Superintendents Rowe and Giltrap arrived in Shaba to help clear up the investigation. Nothing significant was revealed in their search round the camp area other than a *rungu*, which was hidden in the bush near where the body was found.

On a hot day with the sun high in a cloudless sky, Joy was cremated at Langata Crematorium, near the game park and Lone Tree plain, home of the lions where she and George used to camp. The funeral was simple and moving, but only a handful of people bothered to turn up at the service. A small cluster, mostly journalists, photographers and friends of the wild animals and their country, grateful for all Joy had given, sat behind George. He was shattered. As the minister delivered his eulogy, George, unaccustomed to wearing a suit, continually wiping away tears from his eyes, appeared a forlorn and lonely man. He felt a deep and painful regret that he had not been able to spend Joy's last Christmas with her. He had loved her and had tried for so many years to bring some sort of peace into her stormy life. He felt a profound sadness that it had never been achieved.

On hearing the news of his former wife, Peter Bally remarked, 'The whole world mourns Joy, except her three husbands.' This was not true of her last. Long ago Joy had made George promise that when she died, her remains would be sprinkled over the graves of Elsa and Pippa. After the cremation, George flew with Peter Johnson and Jack Barrah in Peter Jenkins's plane to Meru with Joy's ashes, to the place from where Joy had once been forced out. It was a sad though triumphant return. Here her spirit would rest for ever with two of her beloved animals. George had gone to great lengths to clean himself up for the funeral and now he did the same, scrubbing his body and carefully combing his long white hair and beard before the painful ceremony. Jenkins had thoughtfully tidied the lion's and cheetah's graves. The bush had been cut back and weeds and tall grasses had been cleared from around the slabs of stone. First, Jenkins stopped the car by Pippa's grave under the tree in Joy's former camp. The four men, all of whom had either loved, admired or respected Joy, got out and trooped quietly towards the resting place. George silently scattered half of his wife's ashes on the grave in the place where Joy had experienced moments of real happiness and what little peace she could find within herself. The rest he buried with Elsa, the being that Joy had poured more genuine love into than any other.

By now the police, deep into a murder investigation, had begun their intensive interrogation. The culprit would surely be found among those working for her or ex-employees, particularly those with whom she had quarrelled openly and violently. Among the suspects were Pieter Mawson and Paul Ekai, the tall, strong young Turkana she had sacked a month earlier; Gabriel Ekai, Paul's brother who had once worked for Joy and from whom Paul had taken over; and Stephen and Nano. Except for Mawson the other four were all ex-employees.

Pieter, presumably because he found the body and had been alone at the time, underwent an especially tough and intensive interrogation with the police. Makedde and Kifosha seemed beyond reproach, having worked loyally for twenty to thirty years for both the Adamsons. The only suspect who could not be found was Paul Ekai, supposedly hiding at his parents' *manyatta* near Isiolo. One by one, as their innocence was established, the young suspects were released. That left Pieter Mawson and Paul Ekai.

Paul's mother, Tiokko Ekai, is now a broken, unhappy figure, living in a lean-to shack made out of black plastic, tin and bits of torn clothing in Chichilesi near Isiolo. Dressed in dirty rags and beads and chewing *miraa*, the old shaven-headed woman seems worn out by life and the loss of her son. She cried: 'At the time of Joy's murder Paul was staying here with us, his parents. He was a really good boy as a child, even better than my other two children, Gabriel and Erebon. I cannot believe my son did such a terrible thing. I know he didn't do it.' This sentiment was repeated by all who knew the young man in his home area. As soon as he had heard of the murder and knowing he would be a prime suspect, Paul had run away to stay with a relation at Baragoi, towards the Turkana country round Lake Rudolf – two hundred miles away from Isiolo. He was dancing the night away at an *ngoma* when the Maralal police approached him and asked him to hand over his identification card. Recognizing him as being on the 'wanted' list, the sergeant immediately arrested him.

The following day Ekai was removed to Isiolo where Mr Ngansira interviewed him. He denied all knowledge of Joy's murder and spent the night at the police station. The next day he made a full confession. Shortly afterwards he was also seen by his parents and both were horrified – his mother crying out in anguish when she saw his condition. His mouth was split and some of his teeth had been smashed out. There was a large cut on his head and several lacerations on both his legs. 'He had obviously been badly tortured by the police,' she said. Ekai later claimed that he had been burned with a red-hot iron rod, tortured by having a string tied round his testicles, whipped on his legs and hit in the face, in order to obtain a confession.

Ekai apparently confessed to the police that he had been filled with rage when he had been sacked as Joy had not paid him his full wage. She had also accused him of theft. According to the confession, he had walked back to the area where she took her walk each evening, determined to have it out with her. He waited without moving, hidden in the bush for four hours. But when he accosted Joy she immediately became angry with his impertinence, abusing him loudly, and so he stabbed her in a fit of fury. After stabbing her three times, she fell to the ground, crying faintly 'Kifosha, Kifosha,' calling desperately for her cook. Ekai then claimed he tossed his *simi* into the swamp and crept into the camp, put out the lights before going straight for her tent where he knew she kept her tin trunk – the police had not tested the paraffin lamps for fingerprints. He was interrupted by Pieter who had rushed back for his rifle and a blanket in which to wrap Joy's body. Ekai then stepped steathily into the bush, hiding there until Kifosha was left alone to guard the camp. Running quickly to the pick-up truck, he wrenched the battery out – he could get money by selling it in Isiolo – and walked home along a game path, after hiding the battery under a tree some distance from the camp.

Roy Wallace, who had always been fond of Kifosha and his calm, pleasant nature, immediately took him on as cook. Joy had been good to him financially, occasionally giving him loans to send to his family. Long ago he had decided that the longer he stayed with her, the more Joy would leave him when she died. The two men spent many hours sitting on a rock near the camp, discussing the dreadful events. Both men, white and black, friend and servant, were convinced that Pieter had encouraged Paul to kill Joy – either himself or by arranging for some friend to do it – by promising him a piece of the pie in the set-up should the Trust see fit to keep Mawson on at Shaba to continue the leopard project and future books.

Others in Kenya wondered the same thing, especially as Pieter had immediately identified the killer as a lion. The day before Joy died, Mawson's Toyota was noticed in Isiolo outside the Frontier Lodge, a brothel and pick-up joint. Roy had thought it highly suspicious, since Pieter was not known to seek the favours of African women.

Meanwhile the police, dissatisfied with the South African's statement, were on the point of arresting Mawson in Nairobi on a charge of incitement to murder. However, the two investigating CID officers arrived and dissuaded them. 'There would be major repercussions on this throughout the world,' they said. Mawson eventually left for a post in the bush in Botswana, on the undertaking he return for any trial.

A month after the murder the police took Ekai to Shaba but were unable to find the *simi* in the swamp. Perhaps it had sunk in the thick mud? Peter Jenkins's men had previously spent hours wading through the swamp to find the battery, with no luck. Paul took the police directly to the battery hidden in the bush – his fingerprints were not found on the vehicle from which the battery had been stolen. The next step was to lead them to a *manyatta* near Daba, where he produced a knife, scabbard and belt. On 5 February Ekai was charged with murder. On the same day he guided the police to another *manyatta* where he pointed to a sack full of jerseys, shirts and shoes belonging to Pieter Mawson, stolen on 10 December. A Leica camera and telephoto lens were also hidden in a corner in the hut. It was soon established that bloodstains on the sack belonged to Joy's blood group, suggesting that Ekai had handled it shortly after the murder. That day Paul had fresh lash marks on his body, and was sent to Isiolo Hospital. The next morning he was transported to Nyeri for investigation of the lash marks. No explanation was found.

After a preliminary hearing in June, Paul Nakware Ekai was committed for trial. He was still only seventeen and therefore under age for a prison sentence, but remained detained. Nearly one year later, on 26 May 1981, the High Court sat at Nyeri. When Paul Ekai, pleading innocence, came into court he smiled wanly at Roy Wallace and said quietly, 'You know what really happened, Bwana.' As Pieter Mawson, ashen-faced, sat in the row of benches in front of Wallace, the latter leaned forward and accused him directly of participating in the murder. Mawson looked straight ahead.

The young African's defence counsel claimed that Ekai was innocent and pointed out that Mawson was equally capable of having done the deed. Paul Ekai was found guilty but escaped the death sentence as there was doubt as to whether he was an adult at the time he committed the crime. Two out of the three assessors found him innocent. He languishes to this day in Embu prison and was not allowed to be interviewed. On 8 December 1982, Kenya newspapers reported the death of Mawson in a car accident in Botswana.

Few people were surprised that Joy may have been killed by an African. The general opinion was that Joy got what she deserved, treating them so appallingly, forgetting to pay their wages and dismissing them with extreme rudeness and little regard for their welfare. One well-known Kenya gentleman, who knew Joy intimately, felt so strongly about Joy's handling of African servants that, 'When she was murdered I wrote to the advocate defending the man charged and said that if he was running a defence of provocation I would give evidence of the way she behaved towards her servants generally. In the event, he put up another defence.'

Who, then, did murder Joy Adamson and what was the motive? Although the circumstances surrounding the murder were obscure, various points stand to reason. It is unlikely that poachers from the north struck her down in a random killing. There were no rumours of any *shifta* near her camp at that time. Unless Mawson had temporarily lost his reason, it is difficult to believe that he knifed Joy. He could not have darkened the lights or robbed the camp while he was with Kifosha unless he had employed an accomplice.

It is most likely that Joy was killed by an African with whom she was familiar, quite possibly the Turkana, Paul Ekai, who was on intimate terms with the workings of the camp and Joy's daily routine and activities. Turkanas are a tough people, capable of their own dealings with what they see as rough justice. Perhaps Paul Ekai did indeed go momentarily berserk. However, people from the bush, including poachers, rarely act so savagely without financial or material motivation. If indeed Paul Ekai is guilty, the implication of this line of reasoning would be that he did not act alone. Perhaps greed, as well as exploitation of the people of the north, sealed Joy's death warrant.

Towards the end of her life Joy was a lonely, tragic figure – her critics were numerous, her friends few. But perhaps she, like many others, was aware that much of the tragedy was of her own making, the result of a nature based on emotion rather than practicality. Deeply flawed, but ablaze with guts and sincerity, she, more than most, suffered the loneliness of the successful. Her outstanding gift was that she was never content to stand aside without attempting 'the great enthusiasm, the great devotions'. As for the true objective of Joy's life, the protection and understanding of the big cats, no one can deny that through her total dedication to the animals she loved, she engendered and ensured a lasting interest in the survival of the creatures of the wild. For all her heartaches and disappointments, imperious ways and aggressive behaviour, Joy was a woman who remained passionately in love with life – a firm believer that, through animals, man would rediscover his soul.

Swahili Glossary

askari	policeman
banda	hut
baraza	public meeting
bibi	woman
boma	village community
bui-bui	long garment
bundu	bush
debbie	tin can
duka	shop
duthu	spear cover
fitina	trouble
fundi	artisan
kali	fierce
kanga	sarong
kanzu	kaftan
kiboko	leather whip
kikoi	sarong
laibon	tribal leader with mystical powers
lugga	riverbed
manyatta	hut made out of mud and dung
miraa	khat
moran	young warrior
muzungu	white man
ndume	bull
ngoma	native dance
panga	machete
pishi	cook
posho	maize meal
rungu	stick
shamba	plantation
shifta	poachers
simi	dagger
tukana	insult
wananchi	people
zariba	thorn hedge

Select Bibliography

Adamson, George, *Bwana Game* (Collins Harvill, 1968)
——, *My Pride and Joy* (Collins Harvill, 1986)
Adamson, Joy, *Born Free* (Collins Harvill, 1960)
——, *Living Free* (Collins Harvill, 1961)
——, *Forever Free* (Collins Harvill, 1962)
——, *The Peoples of Kenya* (Collins Harvill, 1967)
——, *The Spotted Sphinx* (Collins Harvill, 1969)
——, *Pippa's Challenge* (Collins Harvill, 1972)
——, *Queen of Shaba* (Collins Harvill, 1978)
——, *The Searching Spirit* (Collins Harvill, 1978)
Apter, Terri, *Altered Loves* (St Martin's Press, 1990)
Beard, Peter, *The End of the Game* (Viking, 1965)
Blixen, Karen, *Out of Africa* (Random House, 1937)
Chilver, E.M. and Smith, Alison, *A History of East Africa* (Oxford University Press, 1965)
Douglas-Home, Charles, *Evelyn Baring: The Last Consul* (Collins, 1978)
Fisher, Angela, *Africa Adorned* (Collins, 1984)
Fox, James, *White Mischief* (Jonathan Cape, 1982)
Gall, Sandy, *Lord of the Lions* (Grafton Books, 1991)
Huxley, Elspeth, *White Man's Country* (Chatto & Windus, 1935)
——, *Out in the Midday Sun* (Chatto & Windus, 1985)
——, *Nine Faces of Kenya* (Collins Harvill, 1990)
Kenyatta, Jomo, *Facing Mount Kenya* (Heinemann, 1938)
Markham, Beryl, *West With the Night* (Penguin, 1942)
Miller, Alice, *The Drama of Being a Child* (Virago Press, 1987)
Parker, Ian, *Oh Quagga* (Rodwell Press, 1983)
Reece, Alys, *To My Wife – 50 Camels* (Collins Harvill, 1963)
Ricciardi, Mirella, *African Saga* (Collins, 1981)
Thurman, Judith, *Isak Dinesen, The Life of a Storyteller* (St Martin's Press, 1982)
Trzebinski, Errol, *Silence Will Speak* (Heinemann, 1977)
——, *The Kenya Pioneers* (Heinemann, 1985)

Index